Rethinking Friendship

Hidden Solidarities Today

Rethinking Friendship
Hidden Solidarities Today

Liz Spencer

Ray Pahl

PRINCETON UNIVERSITY PRESS · PRINCETON AND OXFORD

For Robin, Josh and Luke,
Helen, Sara and Kaye, and in
celebration of our friendships

CONTENTS

This is a marvellous book about a marvellous subject. Social theorists often seem most comfortable with more abstract issues than this: the vast and impersonal processes of globalization, or economic change. But most of us live our lives closer to home, both literally and metaphorically, and it is in the intimate private space of friendship that we find some of our greatest joys and greatest disappointments.

While we know a lot about what is supposedly happening to the family, we know far less about the nature of friendship today. Part of the reason may be that, as with so many of the most vital social phenomena, there are acute problems of definition. And part of the reason is that this is a world that is beyond the reach of policy and government.

All of this makes this attempt to stand back and make an assessment of what is happening to friendship all the more valuable. It belongs in a long tradition of sociological study of the bonds of community. Much of that tradition assumed that the grinding forces of modernity and industrialization were smashing the intimate relationships that made life worth living, leaving us atomized, insecure and anomic. The world of mutual commitment was being replaced by a world of impersonal transactions.

But the picture painted here is much more interesting than that. It shows the sheer variety of relationships we have with friends – some absolutely vital to our ability to live, others sources of fun and entertainment; some carried with us from childhood, others acquired and discarded casually. It shows that there is little evidence for sweeping claims of decline and decay, even though there has undoubtedly been a change in the patterns of friendship, driven by bigger changes such as the large-scale movement of women in the workforce or the spread of the telephone.

The detailed analysis also quietly confirms what we know from other research on happiness and well-being about the importance of strong networks of family and friends. Without them we are more likely to suffer from mental illness, and indeed physical illness too. In later life friends become even more important than family in keeping us healthy.

One of the many virtues of the book is that it provides a longer historical perspective. The authors remind us of the fluidity of daily life in the eighteenth and nineteenth centuries, and the complex ways in which class and gender framed how people thought about their friends. A historical perspective also provides a salutary reminder that more than a century ago, when the telephone was first coming into cities, there were many forecasts of the death of community. The more recent villains of the piece are television, the Internet and computer games: yet these too probably do as much to aid as to harm sociability, and the Internet has certainly proved to be a very powerful tool for people to sustain their friendship networks over longer distances.

Much of the book stands in the best traditions of empirical British sociology, particularly those incorporating careful and meticulous ethnography. Drawing on qualitative material and using their own words and stories, it gives an accessible and intriguing account of people's personal social worlds. But it also provides an important set of arguments about theory too. The recent theorists of social capital have tended to give the greatest prominence to relatively formal kinds of mutual involvement, in particular, membership of civic organizations. These have traditionally been seen as more virtuous than circles of friends gathered together for pleasure or mutual help. But here the authors rehabilitate the informal *schmoozers*, who may not join anything formal but who nevertheless may play a critical role in holding friendship networks together and, indeed, in holding communities together, below the radar of any official measures.

This book should appeal to a number of different audiences, from general readers fascinated by friendship to policy makers concerned about community, social capital and social inclusion. I hope that many researchers will be inspired to continue the task of observation and reflection, digging deeper into the micro-worlds of everyday life. The greatest value that any social science can have is to look at something familiar and show it in a new light. This book does that admirably.

GEOFF MULGAN
Director, The Young Foundation
London

ACKNOWLEDGEMENTS

We owe a debt of gratitude to the many people who have provided inspiration, insight, commentary and practical help throughout the creation of this book. Foremost among them are Jane Ritchie, one of the stars of qualitative research, who carried out some exquisitely sensitive interviews, and gave wise and invaluable feedback on the manuscript, and Robin Sadler, who not only contributed to the study on which the book is based, but also coped with seemingly endless disruption, affording priceless support and encouragement.

Particular thanks are also owed to the following: Karen O'Reilly, for inspiring such stimulating discussion when we were submitting our proposal to the Economic and Social Research Council – her ideas heavily influenced the focus of our study; Graham Allan, for showing long-term enthusiasm for our research and giving thoughtful and detailed advice on the manuscript; Mark Vernon, for casting a philosopher's eye on aspects of our analysis and argument; Geoff Mulgan, for writing a foreword; and Brian Spencer for generously reading and commenting on the entire book, with the interests of the general reader at heart. We are also grateful for the support of friends and colleagues when we were developing our methods, and for the many thought-provoking comments we have received throughout the extended period of this project. Given the nature of our topic, many people have enthusiastically engaged in discussion with us and, while we are unable to acknowledge everyone individually, we appreciate all those who helped us develop and refine our ideas.

Janice Webb deserves a special thank you. Not only has she been involved throughout the project, showing great interest in the study, and preparing the manuscript with infinite care and patience, but she has also been more like a professional PA in dealing with the media and countless other matters connected with our joint enterprise. We warmly appreciate her generous and willing support, and unfailing good humour.

Our sincere thanks also go to The Institute for Social and Economic Research at the University of Essex, for providing a world-class base in which to do research. Judi Edgerton and her colleagues in the Research Resources Unit provided an exemplary service, finding obscure references with unfailing patience, no matter how inadequate the details of our requests sometimes were. Jay Gershuny and Nick Buck were particularly supportive to Ray Pahl during a difficult period in the middle of the project; their consistent commitment to our research has been immensely encouraging.

We are also grateful for IT help and support at various stages in this venture; Josh and Luke Sadler deserve a special mention for bringing our IT skills into the twenty-first century.

We acknowledge with gratitude the support we have received from Ian Malcolm, our editor at Princeton University Press, who encouraged us to stick to our beliefs about the overall conception and thrust of the book. While defending our approach against strongly held counter views from an anonymous reader substantially delayed publication, we readily admit that the struggle has been worth it. We would also like to thank Jon Wainwright at T&T Productions Ltd for his meticulous care and commitment during the production process, and for showing such respect for our concerns about the overall feel of the book.

Finally, we express our heartfelt thanks to the people who took part in our study, generously giving us their time and telling us their stories. Without them, none of this would have been possible.

Rethinking Friendship
Hidden Solidarities Today

A faithful friend is a strong defence, and he that hath found such an one
hath found a treasure. . . A faithful friend is the medicine of life.

— Ecclesiasticus

This book is about friendship in its rich and varied forms, but it is
also about the role of friendship in contemporary society. Not only
do we investigate and describe relationships between friends, we also
examine the relevance of friendship for current debates about social
integration and the state of community today. Using the findings of
our study we reveal the persistence of *hidden solidarities* and question
some of the gloomier analyses of our times.

We began with a problematic involving both public issues and private troubles. In the private sphere, there are fears that relationships
today have become fleeting and transient, that people have become
socially isolated. Depression and other mental health problems, for
example, have been claimed by the World Health Organization (WHO)
to be the most rapidly growing form of ill health in recent years.[1] In the
public sphere, politicians and policy makers have been alarmed by a
supposed lack of civic responsibility and a retreat into self-absorbed
individualism. Our interest in friendship, therefore, has been fuelled
in part by a feeling that, although friends have been studied at the
level of individual relationships, the role of friendship in providing a
kind of social glue has largely been ignored. Consequently, we set out
to examine friendship in depth and to rethink its broader sociological
and political significance.

FRIENDS, FRIEND-LIKE TIES AND PERSONAL COMMUNITIES

As part of our study of friendship we have, of course, probed the nature
and quality of relationships between friends who are not related to

each other by blood or marriage – but our study is not confined to these non-kin ties. Because friendship may be found between spouses, partners, siblings, cousins or parents and their children, we have also explored friend-like qualities in a broader set of social relationships. We compare cases where friends and family play rather similar roles with cases where they occupy a distinct and separate place in people's lives.

So this book is about friendship in its broadest sense, but it is also about friendship in the context of the significant others who inhabit our micro-social worlds. We call these sets of significant others *personal communities*[2], and examine the role of friends and friend-like ties within them. Because of this focus, our book deals with those friendships that are considered important in people's lives; our research does not tell us much about the dark side of friendship, about unsatisfactory, competitive or destructive relationships, though this is undoubtedly an important theme. Our study has also focused on adult friendships, rather than friendships among children, adolescents, and in old age, since these have been the subject of many other studies.

Friendship in the Wider Social and Political Context

Given our interest in the role as well as the nature of friendship, we have set our findings against the backdrop of contemporary fears about a decline in the quality of personal and communal life. Perhaps it is part of the human condition to claim that things 'ain't wot they used to be'. Perhaps it is a way older generations claim authority by asserting that the quality of social life has deteriorated markedly since their youth. Perhaps governments need to create a degree of dissatisfaction and unease to justify the continuation of their power and authority over us. Perhaps, finally, we are indeed living in a world which can be shown – with the aid of hard empirical evidence – to be in many significant and important aspects qualitatively different from a better world we have lost or may be in the process of losing.

It is not hard to show that, for as long as recorded history, there has been a perennial concern with the way people live, which has provided the motivation and the power of priests, shamans and prophets. Now, in a more secular age, social science has added new voices. It is true that the traditional vocabulary of sin, falling from grace, and the hope of salvation still has considerable resonance in many quarters – some would even argue that the idea of the loss and recovery of community lies at the heart of Western millennial thought[3] – but a new vocabulary of social disorder and disruption emerged with the rise of social science in the nineteenth and twentieth centuries. Furthermore, the development of various rigorous research techniques has made possible the generation and collection of empirical evidence to support or, indeed, refute such perceptions of social ills. However, as we shall see, much depends on what is measured and on how we interpret the evidence.

Our aim in this book has been to challenge the views of those social theorists and commentators who have adopted an overwhelmingly pessimistic, if not despairing, response to the society they describe. Inevitably, this has meant that we have concentrated on commentators who take the most negative readings, giving less attention to others who have questioned such dark interpretations. However, lest some accuse us of Panglossian complacency, we recognize that our stance is more one of modification than of complete rejection. To claim that society is eternally enduring and unchanging would be absurd. However, we feel that there has been a serious misunderstanding of the dynamics of micro-social worlds, and particularly of the role of friendship and trust. Such issues have not figured greatly in the magisterial sweep of theorists of social change, who have, perhaps, concentrated more on identifying the overarching spirit of the age.

Of course, we recognize that there are good reasons for this. Detailed ethnographies of different social groupings and communities did not develop until well into the twentieth century. Initially, these were little more than elementary social surveys, spliced with gossip, and it was only with the rise of a rigorous social anthropology that a more nuanced and subtle understanding of the complexities of micro-social worlds could emerge. One only has to read the essay by William Foote Whyte, reflecting on his classic study, *Street Corner Society*, which he began in 1937, to see how untrained he was, and how 'baffled' he felt on finding his way into an inner city 'slum'. Whyte recalled that, at that time, studies of 'the community as an organised social system did not exist'.[4] While the collection of detailed ethnographies still remains relatively sparse, these kinds of studies unquestionably provide a more rooted view of society than was available to earlier generations of social commentators, particularly those of the nineteenth century.

We also believe that the broad sweep of classical social theorists should be challenged because of the dramatic and exciting developments in historical demography and historical anthropology over the past forty years.[5] Evidently, the founding fathers of social science did not have the detailed understandings of families and communities in former times which are now available, but, even today, some contemporary social theorists show little recognition of this body of knowledge in their work, relying on unspecified notions of traditional society when referring to the past.

A QUALITATIVE APPROACH

It is important to recognize that the empirical findings reported in this book take the form of qualitative rather than quantitative data. We adopted a qualitative approach partly because, in attempting to rethink the contemporary salience and significance of friendship, we had to confront the fact that there is no clear agreement on what precisely the term 'friend' means. In some studies this problem is simply ducked. For example, people may be asked how many friends they have, or invited to give details about frequency of contact with their three closest friends, or the age, sex, occupation or ethnicity of those friends, but the word 'friend' is not defined, nor is any check made on how the term is being used. This is why it is difficult to make sense of conflicting statistics about the average number of friends we are supposed to have nowadays, and why we, perhaps, should take with a pinch of salt claims made by some in the public eye that they have the names of over a thousand 'friends' in their email address books.

Alternatively, in other studies, people are asked to define in detail what they mean by the term 'friend' and to list the qualities they associate with friendship. In most cases, however, these qualities refer to some general or idealized concept, or to cultural stereotypes, rather than to actual flesh-and-blood relationships. Our challenge, therefore, was to look at friendship in depth, to establish how people use the term, and to examine the content of particular relationships. A qualitative approach also gave us the flexibility to explore the complexities of friend-like ties, where categorical labels like brother, sister, parent, cousin, colleague or neighbour might mask additional friend-like qualities. Through open-ended, in-depth interviews, we were able to identify cases where family members are also considered to be friends, and, indeed, where friends take on a family-like status.

In the main study we conducted a total of sixty interviews with men and women of different ages, at different stages in the life-course, from different socio-economic and ethnic backgrounds, and living in different parts of Britain, including the northwest and southeast of England as well as the Welsh borders. With this purposively selected sample, our aim was to paint as broad a picture as we could in order to understand the nature of friendships and the diversity of people's personal communities today.[6] We made a special effort to include some people who were at risk of being socially isolated, as well as those with robust personal communities, and interviewed two young people brought up in care, a woman with mental health problems, a man who suffered from aphasia following a stroke, and a young man with drug and alcohol problems. We did not, however, interview homeless rough sleepers, travellers, asylum seekers or international jet setters, so our study may fail to capture the personal communities of the most isolated or the most global citizens.

Given the rich diversity of cultures and backgrounds in Britain today, we also had to make some key decisions about the range of ethnic groups we could incorporate. We concluded that it would be better to understand a few situations well, rather than spread our resources too thinly, and, consequently, we interviewed people from white British and from black African and Caribbean backgrounds. Although this means we have no data for other minority ethnic groups, because of the way we present our evidence, readers from other backgrounds should be able to judge the extent to which our findings are applicable to them.

The fact that our data are qualitative has implications for the kind of evidence we portray, and for the way readers should judge its wider relevance. In each of the chapters that describe our findings we present two different kinds of material: a set of analytical concepts and cases which illustrate these ideas. It is important to stress that the themes and concepts presented throughout the book have emerged through clear and explicit procedures of analysis, which are fully explained in the appendix. If these themes and concepts have resonance, we believe this is because they reflect people's experiences; but their easy acceptance should not mask the fact that they have been rigorously devised. There are no numbers, percentages or statistical tables. Although we aim to identify recurrent patterns, we do not rely on traditional variable analysis, where the aim is to account for most rather than all of

the variance. On the contrary, we are interested in the range and complexity of people's situations and relationships: this means we also
investigate the outliers, since apparently atypical or negative cases
can sometimes hold the clue to patterns which recur in the data.

Readers may well ask whether British data can have relevance for
other societies, particularly the United States, which is sometimes considered to be the embodiment of an individualized, isolated society.
They may further question the wider relevance of a nationally focused
qualitative study. We argue that our study does indeed have broader
relevance, precisely because it is qualitative and because of the nature
of generalization within qualitative research. In small-scale, purposively sampled studies, the reader makes a qualitative judgement
about the wider applicability of the findings based on the detailed
description of concepts and cases. Essentially, the reader decides
whether the concepts have wider analytical or explanatory power by
looking in detail at both the setting of the initial study and other settings where the findings might be applied, by comparing those contexts, and by judging whether the analysis and interpretation found in
the initial study can help make sense of other social milieux.

We are not making any claims about the frequency or ubiquity of
any particular kind of friendship or personal community, simply that
a range of types and patterns exists. We are mapping the territory, if
you like, and the reader's main concerns should be: Can I recognize
the map? How well does the map fit my situation or are some parts of
the map less relevant? Are some parts of the map missing? By giving
details of how the concepts and patterns were identified, and illustrating each with cases from our research, we enable the reader to check
the wider applicability of the map. It is important to remember that,
even in the case of a large quantitative study carried out in Britain,
there could be no automatic generalization to other countries, since
a British sample would not be representative of other populations. In
this case, the reader would still have to make a qualitative judgement
about the transferability of findings, and might well have less detailed
information on which to make such a judgement.

A Guide to this Book

From conversations with our colleagues, friends and families, we have
gathered that the subject of friendship and personal communities fas-
cinates others and well as ourselves. We have therefore written this

book with both a general and an academic audience in mind. To make it more accessible to general readers, we have tried not to clutter the main text with too many references to the literature. For academic readers, however, we have put a great deal of very detailed information, as well as many interesting references, in the endnotes for each chapter.

A guide to individual chapters, however, might help different readers navigate their way through the book. Chapter 1 explores some of the main concerns that have been expressed about the state of society today, outlining some of the moral panics over the quality of our social life as we move through the twenty-first century, and making the case for a detailed study of people's micro-social worlds that focuses on the role of friends and friend-like ties. Chapter 2 gives an account of some of the factors that influenced the way we carried out our study, and gives an initial picture of the kinds of personal communities we identified. Both these chapters inevitably contain some discussion of theoretical ideas, but we have tried to keep this discussion interesting and accessible. Readers who are mainly interested in learning about friendship may prefer to skip this part of the book and begin with chapter 3, perhaps returning later when they have satisfied their curiosity.

Chapters 3–6 present the main body of our findings, illustrated through case descriptions, but putting more technical matters and references in the notes rather than the main text. Chapter 3 explores the nature and diversity of friendship and introduces the idea of a friendship repertoire, or the range of different types of friends that people have. Chapter 4 looks at friendship over the life-course and at different patterns of friend-making. Chapter 5 examines friendship and family relationships, exploring the notion of suffusion and the extent to which family and friends play distinctive or overlapping roles. In chapter 6 we then take the ideas discussed in earlier chapters and present a set of seven different kinds of personal community. Chapter 7 addresses the question of how personal communities may in general be shaped by factors such as age, gender, social class and geographical mobility. Finally, in chapter 8, we consider the wider implications of our findings, returning to debates about community, social capital and social integration. Again, these two final chapters incorporate some references to the literature, but we hope that our overall discussion of these key themes will appeal to both our audiences. For those who would like to know more about how we carried out the study, there is a full appendix.

The order in which the authors' names appear should not be taken to imply that one of us has made more of a contribution than the other. It is simply that we have written a number of papers together on this subject and Ray Pahl's name has appeared first on other occasions. It is true that we have made different contributions, but these reflect our different strengths and interests. Liz Spencer has spent thirty years conducting and championing qualitative research and passionately believes in its power to inform and illuminate. She has taken major responsibility for the analysis and presentation of our findings. Ray Pahl has a breadth of knowledge and scholarship that has enabled us to set these findings against an expansive backdrop, incorporating recent historical and anthropological as well as sociological debates.

Finally, as long-term friends ourselves, we welcomed an opportunity to work together and to pursue a long-held interest. In Ray Pahl's case, friendship is a subject he has already investigated and written about over a period of more than thirty years; for both of us it holds a personal as well as a professional fascination. A grant from the Economic and Social Research Council, and a home at the Institute for Social and Economic Research at the University of Essex, enabled us to carry out the research on which this book is based.[7]

CHAPTER ONE

The Fragmentation of Social Life?

Debates about the waxing and waning of 'community' have been endemic for at least two centuries. 'Declensionist narratives' – postmodernist jargon for tales of decline and fall – have a long pedigree in our letters. We seem perennially to contrast our tawdry todays with past golden ages.

— Putnam

... the rupture of community leaves men preoccupied by the nature of friendship, the allowable bonds of intimacy, the canons of discretion and the limits of loyalty. To traditionalists, in such an age of change, real friendships, confidences, and loyalties can appear as, at best, shards of community that once existed but now is dead, as pieces of jetsam afloat on the seas of economic and political egoism.

— Nisbet

With the possibility of greater levels of diversity in people's experiences and a heightened emphasis on life-style issues, friendships may be recognized increasingly as one of the main sites of activity giving life meaning.

— Allan

As we embark on a new century, is it the case that community has fractured, that people in the Western world are selfish, isolated and irresponsible, turning away from public and private responsibilities? Or is it possible that our pessimism is overstated, even unfounded, that we are, perhaps, looking in the wrong place, basing our concerns on the decline of old solidarities rather than being alert to the possibility of new forms of social cohesion? Are friendships simply 'shards of community', 'pieces of jetsam afloat on the seas of economic and political egoism', or 'one of the main sites of activity giving life meaning'?

In this chapter we explore debates about the nature and quality of social life, citing the critical analyses of commentators who have drawn mainly pessimistic conclusions about the state of society, before going on to review alternative prognoses and examine some of the available evidence. We begin with nineteenth-century thinkers such as de Tocqueville, Durkheim, Tönnies and Simmel, and move on to more recent contributions from Zygmunt Bauman in Britain, and Robert Bellah, Amitai Etzioni, Robert Putnam and Manuel Castells in the United States. These commentators do not, of course, necessarily all agree with each other in detail, but they share a common concern that all is not right with society. Indeed, they believe that there has been something distinctively awry since the beginning of modernity and now, in what is variously described as 'late' or 'post' modernity, some argue that things seem to be getting progressively worse.

Individuals, it is claimed, are not happy; they suffer more from mental ill health; they are less ready to make long and enduring commitments; they are less able or prepared to trust each other. In more extreme analyses they are seen as isolated social atoms, pursing a life of consumer-driven gratification: in a consumer society we are what we buy. Whether as a cause or consequence of this, various indicators are adduced, demonstrating an alleged collapse of family life, civic engagement and communal values.[1]

ON THE NATURE AND ORIGINS OF CURRENT DISCONTENTS

As we shall see, the theme of community lost has 'a long pedigree in our letters'.[2] Much commentary and debate has been prompted by new forms of political organization, for example, the rise of the nation state and the growth of democracy, or by new economic relationships linked to industrialization, the rise of capitalism and, more recently, to post-industrialism. Certainly, throughout the nineteenth and twentieth centuries writers have returned over and over again to the problem of social integration and community, sometimes lamenting the passing of traditional forms of associative life, sometimes wrestling with the impact of new political arrangements on civil society, sometimes fearing for loss of social morality.[3]

For some pessimistic commentators, the notion of 'community lost' is associated with the decline of place-based communities. According to this argument, traditional community was embodied in the pre-modern world, in stable rural communities, where people knew their place in society and social relationships were based on people's position in the family, their sex, age and trade. The growth of the city and increased social and geographical mobility were thought to have disrupted these rural communities and were said to threaten social cohesion. During the first half of the twentieth century, for example, American sociologists, who feared that an urban way of life would undermine traditional ties, began to see community as preserved in local neighbourhoods but threatened by the wider city. For these writers, community was essentially a sense of place, which could only be expressed in relation to small localities.[4] In the middle of the twentieth century, ethnographic studies in Britain and the United States explored the survival of place-based community, identifying examples of tightly knit, cohesive, apparently traditional communities whose continued existence was attributed to their resistance to modernity.[5] More recently, the search for place-based community has continued in newly established estates and housing developments where community is characterized, not as resistance to modernity, but as a sense of shared commitment to the collective common good among people in a particular physical space.[6] The assumption behind some of these studies appears to be that the work situation as a source of common solidarity has given way to the residential situation, but the basis of such an assumption has rarely been confronted openly.

However, the idea of community as necessarily place-based is now being increasingly challenged, especially in the light of apparently ever greater levels of geographical mobility, the process of globalization, and, in particular, the spread of new information technologies. We are told that contemporary postmodern communities are nomadic, emotional, elective and communicative, rather than based on given relationships or tied to physical spaces.[7] The Internet, it is argued, has made possible the establishment of virtual communities and radically reshaped social relations. Some have welcomed this development, arguing that it creates new possibilities for relationships, opening up connections between people who otherwise would have no contact.[8] Where virtual communities exist only online and do not involve any

face-to-face-contact, however, they are not recognized by some writers as communities, in the traditional sense, because they lack most of
the defining characteristics and are based on 'thin', ephemeral, rather
than 'thick', resilient, bonds.[9]

In addition to concerns about the perceived breakup of locally
based communities, fears have also been expressed about a reduction in wider public participation. For example, writing about the
United States in the 1830s, Alexis de Tocqueville argued that, under
democracy, people were focusing on immediate 'little circles' and
neglecting their broader social responsibilities:

> Individualism is a mature and calm feeling, which disposes each member
> of the community to sever himself from the mass of his fellow-creatures;
> and to draw apart with his family and friends; so that, after he has thus
> formed a little circle of his own, he willingly leaves society at large to
> itself.[10]

De Tocqueville maintained that these 'little circles' arise out of what
he called the 'erroneous judgement' of individuals which 'saps the
virtues of public life'. Ironically and paradoxically, it was the coming of
democracy which encouraged individuals to leave 'society at large to
itself'.

> As social conditions become more equal, the number of persons in-
> creases who, although they are neither rich enough nor powerful enough
> to exercise any great influence over their fellow-creatures, have never-
> theless acquired or retained sufficient education and fortune to satisfy
> their own wants... they acquire the habit of always considering them-
> selves as standing alone and they are apt to imagine that their whole
> destiny is in their own hands.[11]

To early sociologists, the world of personal social relationships – de
Tocqueville's 'little circles' – was an insubstantial form of social glue,
and Auguste Comte, for example, went so far as to proclaim: 'Society
is no more decomposable into individuals than a geometric surface is
into lines, or a line into points.'[12]

These concerns have been echoed more recently by political scientists, who are also troubled about a retreat from wider civic and social
engagement. Robert Putnam, for example, is particularly concerned
about a weakening of what he and others call social capital, a concept we discuss in more detail below. Putnam's fear is that a decline in
social involvement, particularly in formal associational life, is eroding
the quality of America's civil society. In his widely cited work *Bowling Alone*, Putnam supports his case with a very closely documented

account of the decline in memberships of churches, trades unions and a host of voluntary associations in the United States, which has taken place in the last few decades of the twentieth century.

Other critics concerned about the state of community today, such as Amitai Etzioni, place less emphasis on associational memberships but look back to small-town values of early nineteenth-century America and preach the need for people to be members of 'well-integrated communities'. In Etzioni's case, however, he emphasizes that 'communities need not be local or residential. The main features are a web of interpersonal attachments and a shared sense of values.'[13] Etzioni affirms, with much empirical evidence to support him, that people in communities live longer, healthier and happier lives than those who are socially isolated. The fear now is that people have withdrawn yet further into their separate 'little circles' or, in even more extreme analyses, have become individualized atoms.

Changes in the quality of primary, informal social relationships, and a supposed increase in social isolation have concerned lawyers, historians and sociologists throughout the nineteenth and twentieth centuries. A number of conservative nineteenth-century thinkers, for example, were preoccupied by a perceived long-term shift away from what Ferdinand Tönnies called *Gemeinschaft* or 'community' to *Gesellschaft* or 'association'. This shift entailed a change from 'natural' solidarities rooted in family life, folkways and religion, to solidarities where social relations were 'rational', impersonal and shaped by various forms of exchange.[14] Writing in 1908, the German sociologist Georg Simmel, who was evidently fascinated by the constituents of communal life such as friendship, dependence, confidence and loyalty, was nevertheless concerned that there had been a fall-off in the quality of friendship as people became more differentiated from each other.

> Modern man, possibly, has too much to hide to sustain a friendship in the ancient sense... The modern way of feeling tends more heavily toward differentiated friendships, which cover only one side of the personality, without playing into other aspects of it.[15]

Concerns about a perceived deterioration in social relations, problems of isolation, loneliness, unhappiness and fleeting, transient ties, remain to this day. In the middle of the twentieth century, for example, David Riesman and his colleagues published *The Lonely Crowd*[16] and, twenty years later, Philip Slater published *The Pursuit of Loneliness*, claiming that

> ...Americans attempt to minimize, circumvent, or deny the interdependence upon which all human societies are based. We seek a private house, a private means of transportation, a private garden, a private laundry, self-service stores, and do-it-yourself skills of every kind. An enormous technology seems to have set itself the task of making it unnecessary for one human being to ask anything of another in the course of going about his daily business... We seek more and more privacy, and feel more and more alienated and lonely when we get it...[17]

> Americans thus find themselves in a vicious circle, in which their extra familial relationships are increasingly arduous, competitive, trivial, and irksome, in part as a result of efforts to avoid or minimize potentially irksome or competitive relationships.[18]

In 1978, Christopher Lasch wrote of a 'culture of narcissism',[19] and others such as Robert Bellah and his associates wrote in *Habits of the Heart* that 'our problems today are not just political, they are moral and have to do with the meaning of life'.[20] Robert Lane has used statistics on mental ill health and survey results reporting decreasing levels of personal satisfaction to suggest that, in the United States at least, there has been a serious loss of happiness through the second half of the twentieth century.[21] In 2005 it has been reported that about one in five Americans now suffers from a diagnosable mental disorder. The National Institute of Mental Health estimates that more than thirteen percent of Americans – over nineteen million people between the ages of 18 and 54 – suffer from an anxiety disorder.[22]

Postmodernist writers have added their voices to the chorus of gloom, seeing people as corks on the tides of social change, bobbing about helplessly in the face of broader social and economic forces such as globalization or the information society. Zygmunt Bauman, for example, maintains that the contemporary '*Homo oeconomicus* and *homo consumens* are men and women *without social bonds*'.[23] Other people are seen as objects of consumption, who are judged by the amount of pleasure they are likely to offer in value-for-money terms. There has been a crumbling away of the skills of sociability. In his polemic on 'liquid love', Bauman maintains

> Much... has happened on the road to liquid modern individualised society that has made long-term commitments thin on the ground, long-term engagement a rare expectation, and the obligation of mutual assistance 'come what may' a prospect that is neither realistic nor viewed as worthy of great effort.[24]

Bauman, however, does not have much patience with those who be-moan the loss of community, regarding this is as a search for some kind of security blanket, a hankering after some mythical or utopian state. Delanty, on the other hand, maintains that the notion of community is still relevant today, even though it may no longer refer to institutional or place-based attachments:

> ... the search for community cannot be seen only as a backward-looking rejection of modernity, a hopelessly nostalgic plea for the recovery of something lost; it is an expression of very modern values and of a condi-tion that is central to the experience of life today, which we may call the experience of communicative belonging in an insecure world.[25]

THE CORRODING EFFECTS OF INDIVIDUALIZATION?

Running through these debates about the nature and quality of social life are two rather separate concerns, which are often conflated. The first concern is that *social connections are taking place at the wrong level or at only one level,* that of immediate personal social relation-ships. Although there may still be informal personal interaction be-tween family, friends, colleagues and close neighbours, this does not appear to connect to wider civic engagement. People are said to with-draw into private worlds and turn their backs on communal or col-lective activity, there is widespread political apathy with few people bothering to vote and a weakening of old solidarities as membership of voluntary associations, such as friendly societies and trades unions, continues to fall.

A second concern is that *the quality of social relationships has deteri-orated and that social connections of all kinds are weakening.* Even the immediate micro-social world of personal relationships has collapsed and all we are left with are transient, casual, self-interested ties and widespread social isolation. People are said to be lonely, to lack trust and suffer various forms of mental ill health. The couch potato, sitting alone watching television, snacking on junk food, is an iconic image of our time.

Both these concerns, however, rest on a more fundamental cri-tique of contemporary society, namely, the growth of what Bellah and his colleagues call ontological individualism, or the idea that the individual is the only form of reality. More recently, sociologists have added the notion of 'individualization' to describe the complex processes in contemporary market capitalism and cultural life that lead to such an emphasis on the individual. For writers like Christopher Lasch, individualism is a manifestation of narcissism in which individual autonomy and creativity are paramount and the individual self is expressed and sustained through patterns of consumption and lifestyle choices.[26] Anthony Giddens, on the other hand, focuses on individual empowerment; through 'reflexivity', a process of self-monitoring, individuals constantly and iteratively shape and amend their life projects.[27]

It is feared that this overwhelming focus on the individual undermines the essential forms of social obligation that are necessary for the development of a 'morally coherent life'.[28] The social supports of collective action have been destroyed and individuals retreat into self-absorbed consumerism.[29] Interestingly, over the past decade, the rhetoric of Labour Party politicians in Britain has changed, shifting from a more collective sounding vocabulary such as 'the working class' to individual 'customers', 'clients' and, above all, 'consumers'. Even at the level of personal relationships, it is argued that individual choice has developed to such a degree that some have questioned whether, for example, the family is 'just another lifestyle choice'.[30]

Part of the condition of late modernity, as seen by commentators such as Zygmunt Bauman or Amitai Etzioni, is that people do not take on responsibilities, relationships and commitments which might curtail their individual freedom. Rather than engage with problematic commitments, perhaps at much personal trouble and inconvenience, the new reflexive self recognizes that it is 'time to move on'. If mothers in a previous generation accepted that 'once you've made your bed you've got to lie in it', their sons and daughters today might simply prefer to leave it. Tracey Emin's unmade bed, an icon of conceptual art, famously exhibited at the Royal Academy in London, could be seen as a powerful contemporary metaphor.

This emphasis on the individual and the widespread prevalence of market mechanisms is coupled with the idea that the individual making rational choices is somehow more free than the rule-bound, sanction-ridden, societally constructed member of so-called traditional societies. Yet, according to some, this freedom may be a wolf in sheep's clothing. Zygmunt Bauman, in his book *Liquid Modernity*, is particularly concerned to emphasize the way society has created more and more choices, and situations where choices have to be made.[31] 'I am what I choose' becomes the mantra of the self-reflexive individual. Yet this individualization is a fate, not a choice: in the land of individual freedom of choice the option to escape individualization and to refuse to participate in the individualizing game is emphatically *not* on the agenda... [The] 'individualized' individual... is a human being who has no choice but to act as if the individuation had been attained.[32]

The consequence of this, according to Bauman, is the 'corrosion and slow disintegration of citizenship'.[33]

This is a very strong argument. Individualization takes place not because individuals necessarily prefer to make choices and reject constraints and obligations, but rather because they have no choice but to make choices. Bauman's prose and style are nothing if not apocalyptic: not only are things bad, they are bound to stay this way; there is no obvious panacea or solution to the troubles created by an unstoppable and irreversible process of individualization. The chorus of gloom has indeed become so deafening we can hardly hear.

MAKING SENSE OF THE EVIDENCE: A HISTORICAL PERSPECTIVE

So what are we to believe about the nature of social change? To what extent are fears about the loss of community justified, or based on a myth of a past golden age? At each stage, it seems there have been alternative interpretations, or other voices, which, somehow, have not been heard as loudly. For example, despite his fears about the neglect of 'society at large',[34] de Tocqueville did not propose that this neglect necessarily led to social isolation. He acknowledged that Americans could be strongly embedded in face-to-face relations and that these informal personal relations could help foster a wider sense of commitment:

> ... to each the love and respect of the population which surrounds you, a long succession of little services rendered and of obscure good deeds – a constant habit of kindness and an established reputation for disinterestedness – will be required. Local freedom, then, which leads a great number of citizens to value the affection of their kindred, perpetually brings men together, and forces them to help one another, in spite of the propensities which sever them.[35]

Similarly, Karl Marx, who was concerned about the way that large-scale reorganization of the means of production had created new types of exploitation, nevertheless optimistically believed that new collective solidarities would emerge from a developing class consciousness, and Engels recognized that home ownership among the working class could increase local community bonds. Durkheim challenged Tönnies's view of *Gesellschaft*, claiming that people were bound in more cooperative and flexible ways in modern society, giving greater personal freedom.[36] More recently, others have also challenged the seemingly endless catalogue of contemporary woes. Herbert Gans, for example, has criticized the pessimistic interpretations of many of his sociological colleagues with a spirited and insightful defence of middle American individualism. He remarks that 'people continue to structure their lives around the family and a variety of informal groups in a pattern I call micro-social, which has changed remarkably little over time'.[37]

Despite cautious or dissenting voices, comparisons with some previous better, happier condition continue to be made. It seems that beliefs about an idyllic rustic community are deeply embedded in our culture. Raymond Williams argues that the folk ideal of a rustic pastoral, which goes back to the Garden of Eden fable, has long been part of the world's poetic tradition. The problem is that sometime in the late seventeenth or early eighteenth century it was somehow offered as a description, and thence an idealization, of actual English country life and its social and economic relations.[38] It is perhaps indicative that classical European sociology has its roots in the period of high Romanticism, when the literary transformation of the pastoral idyll was taking place.[39]

Furthermore, those historians who were most likely to have influenced nineteenth-century social scientists were typically constitutional or political historians, and such economic and social historians as there were looked to the broad sweep. The enormous expansion of the new social history over the past thirty years, however, with its painstaking analysis of local documentary and statistical sources, has dramatically changed our understanding of everyday life in former times, and enabled us to question some of the assumptions which underlie fears about the loss of traditional community.

For example, the idea that, in the past, social life was rooted in stable geographical localities may have been overemphasized. It is very easy to forget how much geographical mobility has been the norm in Britain from well before the Act of Union. Men who voluntarily or involuntarily enlisted in the army were moved about the country in internal wars and, later, on the Continent in France and elsewhere. Those who enlisted in the navy perforce travelled much further and there would be few villages where young men were not taken away to the wars. The growth of trade and commerce and the expansion of large urban markets from the sixteenth century in Britain also led to a degree of internal mobility that some might find surprising.

Even the most remote parts of upland Britain were affected by these economic changes as people herded their sheep and cattle to the huge fairs such as that at Barnet, north of London. In his classic essay on London's importance from 1650 to 1750, E. A. Wrigley concluded:

> If it is fair to assume that one adult in six in England in this period had had direct experience of London life, it is probably also fair to assume that this must have acted as a powerful solvent of customs, practices and modes of action of traditional rural England.[40]

For the last thousand years or so Welsh hill farmers drove their flocks over the mountains and into the eastern parts of England. From the remote Lleyn peninsula, drovers, together with sons of rich landowners in search of adventure, made the annual trek from the uplands to the lowland markets. In his study of Tregaron, a seemingly isolated little community, Emrys Jones has documented the movements of population into the town from South Wales and London; for example, in the nineteenth century, Welsh dairymen in London would return to Tregaron to retire.[41] There are still many 'Smithfield Streets' or 'Smithfield Squares' in remote Welsh towns and villages, reflecting the links with the Smithfield meat market in London.[42] The so-called stable working-class communities of South Wales, the Midlands and the industrial north have been made much of by sociologists who were misled into extrapolating the short-term constraints of occupational communities into a permanent feature of the past.

The more detail we have about supposedly isolated rural communities, the more we learn about the range of external social contact. Young people who left home to be apprentices in the towns or to go into service as maids or footmen in 'the big house' often met their partners from other parts of the country under these circumstances and later returned home with someone who was likely to have strong family links some distance away.[43] Poverty in Scotland, Wales and Ireland in the nineteenth century drove many to Canada, Australia, New Zealand and even Patagonia (in the case of the Welsh) to seek new lives. This, and the rapid expansion of the British Empire, provided global links to even the most remote village. A parallel argument could be made in relation to the American 'frontier thesis'.[44]

Despite the strength of the historical record and the detailed knowledge about geographically scattered personal communities in the seventeenth and eighteenth centuries, the idea of the stable, isolated 'real' community dies hard. In *Pride and Prejudice* Jane Austen wittily exposes some unthinking prejudices, for example, when the well-to-do Darcy remarks, 'In a country neighbourhood you move in a very confined and unvarying society'. Mrs Bennet interprets this as some kind of a slight on their social life and sharp words are exchanged. The tactful Elizabeth attempts to lower the temperature by assuring her mother:

> You quite mistook Mr Darcy. He only meant that there were not such a variety of people to be met with in the country as in town, which you must acknowledge to be true.

Mrs Bennet responds in a way which recognizes that her personal community is not simply limited to a geographical space.

> Certainly, my dear, nobody said there were; but as to not meeting with many people in this neighbourhood, I believe there are few neighbourhoods larger. I know we dine with four and twenty families.

Mrs Bennet is certainly not referring to neighbours defined by propinquity. Dining could involve a long drive in a carriage and often an overnight stay. Furthermore, the characters in Jane Austen's novels moved between wintering in London or spending the season in Bath and their country homes. Arguably, this more dispersed lifestyle has been common for the gentry since London became a centre of conspicuous consumption in the sixteenth and seventeenth centuries.[45]

We do not want to labour the point about the scattered nature of the gentry's social networks and the amount of mobility and 'churning' that took place among 'the lower orders'. Nor do we want to imply that there were not long and enduring family links with the land in pre-industrial society. However, even the poorest and most remote areas had connections with a much wider area, thus extending personal communities. As Wellman has concluded:

> It seems that by looking for community in localities and not in networks, analysts had focused on local phenomena and stability, rather than on long distances and mobility.[46]

Similarly, the idea that traditional communities were tied by family obligations and that people had little opportunity for personal choice or self-expression may also be open to question. The American historian Steven Ozment has provided an enviably clear account of what he describes as 'the loving family in old Europe', based largely on German sources. He argues that even before 1200 it would be wrong to consider medieval society as an 'emotional desert' and he also draws on church records from the thirteenth and fourteenth centuries to suggest that 'couples found sex pleasurable, eagerly pursued it, pondered its consequences for themselves and their offspring, and discussed contraceptive options'.[47]

In Britain, historians such as Diana O'Hara have also contributed to our understanding of marriage choices in the middle mass of society: the elite and the very poor being most likely to be excluded. Drawing on the records of the ecclesiastical courts in the Canterbury Diocese between 1540 and 1570, O'Hara concludes that 'Clearly, love, choice and individual experience existed in the sixteenth century.'[48] The tensions evident in a period of social change were what brought families to the court in an attempt to constrain wayward daughters. However, what is striking is the confidence with which the young women in question spoke up for themselves. 'I must be ruled by my freends', said Elizabeth Fletcher of Canterbury, 'as well as by myself', while other women equally stubbornly refused to take the their friends' advice.[49] In the case of Turner *versus* Hubbard, Marion Hubbard, who was a servant in the parsonage house of Aldington, was questioned about the promise she had made to a fellow servant Richard Turner. She answered 'In deede, I cannot denye, but I have made [him] a promise, the which I meane faythefully to performe, thoughe all my freendes be ageynote yt, and though manye troobles followed the same'.[50]

Finally, the idea that traditional communities in the past were highly integrated and harmonious has also been challenged. For example, Alan Macfarlane has argued in his highly influential book, *The Origins of English Individualism*, 'however one defined "community" there was relatively little of it in the villages... as far back as the sixteenth century'.[51] Likewise Lawrence Stone has remarked:

> In the 'face-to-face society' of the traditional village, whose virtues are often praised in this more impersonal and mobile world of the twentieth century, it was possible for expressions of hatred to reach levels of frequency, intensity and duration which are rarely seen today, except in similar close-knit groups like the Fellows of Oxford and Cambridge Colleges.[52]

Stone goes on to comment that this hostility, based on propinquity in the so-called 'good old days', frequently turned into open violence. This violence was far more likely to be directed outside the family –

in Stone's inimitable phrase, 'The family that slayed together, stayed together'.[53]

Perhaps the most thorough undermining of the myth of a golden age is Raymond Williams's *The Country and the City*, in which the notion of a natural, moral economy is mercilessly debunked. In the world of 'natural' subsistence agriculture, the social order was as hard and as brutal as anything later experienced.

> Even if we exclude the wars and brigandage to which it was commonly subject, the uncountable thousands who grew crops and reared beasts only to be looted and burned and led away with tied wrists, this economy, even at peace, was an order of exploitation of a most thoroughgoing kind.[54]

Williams shows the organic community of 'Merrie England' was always about fifty to seventy years before the time when the writer was bemoaning its loss. Using largely literary sources, Williams moves back from Leavis and Thompson to George Sturt, Thomas Hardy, George Eliot, Crabbe, Goldsmith, Thomas More, Langland's *Piers Plowman*, back beyond the Black Death to the Norman and Saxon invasions: 'where indeed shall we go, before the escalator stops?'[55]

MAKING SENSE OF THE EVIDENCE: A CONTEMPORARY VIEW

Turning to the present, what sources can we draw on to help us understand the nature of social life today? Are we less responsible about our commitments? Are we indeed uncaring, selfish, narcissistic and atomized, living vicariously through television? In Britain, and probably in most modern Western societies, there is a large amount of statistical material on the family and households on which one could draw: for example, the decennial census, the General Household Survey, the Labour Force Survey and many other studies funded by the Government in association with its policy objectives.[56] *Social Trends* appears annually, and an academic volume such as *Changing Britain: Families and Households in the 1990s* provides a good sample of recent academic research.[57]

Sources such as these inform us, for example, that the number of marriages has fallen in the last thirty years while the divorce rate has risen.[58] In the meantime the proportion of women cohabiting has increased dramatically.[59] Clearly, unmarried couples living together is no longer taboo but almost the norm. In 1992, for example, 72% of all newly formed couples were cohabiting rather than legally married.[60]

In 1996 there were 1.6 million one-parent households, that is, house-holds comprising a mother or father living with a child or children under sixteen years of age but without a spouse or partner.[61] In Eng-land and Wales the proportion of one-person households aged be-tween twenty and forty rose from 10% in 1971 to 20% in 1991; by 2020 more than one in three households will be made up of people living alone.

Clearly, family life and households in Britain are changing, but how are we to read these figures? Statistics like these can be interpreted in many different ways. More lone-person households, for example, as a statistical tendency is not necessarily 'good' nor 'bad'; nevertheless, this pattern of living has been interpreted as an indication of a fun-damental change in modern societies, implying the declining impor-tance of the family.[62] It is said that such changes are leading not to 'new' families but rather to 'non-families'. On the other hand, if families are supposedly in decline, how do we interpret a statistic from the 2001 UK Census that there are 5.2 million unpaid carers in England and Wales, including over a million providing care for more than fifty hours a week? Clearly, people can use statistics to read social trends optimisti-cally or pessimistically: for example, recent figures show that while the divorce rate in Britain is rising, depression amongst women is falling.[63] Arguments rage wildly, with both sides adducing evidence to show that their position is the correct one: some of the books about families and households written in recent years are highly judgemental, combin-ing statistical and ethnographic evidence with strong moral opinions about how the family 'ought' to be.[64]

In the case of friends, however, far less evidence is available. There is next to no information about friends in official statistics and friends remain largely invisible to public scrutiny.[65] Of course, there are sur-veys that tell us the extent to which our friends have similar charac-teristics to ourselves,[66] or how frequently we see them.[67] For example, the British Social Attitudes (BSA) survey reported that in 1995 about half of those who took part in the survey saw their 'best friend' at least once a week, but that this figure had fallen since 1986.[68] We also have information about the average number of friends people say they have. However, the 2002 BSA survey found widely differing reports, with a quarter of respondents claiming to have fewer than three close friends and another quarter claiming more than eighteen.[69] However, without knowing how people have interpreted the terms 'friend', 'best friend' or 'close friend' in different studies, it is difficult to interpret statistics of this kind. For example, the same BSA report informed us that eight in ten people had a best friend, but one in six claimed not to have a best friend at all.

It seems that much of our knowledge of friendship patterns in Britain is based on hearsay and anecdote, some of which is actually contradictory. We are told, for example, that the north of England is 'friendlier' than the south; 'real' friendship is a thing of the past, as today people simply collect fleeting, address book friends; only now are men able to have close, confiding friends as they are more prepared to recognize their feelings and emotional weaknesses; only women know how to be real friends; as women get more involved in the male-dominated world of work, so their capacity to make true, deep friendships evaporates; people are afraid to make friends at work as collective collegiality gives way to individual mistrust; the workplace is the best context for people to find and make new friends. And so on. While some of these suggestions are based on relatively sound evidence, others are merely anecdotal, but the muddle between the two confuses people.[70]

On the question of the impact of new communication technologies, recent surveys appear to show that early fears that ephemeral virtual communities would replace those based on family, friends and neighbourhoods are unfounded. There has not been a mass retreat from face-to-face sociability, and it seems that the Internet is mainly used to complement and sustain existing relationships, rather than creating entirely new personal networks.[71] For example, a British study has found that people who spend more time on the Internet also spend more time socializing, concluding that using the Internet

> makes going out more efficient – potentially at least, more pleasant, and more sociable, better focussed on our wants and preferences. And so 'at the margin', as economists say, we might be prompted to do more of it.[72]

Similarly, a Canadian study of a newly built estate, where all the houses were equipped with a series of advanced communication technologies, supplied across a broadband high-speed local network, also supports the view that email complements rather than supplants other forms of sociability. The study compared the social contacts of residents who had signed up for free access to the network and those who had not. After an initial dip while people established themselves, those who were freely connected to the local system reported the same or higher levels of social contact and exchange of support with friends and family after moving. Not only that, counter-intuitively, the wired residents got to know people in a much wider area of the local estate than the non-wired residents, whereas it might have been assumed that their social contacts would be less place-based. The authors concluded that some of their findings were contrary to expectations:

> On average, most North Americans [sic] have few strong ties at the neighbourhood level. Personal communities consist of networks of far-flung kinship, workplace and interest group relations. They are not place-based communities of geography. Yet in Netville, the local computer network facilitated the formation of local ties of various strengths.[73]

Recent innovative research on the use of home telephones, mobile phones and text messaging is particularly illuminating. A study by Christian Licoppe in France examines the impact on patterns of communication of a technology that enables people to engage their body, and the terminal that is its extension, at anytime from almost anywhere in a few seconds.[74] Licoppe's analysis of SMS users indicated that they were often contacting the people whom they saw the most:

> With close friends, the density of the experience shared in an intense and lasting relationship allows the use of codes, allusions, and veiled references, so that this kind of interaction is hardly relevant for an outsider.[75]

Licoppe also notes that the average duration of conversations on a domestic telephone is tending to shrink. A move to more frequent, short calls would suggest that communication is becoming more focused on a kind of continued presence. This, to some extent, modifies earlier research which showed that the more geographical distance there is between people the longer (on average) their telephone conversations are and the longer the interval between their calls will be. The very rapid growth of the use of mobile phones has led to 'reassurance' communication. 'Calling on a mobile phone becomes an act of domestic devotion in which reassurance is experienced as much in the mind as in the body'.[76] The new mode of communication allows, as it were, the possibility 'of multiplying small communication gestures to maintain presence over a distance'.[77]

Finally, the issue of civic participation and fears about the perceived erosion of social capital are rather more difficult to address. Whereas Robert Putnam demonstrates a steady decline in membership of formal associations in America,[78] Peter Hall claims overall levels of participation in Britain are high, but demonstrates that they vary considerably across different social classes and age groups.[79] The British Social Attitudes Survey, for example, shows that political participation has not uniformly declined. In 1986, 34% of people said they had signed a petition; this rose to 53% in 1991 and then fell to 42% in 2000. Over the same period the proportion of people who had gone on a protest or demonstration steadily increased to 10% in 2000.[80]

However, there are far more fundamental problems with diagnosing the state of social capital than simply attempting to reconcile conflicting figures about public participation. Despite its adoption within a number of disciplines and among policy makers around the world, the concept of social capital is extremely contentious. For example, if, as appears to be argued, social capital is a kind of social cement, a social resource which resides in relationships and in interaction between individuals, which can be utilized by individuals or communities,[81] which is associated with high social trust, and linked to beneficial social outcomes such as good health or low crime rates, there is still no agreement about how social capital can be measured, nor about how it actually works in practice.[82] Many of the attempts at definition are circular, contradictory or tautological,[83] and the assumptions about a process of direct causation are not clear.[84]

It is perhaps not surprising, then, that there has been considerable scepticism about the emergence of a

> magic ingredient that not only may provide the social glue to solve the age-old Hobbesian problem of order, but also serve as a kind of social ginseng root, energizing and activating the sluggish parts of the social system.[85]

A particular criticism we make in this book is that commentators like Putnam appear to believe that social capital – defined as engagement in voluntary organizations – produces some clear measurable and beneficial outcome for civil society, whereas this is not necessarily the case.[86] Moreover, although Putnam himself acknowledges the importance of informal personal relationships with friends and family, as well as associational memberships, for building social capital, there is a strong implication in his work that the latter are somehow more beneficial. For example, in *Bowling Alone*, Putnam laments the fact that membership of bowling leagues, along with membership of a host of other associations, has declined.[87] Not only this, the cover illustration of his book depicts an individual player literally bowling alone. This is confusing, however, since people are not, of course, playing on their own, but with friends and family: the implication seems to be that this kind of bowling is less valuable than bowling with a club or league.

So, despite recognizing the importance of *schmoozers* (a Yiddish term referring to those who interact socially, whose easy informal conversation involves a form of communion), in practice, Putnam appears to attach greater significance to the world of *machers*, a world where men and women are active in local clubs and organizations.

FOCUSING ON MICRO-SOCIAL WORLDS AND INFORMAL PERSONAL RELATIONSHIPS

It is the relative neglect of the world of schmoozing we wish to address in this book. Consequently, in attempting to address some of the fears about the decline of community and the fragmentation of social bonds today, we have deliberately focused on the level of informal personal relationships and micro-social worlds, rather than the formal level of organizational memberships and civic participation. We have done so for a number of reasons. Firstly, part of the debate about the quality of social life today points to the alleged lack of commitment and trust in personal relations, and to their supposed transience. This, we believe, is an empirical rather than a rhetorical question, which can only be answered by looking in detail at actual flesh-and-blood relationships.

Secondly, in the light of the rapid growth of depression and mental health problems,[88] we were impressed by evidence suggesting that social capital at the level of informal personal relationships can play a key role in preventing or reducing health problems of various kinds. Indeed, recent research in psychoneuroimmunology has emphasized the crucial importance of informal ties for mental health and well-being.[89] In a very stimulating essay on friendship, consumerism and happiness, Robert E. Lane has remarked:

> The absence of friends and family solidarity is the crucial explanatory variable for depression, just as their presence is a central explanatory factor for happiness.[90]

Interestingly, a study of the relationship between social capital and health carried out in Britain lends support to the importance of micro-social worlds for our health, concluding that social trust in areas with higher health levels is to be found in small-scale groups of friends, relatives and neighbours.[91] The authors concluded that these small-scale local groupings, reminiscent of de Tocqueville's little circles, 'formed the bulk of the social capital available to informants in our wards'.[92]

Further confirmation of the relevance of the micro-social level, and the importance of social support, can be found, for example, in data from a large-scale, longitudinal survey carried out in Britain. The British Household Panel Study uses a variety of measures of social capital, including a number of questions about social support[93] and the data clearly show that those with low social support were far more likely to report common mental illness.[94] Further analysis revealed that low social support not only increased the probability of the onset of common mental illness but also decreased the probability of recovery.[95]

It seems that the same holds true for physical health. For example, the author of a classic study carried out in 1979 concluded that 'Heart disease, stroke, cancer and all other causes of death show increased risks with isolation'.[96] Furthermore, it has been argued that it is the diversity of ties (for example, with family, friends, workmates, close neighbours, associates and so on), rather than simply their number, which is a key factor in retaining good health.[97] In 1997, a distinguished group of American epidemiologists dramatically concluded that

> the relative risk for mortality among those with less diverse networks is comparable in magnitude to the relationship between smoking and mortality from all causes.[98]

What is not clear, however, is how the relationship between social support and health actually works in practice.[99] It is increasingly recognized that it is not necessarily the actual support provided by members of a person's micro-social world that is so important but the perceived support, since perceived support may act as a buffer against stress. People need to believe that they are cared for and loved, that they are esteemed and valued and that they belong to a network of communication and mutual obligation.[100] Such knowledge, of course, is not new: Epicurus (341–270 B.C.) noted that 'It is not so much our friends' help that helps us as is the confident knowledge that they will help us'. Of course, in popular perception the importance of friends may sometimes be overstated; for example, an article in *Woman's Journal* (Christmas–New Year, 1997–1998) was headed, 'Your friends can save your life.' Nevertheless, there is some basis to such a claim.

An attempt to synthesize the state of knowledge linking social support and psychological mechanisms was published in 1996. The authors concluded that, although an association between social support and better cardiovascular function appears to hold across a variety of cultural contexts worldwide, the nature and quality of particular social relationships needed more exploration in order to unpack the concept of social support in more detail, and to throw light on how the association with health actually works.[101] These and other findings underscore the crucial importance of distinguishing the actual functions played by family and friends.

Thirdly, the makeup and resilience of people's micro-social worlds are also of considerable interest in the policy arena. Politicians, policy makers, social workers, church leaders and a host of social commentators are keen to know more about the nature and quality of our informal personal relationships and about social capital at this level.[102] Policy advisers have recognized the considerable influence of micro-social worlds, of family and friends, in people's lives. For example, in November 2003 the UK government's Strategy Unit published its *Strategic Audit: Discussion Document*, which usefully brought together recent empirical findings on, among other topics, 'Britain as a community'. One striking finding refers to responses to a question seeking to discover what most influenced people on social and environmental issues and how such influences have changed between 1996 and 2001. It appears that the public is increasingly influenced by friends and family rather than government or other large institutions.[103]

Fourthly, people's informal personal relationships are also a subject of fascination among the wider general public. Hardly a week goes by without some newspaper or magazine article holding forth about the state of the modern family, or the fate of modern friendships, and we were keen to enable people to look more critically at some of the pessimistic portrayals of social life today. In any case, it seems we all love gossip. Those who watch television series such as EastEnders, Friends, Frazier or Neighbours get a vicarious satisfaction from sharing the day-to-day vicissitudes of life with their characters. People are also intrigued by the world of the rich and famous and the current obsession with the so-called private lives of celebrities is evident from the circulation figures for magazines such as *Hello!* and *OK!*. Others, who might dismiss these as populist trivia, still read with avid interest the diaries of, say, Samuel Pepys or Alan Clark, or the personal letters of Ronald Reagan, which reveal with explicit directness the details of their authors' intimate lives. This curiosity about other people's private and personal worlds seems widespread in modern societies.

Not only do we want to know how others live, we like to compare our lives to theirs. We want to know whether the way we live now is distinctively different from how it was in the past, or in other parts of the world, or within diverse contemporary subcultures in our own society. Tales of the large Edwardian country house with its upstairs and below stairs ways of life are paralleled today with genuine or fictitious accounts of footballers' wives – and other real or imagined celebrities – contrasted with similar accounts of single mothers on so-called sink estates or journalists living incognito and with considerable difficulty on the national minimum wage. When we look to the past we find that historians have become exceptionally skilled at reconstructing the minutiae of everyday life, whether in a medieval French village such as *Montaillou*, or in an eighteenth-century English village, *Myddle*, in Shropshire.[104] In the latter study, a perceptive clergyman recorded the various social groupings and activities of his parishioners, moving systematically, pew by pew, through his congregation. When we look to other cultures we find that anthropologists provide us with structured gossip from faraway places which most of us would otherwise never penetrate. Through the work of historians and anthropologists, we can respond to the world we have lost in our own country, and to other worlds that are currently being lost as development and modernity flow over the most remote tribal or peasant communities destroying their distinctive cultures. We enjoy recognizing both the parallels and the differences between ourselves and people of other cultures and in other times. Sharing vicariously common woes and excitements across time and space helps us reaffirm our common humanity, but also makes us more aware of the many different forms contemporary community can take.

Finally, focusing at the level of family and friends also chimes well with twenty-first century conceptions of community as a search for identity and belonging in an insecure world, as something found in personal networks, involving cross-cutting commitments, rather than simply in institutional or place-based allegiances.

> The suggestion is that postmodern community is to be found in forms of sociation sustained in everyday life, in forms of consumption and in informal friendship networks.[105]

Interestingly, while the role of family in social cohesion has been acknowledged for centuries, friendship as a form of social glue has been given far less attention. In our study of people's micro-social worlds, we have attempted to explore Gerard Delanty's recent speculation that

Friendship may thus be seen as a flexible and de-territorial kind of community that can be mobilised easily depending on circumstances, and can exist on 'thick' and 'thin' levels, for friendship comes in many forms.[106]

CONCLUDING REMARKS

Our review of some of the issues, facts and fallacies surrounding society's imputed malaise cannot be in any way definitive: to give full justice to the arguments we have mentioned would require another book. Furthermore, although the assertions and conjectures of social prophets, moral guardians and other commentators must, in principle, be open to the possibility of refutation, our review of some of the evidence available simply demonstrates how difficult it is to support or to refute such claims. Ethnographers, social statisticians and the new social historians have, in their different ways, contributed to the debate, as have the different disciplinary perspectives referred to in the next chapter. Our own contribution will be judged on the quality of the research and the evidence we present throughout this book. Once they have learned of our method, followed the development of our analytical framework, and discovered more about the micro-social worlds of our participants, readers will then be in a better position make this judgement.

CHAPTER TWO

Capturing Personal Communities

> Community life can be understood as the life people lead in dense, multiplex, relatively autonomous networks of social relationships. Community life, thus, is not a place, or simply a small-scale population aggregate, but a mode of relating, variable in extent. Though communities may be larger than the immediate personal networks of individuals, they can in principle be understood by an extension of the same lifeworld terms.
>
> — Calhoun

As we argued in chapter 1, exploring empirically the complex web of informal personal relationships in which people are embedded can, we believe, make a contribution to some of the longstanding and intransigent debates about the state of society today. Before describing the diversity of people's micro-social worlds, however, and the place of friends and family within them, we discuss some of key ideas which have shaped our study, propose an alternative way of thinking about *given* and *chosen* ties, and introduce the notion of a personal community.

Some readers may be curious to compare their own private social worlds with those presented in this book; some may even wish to carry out a similar study. Our aim, therefore, is to provide a clear road map for others to follow, whether out of personal or professional interest. Consequently, in this chapter we give a brief description of the way we captured people's personal communities; a much fuller account is given in the appendix.[1] Finally, we present some initial findings about their composition to illustrate the range of personal communities we encountered in our research.

Meanings and Definitions

Exploring the composition of people's micro-social worlds involves a number of difficult challenges, but there is much we can learn from other studies and fields. We cannot emphasize too strongly, however, that our discussion here is not intended as a comprehensive review of the literature on family and friends (even from a sociological perspective – our own particular discipline – since this is not the place, and nor is there space), but rather a brief resumé of some of the issues we have had to address in developing our approach.

The Meaning of Friend *and* Family

A major problem when studying informal personal relationships, and, in particular, people's relationships with their friends and family, is establishing what is understood by these terms. At first glance this might seem straightforward with regard to kin, since, in Britain at least, terms such as brother, sister, mother, father, son, daughter, cousin and so on are generally understood to delineate particular relationships. But, of course, just knowing the type of family connection tells us nothing about the quality of the individual tie. Siblings, for example, can be the closest possible soulmates, or they can be indifferent to each other, or even estranged. Cousins may be considered good friends, or distant relatives whose names, and existence, are sometimes forgotten.

With friends, establishing the meaning of the term is even more difficult. Although the word 'friend' appears to have a common-sense meaning, in practice, there is no agreement about precisely what is meant or how the term should be used.[2] Some people describe their spouse or partner as a friend. Some reserve the word 'friend' for a select group of individuals, while others use the term in an expansive way to include all those whom they know well enough to call by their first name. Without a common reference point, what does it tell us if we discover that some people have three friends while others have thirty? How can we make sense of headlines that inform us about the average number of close friends people have nowadays when we do not know how the term 'close friend' is being used?[3] While writing this book we have been approached by journalists and presenters of radio programmes who are pursuing a specific line and require some illustrative soundbites about friendship today. Very often, however, we have found ourselves simply talking past each other because the word 'friend' is being used in so many different ways.

People talk about friends without saying what they mean, and we only have a single term to describe a variety of relationships. Even when people offer some qualifying adjectives, these are also open to a range of meanings. What is a 'best friend'? Does everyone have one? Do they all mean the same thing? Some people make a distinction between a friend and an acquaintance but do we agree on what the nature of the distinction might be? One person's choice of adjective to describe a particular set of qualities and attributes may not coincide with that of another.

The subject of friendship, and, in particular, the notion that friendship can take different forms, has exercised the minds of philosophers and theologians such as Plato and Aristotle, Cicero, Seneca, Thomas Aquinas, Kant and Emerson, and there is much to learn from this rich tradition. Perhaps the most famous exposition on friendship is that by Aristotle, who distinguished between 'friends of utility', who help each other and provide practical support in much the same way as family do, 'friends of pleasure', who share activities and enjoy each other's company, and 'friends of virtue', who know us as we really are. According to Aristotle, friends of virtue are ultimately friends of communication: our friends who stimulate hope and invite change are concerned with deep understanding and knowing. Each grows and flourishes because of the other in a spirit of mutual awareness. This deep communicative friendship is qualitatively different from friendships of utility and pleasure, which involve far less intimacy and trust.[4] We do not have a separate word in English for this form of friendship, but there is a Russian word, *droog*, that has connotations of Aristotle's third type of friend.

In making a clear distinction between different kinds of friendship, Aristotle's work still illuminates. Psychologists have also paid a great deal of attention to the question, 'what is a friend?', identifying a number of key dimensions and qualities. For example, friendship has been characterized as a relationship which involves participation between equals who enjoy each other's company, who help and support one another, who respect and accept the other, feeling free to be themselves in the other's company, and who trust each other, sharing intimate confidences. These characteristics, however, have often been described in relation to a generalized or archetypal notion of friendship, rather than necessarily applied to actual flesh-and-blood relationships.[5]

Equally, the nature of family ties has also been the subject of much debate. Anthropologists, for example, have been questioning the meaning of kinship and the way kinship has been conceptualized and researched in the past. A recent collection of essays describes how, from the early 1970s, anthropologists have been cautious and sceptical about the study of kinship, a topic perceived by outsiders as the core of their discipline.[6] This scepticism relates, in part, to the fixed concept of kinship – reflected in rigid genealogical diagrams – based on the assumption that biological relatedness was of paramount importance in people's understanding of kinship and that kinship was taken to be the social recognition of such biological links. Yet relatedness can be as strongly social or cultural as biological, and anthropologists have long been aware that not all cultures recognized, for example, that sexual procreation was necessarily central to their local idiom of relatedness. Recognition of such ethnocentric assumptions has led some anthropologists to the rather stark conclusion that 'there is no such thing as kinship'.[7]

Perhaps the most perceptive writer on the ambiguities of kinship is Marilyn Strathern, whose book *After Nature* did much to bring these issues to a wider audience.[8] Not only does she explore the implications of reproductive technology and surrogate mothering, but she also recognizes the interrelationships between cultural and biological 'closeness'. In a study of 'Alltown' in Lancashire, she and Jeanette Edwards note the following:

> 'Closeness' summons affective ties, the obligations and duties such ties entail, and the warmth and mutual care with which relationships are sustained... 'Closeness' also points to distance and 'distant relatives' are those with whom interaction is infrequent, with whom obligations are at a minimum and with whom confidences are unlikely to be shared. From this perspective, close relatives can become distant ones.[9]

This new focus on relatedness by anthropologists means that the core aspects of affection, shared sustenance and nurturing may be ranked on a continuum to show degrees of relatedness, depending on the presence or absence of particular elements.

Meanings and Forms of Relationships over Time: The Importance of Historical and Social Contexts

In addition to the problem that there are different kinds of friendship and that family is not an unambiguous concept, there is also the

question of whether the meanings of particular categories of personal
relationships are widely shared or remain stable over time. Historians, for example, are especially alive to the problem of what the terms
friend and family really mean in particular contexts and alert us to
the dangers of reading the past in an oversimplified way. Although we
may initially associate history with the public rather than the private
sphere, the growth of interest in detailed documentation of everyday life, and the reassessment of such sources as letters and personal
diaries, have enabled us to learn much more about the meaning and
significance of family and friends in the context of individual lives. For
example, there is a very full account of friendship in medieval times in
Friendship and Community: The Monastic Experience 350–1250, where
the author even claims that the twelfth century was 'the age of friends'
(though the book focuses on male monastic scholars and cannot tell
us about women's friendships in the early modern period).[10] Analysis
of diaries, such as those of the clergyman Ralph Josselyn in the early
seventeenth century,[11] and of Thomas Turner, a Sussex shopkeeper,
in the eighteenth,[12] provides us with a meticulous account of people's
personal social worlds.

What is intriguing about these historical studies, and of immense
importance in contemporary explorations of people's private social
worlds, is the way in which the terms 'family' and 'friend' were used.
It seems that 'friend' could also cover kin and, conversely, that 'family'
could encompass both kin and non-kin ties. For example, Ralph Josselyn regarded his servants as members of his family, and, speaking of
a farm of 800 acres, John Arbuthnot wrote in 1773:

> If the tract is in the hands of one man, his family will consist of himself, a
> wife, three children, twelve servants, and ten labourers, each with a wife
> and three children.[13]

Apart from different historical meanings of 'family' and 'friend', there
are also debates about the extent to which different types of personal
relationship might be found amongst all sectors of society, at different times, or in different cultures. Through early ethnographic studies
of particular geographical communities[14] and more recent surveys of
family networks[15], sociologists have investigated patterns of family life
in different social classes and ethnic groups, exploring the effects of
geographical mobility, changes in gender relations, the greater representation of women in the workforce, later marriage, the rise in
cohabitation and divorce, and the increasing number of stepfamilies.[16]

Debates have revolved around the extent to which the nuclear family consisting of parents and their children has universally replaced the extended family in importance, or whether the nuclear family itself has been displaced by new varieties of family life, or, indeed, whether there has been a breakdown of families altogether.[17] For example, with lone parents being statistically much more widespread, some argue there has been a strengthening of the blood family, in particular the link between mothers and grandmothers, at the expense of affinal links.

From the point of view of this book, we are particularly interested in Peter Willmott's idea that there are several types of kinship system in Britain today. From his own research, Willmott identified: local extended families, where most members live together or in the same neighbourhood; dispersed extended families, where members maintain contact over considerable geographical distances; dispersed kinship networks, where contact is mainly with members of the nuclear family, some of whom do not live near each other; and residual kinship networks, where there is little direct contact with family members other than between those living in the same household.[18] Increasing ethnic and cultural diversity in Britain since the time Willmott was writing, would suggest that patterns of kinship are likely to be even more varied today.

Turning to friends, some writers have argued that different kinds of friendship are not universally found throughout society. Philosophers, for example, have claimed that not everyone is capable of or should be encouraged to have certain forms of friendship. Aristotle did not just classify friendships but also believed that friendship of virtue was supposedly the highest, truest form. He maintained that virtuous friendship involves a relationship between whole persons and enables people to know themselves and others fully. Our friend, in this context, becomes our 'second self':

> To perceive a friend, therefore, is necessarily in a manner to perceive oneself, and to know a friend is in a manner to know oneself... The excellent person is related to his friend in the same way as he is related to himself, since a friend is another himself.[19]

Cicero also saw this kind of friendship as the finest. Describing it as 'the one good thing', he argued that it

> Sends a ray of good hope into the future, and keeps our hearts from faltering or falling by the wayside. For the man who keeps his eye on a true friend, keeps it, so to speak, on a model of himself. For this reason, friends are together when they are separated, they are rich when they are

poor, strong when they are weak, and – a thing even harder to explain – they live on after they have died. So great is the honor that follows them, so vivid the memory, so poignant the sorrow.[20]

Such virtuous friendships involve a high level of self-awareness and, it would seem, of self-love. Consequently, Aristotle maintained that only the good and virtuous should be encouraged to develop virtuous friendship, because only the good and virtuous should love themselves. Virtuous friendships are also very intense and this raises the question of whether it is possible, if people have them at all, to sustain many relationships of this kind. Aristotle argued that it was not:

> Clearly, you cannot live with many people and distribute yourself among them... It also becomes difficult for many to share each other's enjoyments and distresses as their own, since you are quite likely to find yourself sharing one friend's pleasure and another's grief at the same time... it is impossible to be many people's friend for their virtue and for themselves. We have reason to be satisfied if we can find even a few such friends.[21]

> Those who have many friends and treat everyone as close to them seem to be friends to no one, except in a fellow-citizen's way.[22]

The idea that some people are not capable of developing intimate forms of friendship also has currency in the field of psychoanalysis. Karen Horney, the eminent post-Freudian, wrote in the 1930s about the neurotic need for affection in her classic study *The Neurotic Personality of the Time*.[23] Those with certain kinds of neuroses may be incapable of forming the virtuous form of communicative friendship that has been celebrated since classical times. In the same way that some people are unable to give or to receive unconditional love, so some are simply unable to be close friends. The recognition that people have different psychological capacities to make deep and fulfilling relationships is a commonplace in the field of psychoanalysis. Some psychologists, however, go even further and claim that whole cultures can suffer from a failure to be able to love fully and completely. American culture, for example, has been singled out as being peculiarly dysfunctional. 'In fantasy Americans remain perpetual adolescents, while adult commitments represent the defeat rather than the fulfilment of the quest for identity. People are "trapped" into marriage, work is a loss of freedom, a shameful settling down.'[24] From this perspective Americans are more likely to have an adolescent-type view of friendship; there is a premature closing off of the self and an incapacity to develop into mature adulthood.

The way friendships develop has been the subject of much detailed research. For example, psychologists have attempted to understand the role of attraction in friendship formation,[25] and to demonstrate that competency in developing mature relationships in childhood will bear some significant correlation with adult capacities to make and maintain mature relationships.[26] However, among psychologists themselves there is now some debate about the possible over-reliance of social and developmental psychology on experimental studies using students or schoolchildren, and some writers call for observational studies to be carried out in more natural contexts.[27]

The development of intimate friendships, in particular, has also been examined by modern philosophers. One key idea is the contrast between the 'mirror view' and the 'secrets view' of friendship.[28] Both these approaches assume that central to the trust and intimacy of close friendship is the disclosure of the self: either my self is disclosed in the other or I disclose my self to the other. So, the mirror view is concerned with the degree to which one's own traits are reflected in the friend, and, in this sense, this is close to Aristotle's view of virtuous friendship, whereby in choosing a friend we choose another self. By contrast, in the secrets view of friendship, bonds of trust and intimacy are cemented through acts of self-disclosure (rather than through recognition alone), and the greater the friendship, the more we are prepared to disclose. The mirror view of friendship can perhaps be criticized for being too static and passive, as though we present ourselves ready-made to potential friends, and that simply having virtue or interests in common generates the friendship. The secrets view, on the other hand, emphasizes the development of relationships.

The notion of recognizing or revealing the self in intimate friendships raises the question of whether we can expect to find classical Western models of friendship in non-Western and tribal societies. Aristotle's idea of seeing the friend as 'another self' would not have much meaning if the idea of having an autonomous self is problematic. For example, the anthropologist Marilyn Strathern explores the question of whether the people of Melanesia can be held to have an autonomous self.[29] She argues that Melanesian selves are constituted through social relations – there is no individual sense of self prior to this, consequently, there is, as it were, no internal source for the creation of personal, spontaneous affection that is characteristic of some forms of Western friendship. Melanesians will, of course, have certain affective relationships but they would be unlikely to think of these relationships in terms of classical notions of friendship. Rather they would speak about them in terms of a common situation or structure of relationship that encompasses the people involved.

For anthropologists, then, the critical issue seems to be that the autonomous reflexive self is not universal across all cultures. Of course, these cultures can change as a result of modernization, globalization, and with the development of the impersonal mechanisms of the capitalist market. Some might even argue that the spread of Western ideas of friendship are part and parcel of political and economic development.[30]

The notion of differing individual capacities for friendship, however, has not generally been of interest to sociologists, who, instead, have turned their attention to the way friendship varies with age, class, stage in the life-course, religion, ethnicity, gender and so on. The fundamental assumption is that friendship is socially patterned and must be understood in context. Ties of friendship are inherently social rather than personal and friendship is not a fixed, universal relationship, but takes its shape and form from the specific context in which it develops. For example, Allan Silver has claimed that a new form of friendship appeared during the Enlightenment in the eighteenth century in the context of the market-driven economic rationalism of the emerging commercial society. He argues that, prior to that period, friendship was based more on a strict calculation of interest rather than compatibility.[31]

Graham Allan, in a series of books and articles over a period of twenty years or so has done much to clarify and to establish a distinctively sociological approach to friendship. He has recently presented his ideas in a particularly strong form claiming that it is wrong to see friendship as being 'based solely upon individual choice, feelings and commitment. Rather its form and content are inevitably influenced by the circumstances, or context, under which it is constructed.'[32] The implications of this are that if, for example, gender relations change, so too would the pattern and form of friendship. Similarly, the sharper class divisions of interwar Britain would have produced different forms and styles of friendship than is the case today. The same would apply to different work contexts: coal miners' friendships would be different from those of computer programmers; young marrieds' friendships would be different both from what they might have been for earlier age groups and what they may become for themselves when they are old.

Unpacking Commitment and Choice

If the terms 'family' and 'friend' do not have shared or stable meanings, then any exploration of contemporary social life must take account of the basis of different kinds of tie, rather than simply rely on categorical labels. Our study, therefore, required a more open-ended approach, one that enabled us to capture the way people experience and talk about their important social relationships. In addition to this, current debates about the supposed transience of modern ties led us to focus on issues of choice and commitment.

Consequently, the first distinction we make refers to the degree to which relationships are (or are perceived to be) *given* or *chosen*. Given ties are essentially ascribed: people are reciprocally related, through blood or marriage in the case of family members, or through mutual roles in the case of contiguous neighbours or immediate work colleagues, for example. With chosen ties, on the other hand, there is no automatic relationship so the bond has to be formed and developed, as most people would recognize in the case of friends. Sometimes, however, given ties can take on an element of choice – for example, a neighbour is also considered a friend. Similarly, chosen ties can acquire an almost given status, such as when a friend is treated as part of the family. We called these ties *given-as-chosen* and *chosen-as-given*, to signify their more complex hybrid nature.

The second dimension refers to the strength of the bond, and, in particular, the distinction between relationships which are high and those which are low in commitment. Highly committed ties may involve strong long-term support, or values in common, or personal confiding, or intimacy. By contrast, ties that lack commitment are usually more casual, involving simple pleasantries, or common interests, or small favours, or simply fun, but they lack intimacy and some may not endure. Taken together, these two dimensions yield a set of distinctive relationships as shown in Figure 2.1. Of course, in practice, actual relationships will vary along a continuum of commitment and do not necessarily fall neatly into high or low categories, but we offer the grid simply as an heuristic device to help unravel the diversity of informal personal ties. Similarly, to do justice to the complexity of actual relationships, we would ideally need to add at least two further dimensions, dealing with the extent to which people like or love each other, and the progress of a relationship over time.

	High commitment	Low commitment
Given	Solid/foundational	Nominal
Given-as-chosen	Bonus	Neglected/abandoned
Chosen-as-given	Adopted	Heart sink
Chosen	Forged	Liquid

Figure 2.1.   Commitment and choice in personal relationships.

Among *solid, foundational* ties (see Figure 2.1), we expect to find immediate family, for example, parents, children and siblings, who enjoy a close bond. Of course, we might also find ambivalent relationships where, despite disliking, possibly even hating, a member of their family, people nevertheless feel a great sense of duty and responsibility. *Nominal* ties are likely to refer to more distant relatives who, for whatever reason, are on the periphery of each other's social world, such as cousins or step-relations whose existence we scarcely register. With *bonus* relationships, given ties become *as chosen*; here we find cases where the special quality of certain given relationships is recognized and, for example, a favourite sibling is seen as more than a brother or sister and assigned the honorary status of friend. By contrast, with *neglected* or *abandoned* ties the element of choice serves to weaken rather than strengthen the relationship (which is still given): here we find relatives who have fallen out because of irreconcilable differences in values or social position, or parents who have lost touch with their children after a messy divorce. The number of people who try to trace their biological parents after being given up for adoption is perhaps an indication of the importance some of us may attach to even the most neglected of family ties.

Adopted ties are highly committed chosen-as-given relationships, such as very close friendships which have taken on an almost family-like status: for example, a friend may also be considered a sister or brother. Also in this category are fictive kin: the unrelated 'uncles' and 'aunts' who may be part of a child's given social world. With *heart sink* ties, on the other hand, the given-like quality of ties is a matter of obligation rather than closeness or familiarity, and here we might find people who feel like family because of a strong sense of duty, for example, the friends you feel 'stuck with'. Adopted and heart sink ties might also refer to people who work with and live in other people's households. In earlier times, service or apprenticeship brought a transference of familial ties,[33] and even today, in certain circles, maids, nannies and au pairs may have a given-like status where the relationship continues long after any formal service role has ceased. *Forged* relationships, on the other hand, are strong chosen ties and this is where we would expect to find close, established, lifelong friendships. Finally, *liquid* ties are likely to be light-hearted, casual friends and acquaintances, or, alternatively, casual sexual partners.

Of course, one could identify, label and elaborate many more types of informal personal relationships, but our purpose here is not to be exhaustive but, simply, to demonstrate that apparently tarring all relationships with the same brush masks rather than displays social reality. Interestingly, in the light of Bauman's thesis, mentioned in the last chapter, only *neglected, abandoned* and *liquid* relationships fit the postmodern prototype, said to be the product of growing individualization, where rampant and irresponsible individuals slip promiscuously between relationships, discarding older models for new ones and being content with fleeting, superficial contacts. The idea that there has been a decisive shift from given to chosen or committed to uncommitted ties is open to empirical question, and is something we address in detail later in the book.

By setting up these different dimensions and categories, however, we now have a more finely grained and complex tool for exploring the inhabitants of people's personal social worlds. This is the first step in a rather complex journey described in the following chapters. We aim to avoid glib generalizations about 'the breakdown of the family' or about people choosing to live in 'families of choice' based on friendship. Rather, our focus is on the content of specific relationships that in any individual's case might include examples from all eight boxes in the diagram. In this way we can begin to examine the nature of commitment in private social worlds today rather than uncritically subscribe to moral panics about its demise.

A Focus on Personal Communities

Finally, when considering the design of our study, we did not want to focus purely at the level of individual relationships but, as the reader may recall, to locate them in the wider set of significant ties in which people are embedded. We needed a way of referring to this collective and adopted the term *personal community*. Barry Wellman has used the term to refer to people's 'intimate and active ties with friends, neighbours and work mates as well as kin', encapsulating precisely the phenomenon we wished to explore.[34]

We realize that some readers may be surprised by our use of the term *personal community*. The juxtaposition of the words 'personal' and 'community' may perplex those who come to the topic with specific notions of community based on shared fate. This shared fate might be geographically circumscribed, as in the case of place-based communities, or socially determined, as would be the case for those collectively involved in primary industries such as agriculture, mining or fishing, or in isolated concentrations of workers in heavy industries. These communities of shared fate remain deep in our consciousness; and it is true that many of the classic community studies carried out by sociologists and social anthropologists in Western societies were based on these kinds of social groupings.[35]

However, social theory has developed in the last thirty-five years in its attempt to understand the conditions of late modernity, and this has led to a shift away from a focus on neighbourhood or occupational bases for a sense of belonging and personal identity to a more complex and individualized approach. Anthony Giddens[36] and Zygmunt Bauman in Britain, or Craig Calhoun and Manuel Castells in America, have been among those most concerned with these issues. Calhoun, for example, maintains that community is 'not a place or simply a small-scale population aggregate, but a mode of relating'.[37] Castells, for example, concludes that

> In a world of global flows of wealth, power, and images, the search for identity, collective or individual, ascribed or constructed, becomes the fundamental source of social meaning. This is not a new trend, since identity, and particularly religious and ethnic identity, have been at the roots of meaning since the dawn of human society. Yet identity is becoming the main, and sometimes the only, source of meaning in a historical period characterized by widespread destructuring of organizations, delegitimation of institutions, fading away of major social movements, and ephemeral cultural expression. People increasingly organize their meaning not around what they do but on the basis of what they are, or what they believe they are.[38]

Gusfield has even gone so far as to suggest that

> rather than conceiving of 'community' and 'society' as groups or entities to which persons 'belong', it would seem more useful to conceptualise these forms as points of reference brought into play in particular situations and arenas.[39]

While we have reservations about these and similar formulations, we nevertheless concluded that it was appropriate to link the terms 'personal' and 'community' for the purposes of this study. As we describe in more detail below, we use the term 'personal community' to refer to a specific subset of people's informal social relationships – those who are important to them at the time, rather than all the people they know no matter how tenuous the connection.[40] Consequently, personal communities represent people's significant personal relationships and include bonds which give both structure and meaning to their lives. As such, personal communities provide a kind of continuity through shared memories, and help to develop a person's sense of identity and belonging; although their composition may alter as an individual moves through the life-course, a core part of their reality does not change. Personal communities act as a reference point helping people define themselves even though the collective may only be directly observable in public rituals such as weddings, special anniversaries or funerals; even then, not all members of a personal community may be present. As collectivities, however, these personal communities are more 'communities in the mind' rather than communities on the ground, but, as most sociologists would acknowledge, 'where men define situations as real, they are real in their consequences'. People relate to each other in personal communities on a range of different dimensions and levels – as would have been the case in communities of fate – but the framework of belonging may not always be as visible. This is because the framework is provided by the individual's biography rather than by his or her membership of a particular, readily identifiable social grouping. Some of the solidarities we describe are largely hidden – hence the title of this book.

Of course, we realize that the concept of network is often used in this context, but we were reluctant to adopt this term. On one level we were concerned that in some network studies there tends to be greater emphasis on features such as the size of the network or the frequency of contact between members, rather than on the content of the relationships, whereas one of the major aims of our study was to explore the meaning and nature of informal personal ties.[41] More fundamentally, however, our reluctance was based on the fact that the word is used in confusingly different ways. At one extreme there is the popular notion of networking, which seems to amount to little more than adding social contacts to an address book.[42] Then there is the notion of a network as clusters of people who know each other within local communities or organizations.[43] Sometimes a network means the entire set of personal relationships of a particular individual.[44] In each of these cases, networks can be affectively neutral, including all contacts regardless of personal significance, whereas personal communities, as we have defined them above, contain only those who are considered important in people's lives.

We should point out, however, that although personal communities are personal and individual – in the sense that they are focused on particular individuals and constructed from information provided by those individuals – this does not mean that they should be taken as an indication of a process of 'individualization'. The concept of a personal community simply enables us to gain access to the meaningful but not necessarily spatially grounded sets of social relations which make up people's personal social worlds. In this way, we have tried to reflect Calhoun's notion of community life as 'a mode of relating',[45] and Delanty's conclusion that community is 'neither a form of social integration nor one of meaning, but is an open-ended system of communication about belonging'.[46]

In this book, then, we attempt to reveal the patterns and processes involved in making sense of people's personal social worlds. Central to this is an understanding of how personal communities are created, grow and develop. As we go through life the people that are most salient to us at any particular period are bound to change. Our parents and other relatives die, certain types of friend come and go. Even those who have rarely moved more than twenty-five miles from where they were born can experience considerable change and dynamism in their personal communities, as we shall describe below. However, at any given time we can, with a little thought and consideration, work out those who really are important in our lives. Such people constitute our personal community.

GENERATING AND MAPPING PERSONAL COMMUNITIES

Having reviewed some of the key ideas that have shaped our thinking, we now describe the way we set about exploring people's micro-social worlds. Given the complexities involved, we designed our study in such a way that we could not only identify who inhabits these worlds – for example, family, friend, colleague or neighbour – but also explore the content of relationships in some depth, looking at their basis and the kinds of interaction that take place. While some studies have used proxy measures for this, for example, frequency of contact has been used as a way of inferring the strength of a tie, we felt these measures were difficult to interpret and failed to capture the nature of personal relationships.[47] In our own study we aimed to ask a series of detailed questions about what relationships were actually like and had to find a way of asking about friends, family, colleagues or neighbours that allowed people to use the terms flexibly, even interchangeably: if a neighbour is also considered a friend, or a friend is also a family member, we wanted to capture this.[48]

Without knowing more about how people use the term friend, or about the respective roles of friends and family, we concluded that it would be difficult to capture the kind of data we wanted using a structured method, for example, a questionnaire. Consequently, as outlined in the introductory chapter, we opted for a qualitative rather than quantitative approach,[49] using a series of in-depth, face-to-face individual interviews.[50]

Identifying members of a personal community, however, presents a number of challenges and many different approaches have been used in the past.[51] In our case we were particularly concerned not to make any assumptions about the kind of relationships that might be included, and to avoid placing undue emphasis on friendship at this stage. Consequently, we simply asked people to list those who were *important* to them now, and to arrange the names in order of importance on a map, placing them in an appropriate place in relation to the centre (see Figure 2.2).[52] We were careful not to hurry people, allowing them time to compare and contrast their relationships, and to reconsider placements, sometimes rearranging them as the map began to take shape.

During the course of an interview we learned about the quality of different relationships in a number of ways. When people talked us through why they had included certain friends, relatives, colleagues or neighbours, and why they had placed them in particular positions on the map, they inevitably described and compared distinctive features of relationships. We also asked to whom people would turn in particular circumstances,[53] which enabled us to identify different sources of help and support, and to see the extent to which family members and friends played distinct or overlapping roles. Building on this, we also asked people to select names from each of the rings, focusing mainly, though not entirely, on different kinds of friends, and to tell us in detail about the basis of the relationship and what it meant to them. Finally,

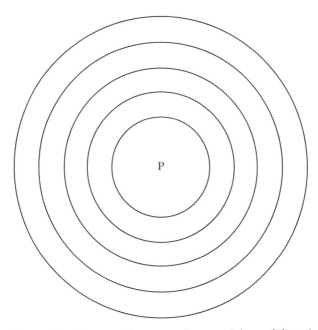

Figure 2.2.   A personal community map (P is participant).

we asked people to make direct comparisons between friendships and family ties. (The process of generating and exploring personal communities is described in considerable detail in the appendix.)

PRELIMINARY FINDINGS: THE DIVERSITY OF MICRO-SOCIAL WORLDS

Criteria for Inclusion: The Meaning of Importance

Given the approach we adopted, we were keen to understand how people interpreted the instruction to include those who were important to them now, and how they went about constructing their personal community. Not only did we discover a raft of different interpretations, we also found that importance is not necessarily judged in the same way for family as for friends. Throughout the interviews it became clear that people had not necessarily considered their personal community in such detail before, and that choosing whom to include and deciding where to place them involved a complex balancing of different criteria.

One of the first criteria for inclusion is that there is a given relationship, usually a family connection, through blood or marriage. In the case of immediate family, such as a spouse or partner, children, grandchildren, parents or a favourite sibling, there may be a strong emotional attachment, in which case there is no equivocation about whether or not to include them. One woman, placing her children and grandchildren in the centre of her map, explained their importance to her by saying, 'they're my life – they're a part of *me*'. In rare cases, however, people exclude their parents, particular siblings, and even some of their own children or grandchildren because of difficulties in the relationship, estrangement after an acrimonious divorce, a feeling of being let down, or simply a sense that they are not important in the other's life. One man described the struggle he went through when trying to decide whether or not to include members of his family.

> There was an issue about family which I found quite difficult – should they be there? By and large they're not there at all... I'm adopted and so I have contact with my adoptive family and I have contact with my birth mother as well... I'm not particularly close to my adoptive family, and with my birth mother that was even more difficult... it would seem extraordinary for her not to be there, given that I'm in regular contact with her... on the other hand it's not going that brilliantly at the moment. And sometimes I wonder how close I really feel to her and what the kind of relative value of contact with her is in relation to friends, and sometimes I think it's probably quite low on the list.

With extended family, on the other hand, we find much more variation. While some people only list aunts, uncles, cousins, nephews, nieces and in-laws where there is a special relationship, others include most or all of their relatives because of strong normative pressures that family should be important, subscribing to the view that 'blood is thicker than water'.

So the given-ness of a tie is an initial consideration but not necessarily a guarantee of inclusion. People also adopt chosen criteria and assess the importance of relationships in terms of their intrinsic quality, particularly in the case of friends. Important ties are ones where there is an emotional attachment: 'these are the people I love', 'they are at the centre of my being', 'I think the world of them'. The exchange of practical and emotional support, being able to share confidences, are also key aspects of the way people interpret importance: 'I know that I would be able to go to any of these people... they would always be there for me.'

Yet, although qualities such as dependability, helpfulness, trustworthiness may determine where relationships are placed on a person's map, it seems that these qualities are not necessarily prerequisites for inclusion in a personal community. For example, unreliable, non-intimate, but fun, friends may still be considered sufficiently important, as 'safety valves', to be included, though they may not merit a central place.

Finally, being known and accepted 'warts and all' is another key aspect of important relationships: 'they've seen the very worst side of you and like you in spite of it... You don't have to put up with any pretence at all, they know you as you truly are.'

Interestingly, loving, liking, trusting and depending upon are criteria that are not always applied to family, some of whom, as we have already seen, can gain a place on the map for normative or cultural reasons.

There are also dynamic factors that help to determine the importance of, mainly, non-kin relationships. Frequency of contact, for example, which may bring a detailed familiarity with the day-to-day minutiae of the other's life, is a key element of some personal ties. In other cases, however, it is the duration and history of the relationship that is valued:

> I think there's no doubt, friends that you make when you're sort of starting out, having left home, I think those relationships just go on and on, because you're experiencing so much all together.

With longstanding friendships, for example, continuity and shared experiences deepen and strengthen the relationship, giving a sense of presence which can be a 'day to day thing... or just that they are there, frequently, in the back of your mind.' With these friendships it is possible to 'pick up where you left off', even when there is minimal contact.

Sometimes people are considered important and included when there is no longer any contact at all. For example, one man insisted that his closest friend was a childhood companion and co-evacuee during World War II to whom he had not spoken in over twenty years. People often asked us if they could place deceased friends and relatives on the map because of the strength of the tie in the past. One person even suggested that the map should be three dimensional so that it could represent the sense of presence and the influence of particular people in his life which continued long after their death: 'I would put these three men actually hovering above me. I sort of feel them as stars shining down on me.'

Finally, and unsurprisingly, people are considered important if they have things in common, or feel 'on the same wavelength'. However, while this is considered almost a sine qua non of friendship, it seems to be an unexpected bonus in family relationships.

Of course, actual relationships may or may not match up to these idealized conceptions, something we explore in detail in subsequent chapters.

Size and Basic Composition

Through the relatively simple method described above, we succeeded in generating a rich diversity of personal communities with wide variations in structure and overall composition. The smallest personal community in our study contains just five people, the largest forty-one; the number of family members ranges from two to thirty-one, of friends from one to twenty-four. In some cases friends outnumber family by as much as ten to one, in others there are four times as many family members as friends. In some maps, friends are placed alongside family in the centre, whereas, in others, friends do not feature until the third ring. Some people put all their friends and family in the first two rings, others make use of all five rings on the map. In addition to friends and family, other relationships such as good neighbours, workmates or colleagues, fellow church members, golfing partners and so on are sometimes listed. Occasionally, a godchild or godparent is included, and some people placed counsellors, care workers, therapists or child-minders on their maps. In a couple of cases people asked if they could include a pet, and one woman was keen to place God in the centre of her map. Figure 2.3 shows two very different kinds of personal community found in our study.

But what can we conclude from these essentially structural characteristics? Personal communities containing large numbers of family sometimes include several generations and, certainly, older people in our study usually listed their grandchildren, even if younger people did not always include their grandparents. Sometimes, the family contingent is boosted by the inclusion of large numbers of extended family such as aunts, uncles, cousins, nephews and nieces. Some of our participants decided to include all their in-laws, and, in reconstituted families, some listed all of their half or step-relations. But can we assume that all these family ties are close? In some cases, as we shall see later in this book, it is clear that strong bonds exist within the extended family, in others, however, people have insisted on including all their relatives, regardless of the closeness of the tie, refusing

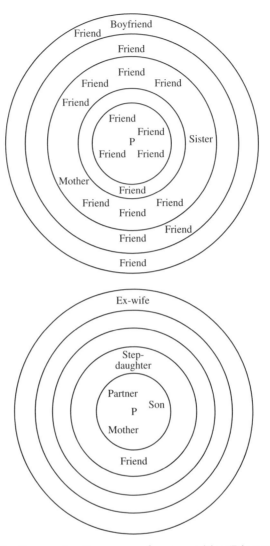

Figure 2.3. Two contrasting personal communities (P is participant).

to make any distinctions or selection. Without knowing something about the quality of family relationships, it is difficult to interpret the significance of different patterns, and a large family component may indicate an extensive close family circle or alternatively reflect people's beliefs about the importance of kin.

Similarly, without knowing something about the quality of different friendships, it is difficult to draw many conclusions from the fact that some people include more than twenty friends, others just one or two. Do those who include a large number of friends have a lot of close and intimate ties or are they including a lot of what others might call acquaintances? Do they have a core of intimates and a wider circle of more light-hearted, casual friendships?

Density

Personal communities also vary in the extent to which members know or are friends with each other. At one extreme, we find very dense personal communities with strong links between friends and family. Sometimes friends are known to members of a person's family, and the personal community contains a number of mutual friends, because friends grew up in the same neighbourhood and visited each other's houses as children. Parents and their children are sometimes friendly with other families as 'family friends' so that different generations know each other. And some people treat friends as quasi-family, or alternatively see family members as friends, including both family and friends in social get-togethers.

> There's none of these people in this whole thing that haven't eaten in my house, or stayed here... the others... all except Sarah because she lives so far away, have certainly been here at any type of function that we've had... They all know each other, yes... so they all certainly, for instance, have been invited to my fortieth last year.

At the other extreme, there are more disparate patterns with few connections between members. Where few if any friends are known to family members, there has usually been considerable social or geographical mobility, childhood friends have fallen away, or close family members have died or become estranged. Again, to make sense of these patterns we needed to know something of the content and development of relationships.

Personal or Geographical Communities

There is also considerable variation in the extent to which personal communities are place-based or contain a more geographically dispersed set of ties. While some people are very embedded in their local neighbourhood, with most of their friends and family living within one or two miles, others sustain significant relationships across hundreds and even thousands of miles. Of course, people's ability to retain dispersed contacts has been aided by the expansion, and the reduction in cost, of communication technologies, but we need to understand which kinds of relationships tend to be local and which can be maintained without immediate access or face-to-face contact. These issues, and the relationship between personal and geographical communities are explored in later chapters.

DIGGING BENEATH THE SURFACE

Our aim, however, was to move beyond a surface description of the structure of people's personal communities and to present a richer and more nuanced picture. As discussed earlier, the detailed descriptions people gave us of the quality and content of their relationships enabled us to develop the analytical ideas presented throughout this book.[54] The idea of *friendship repertoires*, came out of our exploration of the bases of actual friendships where we found that, not only did people have different types of friends, but they also varied in the range or constellation of friends they included in their personal community. Similarly, the idea of *friendship modes* emerged from our analysis of the development and duration of friendships and refers to the way people form, maintain or lose friends at different stages in the life-course. The idea of *patterns of suffusion* was developed after we had examined the extent to which friends and family play similar or specialized roles. These concepts inform the classification of personal communities described in chapter 6. When we present these key ideas in the following chapters, they are illustrated using a series of different cases: the accounts and experiences of more than forty of our sixty participants are used in this way. Annexe 1 gives an overview of these cases, though people's names and some individual details have been changed in order to protect their anonymity.

PERSONAL COMMUNITY AS A LENS

Finally, we believe that the concept of a personal community provides a kind of lens through which we can look in a fresh and more focused way at current issues surrounding family and friends. We identified seven main forms of personal community which reflect the degree to which people, as adults, still rely heavily on kin, keeping their friendships at a lighter more casual level, or develop intimate and supportive relationships outside the family, and, indeed, in some cases, look to friends rather than family in times of need.

Essentially, the idea of a personal community is an analytical tool and we certainly do not expect people to adopt our terminology in everyday speech, referring, for example, to the bringing together of different personal communities at various social functions. However, the general idea of a personal community is implicitly understood and acknowledged. In Tim Lott's novel, *White City Blue*, Frankie, the leading character, is discussing his friends with his new partner, who asks him how many friends he has in all. He replies:

> The average would be... what? Ten really good ones. Ten more peripheral. A score or so right at the outside edge, virtual acquaintances. A few left over from school, a few more from college, a few picked up at work, perhaps an ex in there somewhere. One or two borrowed or stolen from other friends. An ex flat-mate or two. Not as many mates as I used to have, that's for sure.[55]

However, neither the fictional Frankie nor our real-life participants would be likely to introduce two people by saying, 'You two don't know each other but you're both in the same ring of my personal community.' They might, however, introduce two very close personal friends to each other by acknowledging their individual importance and explaining why, despite this, they have never met. Friends from a previous phase of life or friends separated through geographical mobility could be introduced in this way.

As we argued above, personal communities are essentially communities in the mind. Unlike entirely kin-based or place-based communities they cannot necessarily be observed directly as social entities by outsiders; even at public rituals, such as weddings or funerals, there are all sorts of reasons why those present may not fully represent a person's personal community. Identifying personal communities requires self-conscious reflection on the part of the individual at the centre who orchestrates the distribution on the paper map or the map in the mind.

It may be argued, however, that we imposed the notion of personal community on our participants and that, if people do not spontaneously think about their pattern of social relationships in this way, we have simply created a construct that does not reflect their perceptions or experiences of social life. Although one person commented during the production of her map that it was exactly what she had done for the seating plan for her son's bar mitzvah, she was exceptional; a more typical response was for people to recognize and confirm their map as a representation of their significant social world once it had been constructed.

Not only this, when people constructed and mapped their personal communities, deciding which friends, family members, neighbours or colleagues were considered sufficiently important to be included, they actually mentioned factors which are regarded by some theorists and commentators as the key ingredients of community in the twenty-first century. For example, personal communities contain people who contribute to our *sense of identity and belonging*. With family, key members have been described as 'part of me' or 'one of the foundations of my life'. Close friends, who have 'seen the worst side of you' yet accept you, provide a powerful affirmation of who we are. We also gain affirmation of our identity from members of our personal community with whom we share similar values and interests, people who are 'on the same wavelength' as us.

Personal communities also give us a *biographical anchor*. When we include in our personal community people we have known since childhood, or since our early adult years, it is the continuity and sense of shared history that makes the relationship particularly important; these are people who 'know you inside out', 'they know what you are bleeding on about'. As we saw earlier in this chapter, there can be a sense of continuing presence when there is little current contact, lasting even after these significant people have died and are now 'stars shining down'.

There are also *moral* and *normative* dimensions to personal communities. We include those for whom we feel responsible, and those who will support and help us: 'they would always be there for me, and I would always be there for them.' We may also include people because we feel we should, because 'blood is thicker than water'.

Nevertheless, some may still resist our approach, objecting that, in the process of classifying and codifying relationships, we somehow diminish the richness and complexity of people's private lives. Yet this is far from our intention. By describing an important social phenomenon, and enabling people to construct their own personal communities, if they wish to, our aim is to help them become conscious of the processes of which they form a part and to be more in control of their lives. They have a tool with which they can consider their own pattern of social relationships and compare it with that of others. We do not expect the term personal community to supplement the more unfocused phrase 'friends and family' but if it helps us to recognize that people are embedded in a range of different sets of relationships, involving varying degrees of choice and commitment, and diverse sources of support, our study will have made a contribution to understanding the nature of people's micro-social worlds.

CHAPTER THREE

The Nature of Friendship

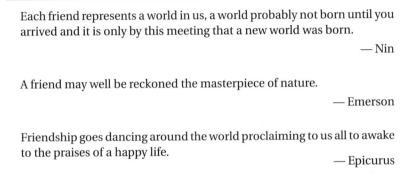

Each friend represents a world in us, a world probably not born until you arrived and it is only by this meeting that a new world was born.

— Nin

A friend may well be reckoned the masterpiece of nature.

— Emerson

Friendship goes dancing around the world proclaiming to us all to awake to the praises of a happy life.

— Epicurus

As we saw in chapter 2, friendship has long been a subject of fascination, and a strong literary, historical and philosophical theme. But does it make sense to talk about friendship in general, as a universally understood and recognized relationship? Not only are there different kinds of friendship, but the meaning of the term may change at different times and in different cultures. Some historians and social scientists even argue that certain types of friendship may be specific to particular social and economic conditions, or that the notion of self in some cultures may preclude intimate, 'knowing' forms of friendship.[1] In the preface to a collection of writings on anthropology and friendship, Raymond Firth concluded:

> Friendship is of a very diverse and complex, even ambiguous nature...
> The concept... can vary greatly in intensity, from simple well-wishers
> to familiar, close, dear, intimate, bosom, boon-companion friend, each
> with its own subtle quality.[2]

Even from everyday observations, it is clear that the word 'friend' encompasses a dizzying array of relationships. For example, those who work at building extensive networks, filling their address books or databases with useful contacts, may refer to these contacts as friends.[3] Primary school children excitedly tell their family they have made a new friend when someone offers them a sweet or invites them to join in a game. World leaders describe each other as friends when they form alliances, even though they have little informal contact outside their roles and spend little time in each other's company.[4] People use the term 'friend' to refer to those with whom they simply have a pleasant association, for example, through neighbourhood, work, joint interests or common activities. People also describe as friends those with whom they have shared a lifelong relationship and to whom they feel closer than a brother or sister. Even our attempts to qualify the term 'friend' lack precision: good friends may be soulmates or simply acquaintances.[5]

Clearly, if we are to make sense of our finding that some people include just one or two friends in their personal community while others list more than twenty, we need to understand how people are using the term. Are people talking about the same kind of relationship? Are the one or two friends selected for inclusion more intimate and valued than the twenty? When people include twenty friends, are these all of a similar type or quality?

In this chapter, the first of two explicitly on friendship, we examine what it means to call someone a friend. In addition to reviewing some common stereotypes or idealizations of friendship, we explore the nature of actual relationships, describing in detail some of the friendships we encountered in our study. Understanding that friendship can take many different forms and that the term 'friend' is used to refer to very different relationships goes some way towards helping us appreciate why personal communities vary so much in the number of people who are designated as friends. But in order to understand the role played by friends within a personal community, we need to look at the range of types of friends people included, something we refer to as their *friendship repertoire*.

In chapter 4, we look at the way different stages in the life-course provide both opportunities and threats to the development and maintenance of friendships. We discover that people vary in their friend-making pattern, in the way they develop, nurture or lose friends throughout their lives.

WHAT IS A FRIEND?

So, what is a friend? In the abstract, it seems that friendship is associated with a whole raft of qualities, and our own research confirmed
the findings of many other studies in this field.[6] For example, one
of the first qualities people mention is that friendships have to be
established; unlike family ties, workmates or neighbours, friendships
are chosen rather than given. Indeed, the fact that people decide to
be friends with each other is a highly prized aspect of friendship,
because it affirms that someone has chosen you for 'who you really
are'.[7] Friends are sometimes defined as people who have something in
common, perhaps the same sense of humour or similar interests, or
they belong to the same organization, live in the same locality, come
from a similar background, lead a similar lifestyle, work in the same
occupational field, or are at the same stage in their lives. Friends are
people who enjoy each other's company, sharing activities, going out
together, chatting on the telephone, emailing, or visiting each other's
home. A core conception of friendship is the idea that friends are people who like each other, who 'get along', though of course the strength
of the attachment can vary a great deal. The tie between friends is
defined as an informal one: friends are people who can relax with
each other, who feel comfortable in each other's presence; there is a
sense of being off duty with friends, free from work or family responsibilities. Friends are also perceived as people who offer each other
practical help, or give emotional support, sharing in each other's highs
and lows, and friends are often defined as people who can confide in
one another, who know each other's secrets. Finally, there is a narrative
dimension to friendship and friends are sometimes defined as people
with a shared history who have 'been through things together'.

But do people expect their friends to match this cultural stereo-
type? Can someone be a friend if the relationship lacks any of these
key qualities?[8] In practice, we find the word 'friend' used to describe
a wide range of ties, many of which are based on only a few of these
ingredients. It seems that actual friendships are valued for particular
attributes, and these attributes can compensate for other shortcom-
ings, so that friends may be fun but unreliable, trustworthy but dull
and so on, and it is the particular combination of qualities, as Raymond
Firth noted, which gives each friendship its distinctive character.

However, when we look at the content of friendships – or main form
of interaction on which they are based – we find some recurring types

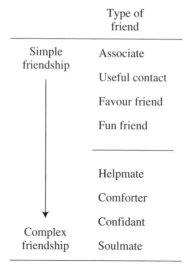

Figure 3.1.   Some recurrent types of friendship.

which we describe in some detail below, illustrating each with the story of particular relationships. Of course, on one level, every relationship is completely unique, our description may miss some nuances and complexities, and there may be other combinations of qualities. We are not claiming that the range of friendships we portray is in any way exhaustive; these are simply the most common forms we encountered in our study. In any case, our purpose at this stage is to highlight the fact that friendship takes many different forms.†

THE DIVERSITY OF FRIENDSHIP

Clearly, the dimensions of friendship on which each type is based are not new discoveries but confirm what other studies have shown.[9] What this chapter sets out to do, however, is clarify the way that friendships vary in their complexity and in terms of their particular combination of elements. While some friendships are simple, based on just one main form of interaction, others are more complex, multifaceted relationships, involving several different ways of relating.[10] Figure 3.1 shows the main types of friendship we identified.

In simple friendships, friends play well-defined and somewhat circumscribed roles. The friends may be *associates* who share a common

---

† The fact that we only asked about friends who were considered 'important now' may mean that we have missed some more casual types of friendship.

activity, *useful contacts* who exchange information and advice, *neighbourly* or *favour friends* who help each other out, or *fun friends* who socialize together. Of course, other friendships also involve fun and favours, but the key feature of simple friendships is that the relationship is limited to one main form of interaction.

Associates are friends whose relationship is based entirely on sharing a particular interest or activity, for example, golf, tennis, bridge, darts, model boats, meeting in a particular context such as the workplace or pub, or belonging to a particular organization such as club or church. These relationships are 'tightly framed', and the friends do not meet outside the shared activity or context.[11]

Terry's friendship with Jack and Brian clearly illustrates an associate relationship. Terry is in his mid sixties, retired, married with one adult daughter and a grandson, and, apart from his time in the services, has lived his whole life near Stockport in Greater Manchester. He and his wife Doreen own their small terraced house and their daughter and grandson live less than a mile away. After leaving school Terry worked initially in a butcher's shop before joining the Royal Air Force and training as a fitter. After completing his National Service, he worked for an engineering company and then became a taxi driver. Terry still has friends from school days and more recent friendships made through the taxi business.

Terry met Jack and Brian six years ago at a model boat club and the friendship very much revolves around this common hobby. The three do not socialize apart from when they meet through the club and have not been to each other's houses.

> Jack doesn't know where we live – well he does, he's got me telephone number, but he's never been. . . We go to exhibitions and things like that, you know. . . Say there's a small coach going you can rely on those two to go. . . I don't really know a lot about them apart from being at the club. I know Jack is a widower but I don't know how long his wife has been dead, and I know he was in electronics. And I know Ron was an engineer because we talk about things like that.

Terry admits that he would not think of asking Jack or Brian for help, or of confiding in them, as 'I only know them from the club. . . I would feel as though I was imposing.' However, Terry is also friends with other club members but these are more than associates: he knew them before he joined the club and sees them socially through mutual friends.

Useful contacts, on the other hand, are relationships which are based on exchanging information or using influence on a friend's behalf. These are not usually affectionate or committed ties, but there is a willingness to give advice or pull strings. For example, people may tell each other where they can buy something cheaply or find a local service, or put each other in touch with a third party, or let each other know about job opportunities. Again, other kinds of friendships may also involve doing a good turn but, with these contacts, this is the main basis of the relationship. People who put a lot of effort into networking are often cultivating friendships of this kind.

A number of people in our study had friends who were useful contacts and Patrick's relationship with one of his professors is a case in point. One of six children, and in his forties, Patrick was born in Ireland. His father had been a professor of paediatrics and Patrick also took up a career in medicine. After studying in Belfast, Patrick moved to England to continue his medical training and now works as a hospital consultant in Manchester. He is single but has a 'serious' girlfriend. Patrick admitted that he did not tend to nurture friends and had found it hard to find non-family members to include in his personal community:

> The folk I know are through my girlfriend... I'm obviously a sorry lost individual, and I realize that I socialize through her.

Nevertheless, apart from friends made through his partner, Patrick listed an old friend from childhood, a friend from medical training, and a number of professional colleagues, including one of his professors. Patrick greatly admired this professor, seeing him as a champion in his field: 'so he's been very powerful and influential in supporting me and what I've been trying to do.'

No longer based at the same hospital, the colleagues do not socialize together – 'I keep a respectful distance... just out of respect for his position of authority' – but Patrick felt that his professor was certainly someone he would contact if he were looking for another job: 'because of his status and position, and, if he says he wants something, he gets it.'

With *favour* or *neighbourly friends* doing good turns for each other is also the basis of the friendship, but in this case the good turn is usually some form of practical help. Although these friends are not always neighbours, they usually live locally and play a good neighbourly role, for example, lending household items, watering plants, putting out rubbish, taking in parcels, giving lifts, or helping with occasional DIY jobs. While other friendships may also involve this kind of help, the key characteristic of favour friends is that the relationship is quite tightly framed and does not involve going out together or socializing. These kinds of friendship tend to be quite time and place bound, and may evolve into more complex or intimate relationships over time, or fade if circumstances change or people move to another area.

Brenda is an example of someone with a number of neighbourly friends. In her sixties, twice divorced then widowed, Brenda has moved around the country during her married life, but has now returned to live near Manchester, in the town where she grew up. She works part-time as a barmaid and cleaner and has established a number of friendships through work, through hosting catalogue parties and through the local neighbourhood. Brenda's neighbourly friends help her out in different ways, looking after her house if she goes away, walking her dog if she is ill.

Edna and Bill live in the same street as Brenda and have been neighbourly friends for five years. The fact that the couple live so close is an important part of the relationship: 'they're near if I need them or anything like that, and they come.' Bill is particularly helpful around the house – 'he does, like, jobs for me, he's a joiner' – and although Brenda does not pay him, she gives him 'booze' as a thank you. But Brenda would not go out with Bill and Edna socially, nor would she confide personal information.

> No, I wouldn't talk to Bill. But Edna, you know, we talk over certain things but, er, certain things I wouldn't talk about to her... like, I wouldn't tell her about me boyfriend, for one... he's in prison... and she's a bit of a chatterbox.

On the other hand, Brenda has other neighbours, like Harry and Marge, with whom she does socialize.

> I'm going out tomorrow night with them to a fireworks display... And they both come over. Harry comes and, like the other day I came back from shopping, he kind of followed me over so we stood talking a bit. It was a nice day and I said, 'are you coming in for a drink?' He said, 'yeah go on', and he'll come and sit for hours talking to me, and Marge comes, but they work funny shifts you know so, er, sometimes if Marge is on nights she's in bed all day, so Harry'll come for cigarettes for her or vice versa, but they both come and you know if I have a party I invite them.

Finally, *fun friends*, or sociable companions, are simple friendships that revolve around enjoying each other's company, but, unlike associates, these friends socialize in a range of different ways and are not dependent on a single activity or context. Where fun friends do not live near each other, or do not see each other very often, some of their socializing is not face-to-face, but the friends may keep in contact and sustain the relationship by telephone or email. Of course, most friendships include an element of sociability and companionship, but the key point about fun friends is that sociability is the main or only basis of the relationship. Brenda's relationship with Marge and Harry is essentially a fun friendship.

Almost everyone in our study, across all backgrounds, and ages and stages in the life-course, had this kind of friend. Take Harriet, for example. In her mid thirties, Harriet was born and brought up in London where she has lived most of her life, although she has moved several times within the city. As part of her languages degree she spent a year in Germany, and has since worked for five different organizations in the United Kingdom. At the moment she works for a medical charity based in central London. Harriet is single, though she has recently met someone whom she hopes will become a long-term partner. Friendship is very important to her and she has many different kinds of friends. She makes a clear distinction between more serious 'high maintenance' relationships and

> people like William who I have a very fun friendship with. . . So these are all, sort of, good friends but low maintenance, I suppose, kind of on both sides. But it still works really nicely, the sort of no excessive obligations either side, but we have fun.

Several of Harriet's women friends from work come into the category of fun friends. The women go for walks, have lunch together, and chat about everyday things. Harriet also has a number of male fun friends, such as William. Harriet originally met William through work but the friendship developed beyond that context, 'just through him being a ton of fun, he's just the most amazing character to be with and he's a perpetual clown.' The two no longer work together but spend a lot of time in each other's company:

> We drink – that's normally on his instigation, or watch videos. Very boyish. There was actually an extended group of lads where I was an honorary lad, and we'd just sort of go and see boy movies and drink beer – that kind of thing. And these two – William and Gary – were the kind of two left over from that.

Fun friends are essentially light-hearted relationships:

> The people who ... add to my life, they're my champagne bubbles.
> They're the ones who, you know, seeing them is refreshing. They're the
> ones who you go and see if you want to spoil yourself.

Some of these friendships may be quite casual, but they can also be
very warm and affectionate relationships. Even within fun friendships,
some friends are more fun than others, and friends who are especially
good fun are often forgiven for lacking other friend-like qualities, for
example, they may be 'fun but flighty' or 'irresponsible and feckless'
but their good company more than compensates for other shortcom-
ings. Patrick has this kind of relationship with his childhood friend
Geoff:

> I wouldn't ring Geoff for advice, you know, financial, personal difficulties,
> whatever, but I'd hate the idea of him not being around, because he has
> a unique contribution to make to counteracting life's seriousness. He's
> a guy who... any time you take yourself too seriously, he can take you
> down to size.

So, although some contemporary commentators bemoan the decline
of 'true friendship' and dismiss relationships based on sociability and
fun as trivial, we found that, in the context of the stressful pace of
modern life, fun friends can provide an important safety valve:

> Because life is so serious most of the time, you know... it is nice to meet
> people that you can relax with... nowadays everybody works so hard and
> it's so fast, that sometimes you just need to get away from it and have a
> really good laugh together.

Fun friendship is often a starting point for relationships which become
more complex and multistranded over time but some never change
their basic form. Harriet spoke of keeping a certain number of friends
at the sociable only level where 'you don't take their problems home
with you', because it would be too demanding and time consuming to
have a lot of high maintenance friends. As Harriet explained, the key
point about fun friends is the lack of excessive obligations on either
side.

As we have seen, simple friendships have one main basis. Complex
friendships, on the other hand are multifaceted, based on different
configurations of qualities and roles. We describe four kinds of complex friendship encountered in this study.

Helpmates are friends who socialize together and help each other out in a practical way. Helpmates are essentially solid, reliable, dependable friends. Brenda, whose neighbourly friendships we have already described, was someone who had been helped by a friend in times of trouble. She recounted the story of how her old school friend had come to her aid at a particularly difficult point in her life when she had broken her wrist, her dog had died, she had been burgled, and she was struggling financially:

> When Doreen heard about me she came round immediately... she just said, 'I couldn't sleep last night thinking about you.' I said, 'Why?' She said, 'The way you're living.' She asked if she could lend me some money to tide me over. I said no but she said, 'I mean it. Nobody'll know about it... I can't bear to think of you living like you're doing.' ... Anyway she insisted.

Many people in our study had friends who were helpmates, people with whom they could have fun but could also ask for help: 'the kind of people who you can phone up having stuffed the car in a ditch at three o'clock in the morning and say, "Come and get me!".' But people sometimes make subtle calculations about the strength of a friendship in relation to the kind of help being requested. They may also take into account personal qualities and whether friends are seen as reliable, whether they are 'absolute rocks who always come up trumps' or 'lazy friends who only do it if they're pushed.' Alternatively, friends may not be approached because they already have a lot of commitments, or because they have troubles of their own. Finally, friends may be limited in the kind of practical help they can offer because they live too far away from each other.

Not only do friends weigh up whether they can ask for help, they sometimes consider whether they should offer help to their friends. They wonder whether to put themselves forward, whether it is 'that kind of friendship', whether it would be presumptuous on their part. People can also feel hurt if they are not asked for help, or if an offer is refused.

Although they provide practical help, helpmates are not the kind of friends who act as confidants, nor are they looked to for emotional support. Sometimes this is simply because people already have a number of other friends to whom they can turn. Sometimes it is because the friend is seen as 'a frightful gossip', or too easily 'shockable'. Despite her friend's generosity, Brenda did not treat Doreen as a confidante, especially about personal relationships, because Doreen was a rather serious and reserved character who might disapprove of her friend's exploits.

By comparison, *comforters* or *rocks* are friends who not only socialize and help each other in practical ways, but also give each other emotional support, and it is the friend's sympathetic qualities that are particularly valued. This kind of friendship was movingly described by David, who had recently lost his partner through AIDS. David is gay and in his mid thirties. Adopted as a baby, he was brought up by his adoptive parents in Dorset, but went away to university and then settled in London. After working in local government and then as a trade union official, he has now taken up an academic career. David met Lucy fifteen years ago through his late partner and through the trades union movement. When his partner was dying, Lucy played a crucially supportive role. It was not that David talked to her a great deal about his feelings, but simply that she was 'there':

> We were together for ten years and the last six months of his life in particular were very difficult and he was very, very ill, and the last three months were even worse in the sense that his brain deteriorated and that was very difficult. And many friends came and went during that situation ... some people who had been very much part of our lives kind of disappeared... they couldn't hack it, they couldn't handle it. But Lucy... was extraordinary... She placed herself right in the middle of what was going on. I mean I suppose this can be summed up most significantly by the fact that when he died his coffin came home the day before his funeral and we all went in – this is a kind of Catholic thing that one does – we all went into the room to see him, to say goodbye for the last time, and the only people who did it were family and me – and I'm really family in that context – and Lucy. And I think that kind of sums up the kind of contribution she made, really, which was very brave. Because, for me, you know, people have often said to me at the time, 'Well, you know, you were very brave and... you coped wonderfully' and all the rest of it. But I didn't really have a choice in a way, whereas she had a choice, and she made a positive choice to be right there.

Not all friendships involve emotional support, however. Asking for or accepting emotional support involves showing some vulnerability and friendships may lack this level of trust. Also, we found that some people are not emotionally open in their friendships, preferring to rely on family or partners rather than friends for this kind of support.[12] On the other hand, some of the men in our study did not believe in sharing their emotions with others at all, family or friend. One man confessed: 'as you've probably gathered by now, I don't really rely on anyone else,

I'm not that sort of person'; another described his family as one where 'there was no culture of discussing emotional issues. . . no emotional language.'[13]

Confidants are another kind of complex friendship. These relationships involve the disclosure of personal information as well as enjoyment of each other's company, but confidants do not necessarily live near by and so may not always be in a position to offer practical help and support. Sometimes confiding tends to be *cool*, with the friend acting as a sounding board for a discussion of problems and possible solutions rather than engaging on an emotional level; at other times it is *hot*, where emotional support is also sought or given. In either case, a confiding friendship is one which requires a degree of intimacy and trust.

This kind of friendship was described by Roger, a lone parent in his early fifties. Roger had met his wife at technical college, though they did not marry until ten years later, and when the marriage ended Roger got custody of his young daughter. During the early years Roger found it difficult to find time to build his career – he now owns a small but successful publishing business in Essex – and to socialize, as well as caring for his daughter. Nevertheless, he managed to keep up with a number of fun friends with whom he shares a range of interests and hobbies, and has developed some dependable helpmates. In addition to these friends, Roger also has a couple of close confidants, one of whom, Geoffrey, he has known for just over six years. The two friends see each other once a week, tinker with each other's cars, and have been on holiday to South Africa together. Recently, Geoffrey confided in Roger that he had been made redundant:

> I was probably the first person he phoned up when this happened. . . So, I went and saw him on Friday and he came round on Saturday and I phoned him up today to make sure he was all right.

Confiding friendships vary in their degree of intimacy, however: while the closest confidants can be told one's darkest secrets – 'like your wife's left you or you've gone broke or whatever, things that you don't want everybody to know that you've got a problem with' – these secrets might not be shared with less intimate confidants. Harriet, whose fun friendships we have already described, distinguished between confidants whom she could tell anything, for example, details of her love life, and others with whom she shared less personal information.

Whether or not friends confide in each other is often linked to the length of time they have known each other (confidants are usually longstanding friends), and to personal qualities (people distinguish between trustworthy friends and those who are indiscreet). People also vary in their willingness to divulge personal information: confiding, like emotional support, requires trust.

> It's the level of risk. . . you decide to take with another individual. . . and I don't quite know how that comes about, or when you decide that the time's right. I don't know that you do, I think probably a set of circumstances arise, or a conversation is struck up and you decide, you take the risk and you do.

However, people do not expect or want all their friends to be confidants: 'I wouldn't tell my personal business to just anybody. . . I keep my other friends at arm's length.' And, just as some friends are fun but cannot be relied on for help or support, others may be fun, or reliable, but cannot be trusted because they are indiscreet.

Nevertheless, for some people, having friends who are confidants is an essential part of life, providing an important if rather different safety valve from the companionship of fun friends. As one young woman explained:

> If I didn't have friends then I'd just be mad, I think, because everything would be internal, whereas with my friends I can speak to them and just discuss everything and change my opinion if they've got something, you know, some different opinion or good advice. I don't think you can actually live, or I couldn't actually live, without having friends.

Finally, *soulmates* are the most multistranded friendships of all. These are friends who confide, provide emotional support, help each other, and enjoy each other's company. They also share a similar outlook on life, feeling they are 'on the same wavelength'. There is a strong emotional bond, a high degree of commitment, and a keen sense of connection, of knowing one other 'inside out'.

A number of people in our study had one or two friends whom they considered to be soulmates. Harriet has this relationship with her friend Letty whom she has known for over three years. The two women 'clicked' and became friends almost immediately, recognizing in each other a kindred spirit and having a lot of fun together, but

> it took quite a while for her to open up to me – probably about a year. . . And at that stage I discovered that she was having problems with her husband and since then she has actually broken up with him and it's been a really traumatic time for her, and it was a messy break-up. Her father's also terminally ill, her work's going really badly so the stress on

her has been absolutely immense... She doesn't actually open up to anyone, she has pretty much two friends in the world, she doesn't like opening up to people, so the fact that she has entrusted me with that is an awfully big thing for her.

Esther and Sarena also have this kind of friendship. Esther is in her late thirties from a mixed race background. She was brought up in Nigeria and Ghana, but has also spent time in the United Kingdom, where she went to boarding school. She has been working in Manchester for nearly twenty years and manages a dental practice. Sarena, a social worker, was born in England and is from a black Caribbean background. Both women are married with young children, and their husbands are successful health professionals. This is Sarena's second marriage and she also has an eighteen-year-old daughter and two step-sons in their twenties. Esther and Sarena have known each other for twelve years since they met through Esther's husband's work. They quickly became firm friends, and are godparents to each other's children. Both women work full-time so they share a school run. As well as having fun together, they feel they can tell each other anything and consider themselves 'just like sisters'. Sarena also considers Esther's mother to be a friend.

Sarena's husband, Robert, has this kind of friendship with Christopher, a consultant psychiatrist, whom he met through his work. Robert is in his early fifties and was born in Dominica, where he lived until he was twenty-six. After leaving school, Robert went straight to work but later took two part-time degrees and is now a qualified psychotherapist. He is married for a second time and has three children, two from his first marriage and a young son with his second wife. Robert admits that he does not have many close friends:

> I mean if I were to be perfectly honest, I think I have a very, very small number of friends. I know a tremendous amount of people, and many people who would consider me to be their friend, but in terms of my recognition of friendship, because of the depth and the emotional connection, and the sharing that we have, the commonality in terms of what we believe in or we understand, I think I probably just have about three friends really... [and] of all the friendships I have, the greatest friendship is with Christopher.

Robert and Christopher have known each other for eleven years. The two go walking together in the hills, and can confide in each other about financial and relationship problems. They also share a similar set of values, particularly in relation to their work, and have set up joint projects so that they can work together.

> We can engage in very deep and meaningful discussions, and we can disagree without falling out... I would say I have a closer relationship now with... Christopher than I have with my brother... We have sufficient shared interest, you know, shared knowledge, shared understanding of how processes should happen... so we are concerned tremendously about human beings and their care, and so on. So it's value systems, I think, really.

Robert could not imagine their friendship would founder:

> I can't really quite put it into words at the moment because if Christopher did something, not to me, or even to me, and it surprised me, I think we have other bits of ourselves that would keep that relationship intact.

As we have shown – associates, useful contacts, favour friends, fun friends, helpmates, comforters, confidants and soulmates – are based on different kinds of interaction, but friendships also involve differing levels of emotional attachment and commitment. Perhaps unsurprisingly, as we move from simple to more complex friendships, the commitment friends feel towards each other tends to increase, with soulmates as the most committed, solid ties. As commitment increases, we also find a growing sense that close friends are people who accept and affirm who you are. We might also expect to find greater emotional attachment in complex friendships, with liking turning to liking very much, and in some cases to love. However, although very close friends tend to be very fond of each other, this does not always mean that people like their close friends the most.[14] Sometimes more light-hearted fun friends are also more uncomplicated. Strong emotions can also involve negative feelings, such as rivalry or envy, and some people spoke of avoiding certain friends when things were not going well, waiting until their situation had improved before contacting friends: 'you don't want them to see you at your worst, do you?' Sometimes people feel stuck with friends they no longer like, but there is such a long history, or there are too many other mutual ties that it would be too difficult or painful to end the friendship. People sometimes feel ambivalent towards some of their friends, for example, where the relationship is out of balance in terms of reciprocity or commitment. The phenomenon of the *heart-sink* friend, described in the previous chapter, struck a cord with some people in our study: 'when they phone you think, "Oh no, it's..."'.

The quality of friendship also varies in relation to the length of time people have known each other, and the frequency with which they have contact. In order to know more about a relationship we need to know something about the *friendship career*: for example, the basis of the relationship itself and whether or not it evolves or remains the same.[15]

It is clear, looking at the history of friendships, that they can follow a number of different trajectories. We might assume that friendships begin modestly, perhaps as associates, fun or favour friends, evolving into confidants or soulmates. We might also assume that people form more casual ties when they are young, developing stronger bonds as they get older and their friendships mature. Clearly, however, the picture is far more complex: some people in their twenties already have friends they consider to be soulmates and those in their sixties include associates within their friendship repertoire.[16]

Friendships do not follow a predictable path. They usually begin as simple relationships, based on common activities, sociability or small favours, because it takes time to build the level of trust or commitment on which more supportive or intimate friendships are based. But there is no predictable or linear development: many friendships remain casual, only a few become deeper and more intimate; people appreciate different kinds of friends and are happy to keep several on a more light-hearted level; others do not form intimate friendships at all; some friendships fade or are deliberately ended.

In our own study, we found three main forms of friendship trajectory. Some friendships are *fixed* and the basis of the relationship has remained the same. Looking back at the history of a particular tie it is clear that the friendship has always been based on the same kind of activities. Fixed friendships tend to be fun friends and associates where sharing common interests and having fun are the main focus of the relationship. Even though, over time, the friends may know each other better, feel more comfortable together, and grow fonder of one another, they do not rely on each other for help and support. Although these relationships can often be short-lived, especially where people move to a different location or environment, we also know from our study that people can maintain this kind of friendship for years. For example, one woman in her sixties, who had lived in the same town all her life, had been friends with a couple for forty-eight years. She and her husband would make up a foursome with them and go out for meals from time to time, but she did not confide in or rely on these friends.

Then there are *progressive* friendships in which the basis of the relationship changes, with friends becoming more supportive and intimate. Associates or companions become helpmates, confidants or occasionally soulmates. This process may be gradual, where people build a level of trust and commitment over time as they get to know each other and share experiences. Some friendships get off to a slow start; people may know each other as acquaintances for years and then redefine the relationship at a later stage when they meet up again in a different environment, or find they are in a similar situation. In our study, some people had known each other as children or young adults but the friendship only moved on when they worked together or both had children of their own. Some people had been friendly at college, but the friendship became closer when they met up again through third parties, worked together or shared a flat. Alternatively, the development can be fast track where people become close much more quickly. In this case there is usually a trigger situation or crisis where one person needs help or support and the other rises to the occasion. As we discovered earlier it may be that a friend takes a risk and asks for help or decides to confide personal information, or it may be that a friend takes the initiative and makes a gesture of support. We found that people cannot always predict who will actually come through, for example, there were people in our study who were surprised by an unexpected show of support. One woman found that it was a neighbourly rather than best friend who was able to be more dispassionate, sympathetic and available when she was going through her divorce.

Other friendships, however, are *variable* and the degree of support and intimacy may come and go, depending on people's circumstances and commitments. Sometimes, a friend who was a crucial support at a particular stage goes back to being a more casual contact. Some friends play a purely fire-fighting role, coming to the rescue in a crisis but having little everyday contact. Friendships can also be re-established. For example, friends may lose touch, move away, become immersed in work and family, but then reactivate the friendship at a later stage when their situation has changed. As we shall see in the following chapter, people spoke of rediscovering old friends after they divorced, after their children had left home, and after they retired.

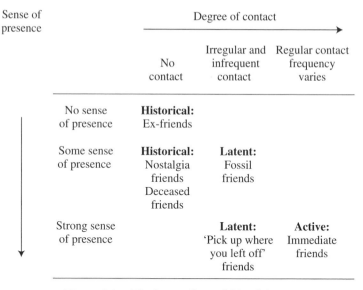

Figure 3.2.   The immediacy of friendships.

Linked to changes in the basis of a friendship are variations in its *immediacy*, in the *frequency and regularity of contact* between friends and in the *psychological presence* friends have in each other's lives. People described this sense of presence as the extent to which friends think about each other, the extent to which 'they're just there, frequently, in the back of your mind', 'you include them in your plans', 'you wonder about their welfare'.[17] Looked at in terms of presence as well as contact, we find that friendships range in immediacy from active relationships to historical ties; between theses two extremes are various kinds of latent friendship (see Figure 3.2)

With active, *immediate* friends there is regular predictable contact, though frequency varies. These are the current friends whom people immediately think of and include in their personal community. But people also include latent friendships where there is still a sense of presence but only irregular and infrequent contact. Some of these latent relationships are 'pick up where you left off' friends, where there is no need to re-establish the relationship and the bond is secure enough to withstand long periods of separation: 'it's as though it was only yesterday that we last met'. Alternatively, latent friendships can be *fossil* friends where there is still some trace or imprint of the relationship but the friendship is essentially on the back burner, to be re-activated in the future or allowed, gradually, to end. Some people described the way in which fossil friends could remain on their Christmas card list for years before more regular contact was re-established or the friends were dropped.

Finally there are historical friendships where there is no contact at all. Some of these are actually ex-friends and the relationship has faded or been deliberately ended. Not surprisingly, these friendships are usually excluded from people's personal communities. But we also found historical friends who still have a positive presence in people's lives. We have called these *nostalgia* friends because it is the memories of shared experiences in the past that keep the relationship in mind. One older man in our study included a friend he had not contacted in over twenty years. The two men had met when they were evacuees together in World War II: 'we spent so much time together as young boys, you know, we were always out and about... I suppose it's the memories, really, and things that we've done.' Nostalgia friends can also encompass those who are deceased and people sometimes asked if they could include these friends on their map. As we saw in chapter 2, one man listed three such friends, describing them as stars above him.

Of course, as the term ex-friend suggests, some friendships come to an end. A recurrent pattern in our study was for the relationship to fade or fizzle out gradually. It is not that friends have fallen out, but they may move away, have competing commitments and attachments, develop different interests, have less in common, and eventually lose touch. Sometimes, they become less comfortable with each other if their lives follow very different patterns and they do not share similar experiences or lifestyles. Sometimes they disappoint each other by not providing hoped for help and support.

There are occasions, however, where a friendship is deliberately ended. In our own study friendships had broken down over religious and political disagreements. We also discovered the phenomenon of the 'confiscated' friend, where a partner disliked, disapproved or was jealous of an old friend and the friendship was eventually dropped. Friends had also been 'dumped' where they had betrayed confidences and told secrets, behaved unethically or dishonestly, where there was chronic lack of reciprocity or friends were too high maintenance, where they had made sexual advances to the friend or the friend's partner, or in one case to the friend's son. As we discuss at the end of this chapter, friendship has a moral dimension.

Friends and Other Kinds of Friendly Relationships

In addition to friends, people also recognize other types of friendly relationships.[18] For example, there are acquaintances, described as people who are pleasant to each other and who might engage in limited sociability, but intimacy is avoided. Acquaintances are kept at arm's length: 'they're people you say "hello" to but you don't tell them your business'. Then there are neighbours who often provide practical support, exchanging favours, but remain 'just good neighbours' if the relationship is confined to this role. Workmates and colleagues are sometimes sociable or give help and support at work but, if the relationship does not extend beyond the workplace, remain 'just someone I work with'.

Of course, these friendly relationships have very similar qualities to the simple friendships outlined above, for example, associates, fun or neighbourly friends, and may vary only in the nature of the emotional bond or the sense of commitment. What is clear, however, is that the term 'friend' is used in more and less inclusive ways. While some people encompass all friendly relationships under the banner of friendship, others make a distinction between friends and acquaintances, neighbours or colleagues, reserving the term 'friend' for more multifaceted, affectionate and committed relationships.[19] However, when introducing a mix of friends and friendly contacts to each other, people may employ the word 'friend' rather loosely in order to avoid any unintended slight.

Best Friends

Best friends are often soulmates, but the term is also applied to friendships which are strongest on whatever dimension is important to the person concerned. So a best friend can be the closest emotionally, the most reliable, the most trustworthy, the greatest fun, the one with whom you have most in common, or the one you have known for the longest time.

Not everyone has a best friend, however. In some cases, people cannot distinguish between several good friends because they value the special character of each relationship. In other cases, people do not have any particularly strong friendships. Sometimes the person they would like to call a best friend does not hold the friendship in the same regard. We also found people who did not believe in best friends, feeling that the concept had childish connotations and was 'something you grow out of when you leave school.'[20]

FRIENDSHIP REPERTOIRES

In chapter 2 we discussed the idea that, according to psychologists, people vary in their ability to make and sustain more intimate forms of friendship. We found that anthropologists believe certain kinds of friendship are unlikely to develop in particular cultures. And we discovered that philosophers like Aristotle went so far as to say that only certain people can and should be friends of virtue. Although our own study is not concerned with psychological capacities or moral judgments, we are nevertheless interested in the kinds of friendships people make. Having identified and explored different types of friendship and friendly relations, we now turn to consider the range of friendships people include in their personal community, and describe four kinds of *friendship repertoire* found in our study.[21]

Basic Repertoires

Some people include only simple friendships, usually fun friends and associates. In this kind of repertoire, friends play limited and specialized roles, sharing interests and activities or socializing together, but they are not treated as confidants or relied on in times of trouble. In our study, people with basic friendship repertoires looked to family members or a partner for more intimate or supportive relationships or, in some cases, preferred to sort things out on their own.

An example of someone with a basic friendship repertoire is Wayne. In his mid twenties, single and living with his parents, Wayne was brought up and has remained in the same small town close to the Welsh border. Having attended schools locally, Wayne now works at a local garage as a finisher. His social life revolves around drinking in the pub or going clubbing with his mates. In his personal community Wayne included a number of friends, most of whom he knew from school days. Wayne thinks of his friends as 'all the same really'; all the friendships are based on going out together and having fun. The only way Wayne distinguishes between his friends is in terms of how frequently he sees them, and 'how much of a laugh' they are. Wayne sees himself as fairly self-reliant and does not look to others – friends or family – as confidants; if he needs some kind of practical help, he relies on his mother and father.

Jackie also has a basic friendship repertoire. In her late thirties, from a mixed race background, Jackie lives in London with her partner and has three young children. Her mother and siblings all live within ten miles and she describes herself as very family-minded. Before having children she worked full-time in a series of secretarial jobs but has recently run a catering business from home, and now works a few evenings a week as a debt collector when her partner or a member of her family looks after the children. Jackie has made friends through secretarial college, work and the local church, but all these friends are strictly fun friends or associates. It is her mother and sisters who act as confidantes and provide practical and emotional support. However, Jackie has not always had this kind of friendship repertoire and used to have a confiding relationship with her close friend Claudia:

> I thought she was a very good friend but we don't talk any more... she was someone I confided in about everything. I've known Winston [partner] for a good sixteen, seventeen years now and there have been a lot of off and on periods with us two, but the things I used to confide in her about that relationship was between me and her... And we went on this business course... maybe in the early nineties... and I had some babysitting problems, the babysitter I had was messing me about, my kids weren't even in school yet, so I had to take a couple of weeks off the course while I was sorting that out. And then when I got back on the course all these people that I'd known nothing about was telling me, 'oh I heard you split up with Winston' and 'oh how did he do this and that to you?' And all my life's spouting out! And I was really mad about that to be honest 'cause not so much, you know, that I'm such a big shot, but to me it was something that I told her alone and she went and blabbed her mouth... and I think it shocked me more because I'd never known her to be that way. It's one of those things that I've just never been able to get over.

After that experience Jackie made a conscious decision to rely only on her family and to keep her friendships on a more light-hearted, casual basis: 'I don't really want to lose any more trust in my friends so I tend not to give them too much more than I want them to know.'

Intense Repertoires

By contrast, other people include only complex close friendships, such as confidants or soulmates, in their personal community. People with intense friendship repertoires make a sharp distinction between 'true friends' and other friendly relationships such acquaintances who are not considered sufficiently important to be on the map.

Ron is an example of someone with an intense friendship repertoire, and was the only person in our study who included just one friend in his personal community. Ron is in his fifties, divorced and living with a second partner, and has one son from his first marriage. After completing an engineering apprenticeship, Ron worked in a number of different capacities, for example, at a local airport and as a fitter in a small engineering company. He has moved a number of times but always within the southeast of England and now lives in Essex. Ron and his great friend Rick met through work when they were in their late teens and their friendship has developed and deepened over the course of more than thirty years. As well as enjoying each other's company, the two men are confidants and supported each other through the break up of their first marriages. Although Ron knows a lot of other people, he feels there is 'nothing personal' about these relationships:

> I am an outgoing sort of person so, yes, I meet lots and lots of people, but really they're, you'd call them just acquaintances I suppose. . . I don't meet them on a regular basis, only down the local pub, and things like that – going to football matches, sort of thing.

Apart from his deep friendship with Rick, Ron has one other very close relationship, his partner, whom he also considers his best friend. Between them, his partner and close friend play a wide range of roles, and Ron does not look to anyone else for support. He has a jokey, sociable relationship with his grown-up son, and rather ambivalent relationships with his mother and step-daughter, the only other people included on his map. He described the whole of his personal community by saying 'that's it, that's my nucleus'.

Focal Repertoires

Unlike basic or intense repertoires where the range of friendship types is narrow, in focal repertoires people include both simple and complex friendships in their personal community, but these repertoires contain a small core of soulmates or confidants and a much larger group of associates and fun friends. Michelle is someone with this kind of repertoire. Now in her mid thirties, Michelle has lived all her life on the borders of northeast London and Essex and made many of her friends in her late teens and early twenties from among 'a local crowd.' Her husband was also part of the same group and she has known him since she was fourteen. Many of Michelle's longstanding friends have remained sociable, fun friends, and the relationship has not become more intimate, partly because Michelle, on her own admission, puts a lot of time and energy into family relationships: with her husband and two teenage sons, her parents, sisters, cousins and in-laws. Over the years, however, Michelle has encountered a few of her long-established friends in other contexts, and this has led to a deepening of the relationship. For example, she discovered that an old friend had opened her own dress shop and now the two friends work together:

> When you're working with someone all the time, you know, obviously you go through things with them, their children growing up and you see all the things that affect them and you know, you just sort of grow together... If she has an argument with her husband on the phone, I'm there and I can hear it all, and the same with me and my husband, you know and you sort of, you get involved because of it, because you're altogether in that close little vicinity.

Being in constant contact, and seeing each other in another environment, has led to the two women becoming close confidantes who support each other in a number of different ways. Apart from a small core of intimate friends, however, Michelle's other friendships are purely sociable, and she relies heavily on her partner and other family members for emotional and practical support.

Broad Repertoires

Finally, broad friendship repertoires contain both simple and complex friendships but people include a wider range of friendship types in their personal community, from associates and fun friends to helpmates, supporters, confidants and soulmates. In this kind of repertoire, fun friends are not necessarily in the majority, and may be outnumbered by helpmates or confidants, though soulmates rarely number more than one or two. Friends play many different roles and people with this kind of repertoire take their friendships very seriously. They tend to appreciate the particular qualities of different kinds of friendship. Some spoke of the need to balance their range of friends, feeling that they could only cope with a certain number of intimate or demanding friendships. Harriet, for example, felt 'there are times when I think I don't have room for this relationship. There really isn't time, I mean there's quite a lot there already who are high maintenance.'

Henrietta is an example of someone with a broad friendship repertoire. In her mid fifties, the daughter of an earl, Henrietta is married to a merchant banker and has four grown-up children. She and her husband live in a large Georgian house with extensive grounds, and

Henrietta herself is a passionate gardener. Brought up in Hampshire, she was educated privately at home before going away to boarding school and then to art college in London; she still has an aura of art school about her, dressing in a colourful, unconventional style. Henrietta describes herself as not having been at all career-minded, preferring to travel and have fun, and giving up work when she married at the age of twenty-four. She included many different kinds of friends in her personal community, several of whom she has known for over thirty years. Some were friends from childhood, daughters of her mother's closest friends, some were from boarding school. In London she was introduced to the sons and daughters of other family friends, meeting some during her season as a debutante, and she has retained many of these friends from her single days. When her children were young she moved from London to live in Norfolk, where friends again put her in touch with other local families.

Henrietta appreciates having a range of different kinds of friends. Some she describes as

> absolute rocks, they'd absolutely sort of come up trumps, you know, every time. . . and I love them partly because I know they're rocks, I'd be deeply disillusioned if they weren't. Whereas someone like Jilly is utterly. . . and incredibly selfish and I love her. . . so I don't expect anything from her ever. . . I mean on the whole the flighty ones are the most fun to be with.
>
> [Felicity] was a kind of rock to me when I was sort of chaotic and hopeless. . . but she's not discreet, she's a frightful gossip, so that holds you back a bit – otherwise she's terrific fun, I love being with her.

Although Henrietta sees herself as very family-minded, she feels a strong sense of responsibility to close friends. Because she wants to be able to support them if they need her, she is not open to forming many more close friendships unless they are either very special or very undemanding.

> I've noticed, actually it's very interesting, I've become much lazier as I've grown older. Most of the people, my new friends, are people who make the effort with me. I don't feel I need any more friends unless they're exceptional nowadays, I've got enough. Do you feel like that? . . . I feel there's not time to see the ones one loves, so unless somebody's very special, I don't make the effort I'm afraid.

Consequently, in her personal community, Henrietta has longstanding friendships which are mainly very close, and some more recent 'special' friendships. Other recent friendships, however, made through children's schools, are entirely sociable and not considered sufficiently important to appear on her map.

THE NATURE OF COMMITMENT WITHIN FRIENDSHIP: A PARTICULAR MORALITY

Although friends are essentially chosen relationships, our exploration of different types of friendship demonstrates that choice per se does not necessarily imply a lack of commitment. As we have seen, friendships range from loose and transient ties to lifelong bonds. Committed friendships are alive and well, but what does commitment in friendship mean? Over two thousand years ago Aristotle maintained that virtuous friendship had a strong moral dimension; virtuous friends enlarge and extend each other's moral experience. The friends are bound together, becoming, as it were, each other, as they recognize each other's moral excellence. Each can be said to provide a mirror in which the other may see himself. It may thus be claimed that this pure Aristotelian form of friendship constitutes the most complete moral experience of which a human being is capable. According to Aristotle, the combination of the loving perception of individuals with the apprehension of their virtue helps us to achieve the good life.

> Friendship derives its moral significance both from the choice that presides at its formation and from the virtues involved in its cultivation. To that extent it signals a concordance between reason, passion and desire.[22]

Nowadays when people talk about what it means to call someone a friend, it seems that part of their conception of friendship still implies a certain kind of morality.[23] Interestingly, many contemporary soap operas on radio and television have as their main theme the responsibilities and limits of friendship. These are frequently highly moral tales. How can we be loyal to our friend who is cheating on her partner who is also a close friend? Should you, as a friend, intervene in a situation of domestic violence when you are the only outsider who knows what is going on? The agony columns of newspapers and magazines provide a stream of examples. It is among our closest friends that we work out together what the right thing to do might be. Part of the function of friendship is to provide the anvil on which we may individually beat out our own personal moralities. In this sense, public debates about friendship raise issues about contemporary morality, even though relationships between friends, in practice, may fall short of expectations.

One element of the moral dimension of friendship is that good friends are supposed to have a sense of allegiance and loyalty to each other. A friend is someone who looks out for you or is on your side. Friends should stick up for one another: 'you shouldn't bad mouth friends'. Friends are happy for you when things go well and if a friend is unhappy, you want to know why, to try and sort the problem.

Constancy is also a component of the commitment between friends. Good friends should remain friends no matter what, and see each other through bad times as well as good. Friendships should also be able to survive ups and downs within the relationship itself, and people described friendships that had endured despite 'blinding rows'. Constancy, however, is not necessarily achieved or even desired in some friendships, which are allowed to fade or, in certain circumstances, are deliberately ended.

Friends are supposed to be trustworthy and not betray secrets. As we have seen, of course, not all friends are treated as confidants, but when people do confide, they expect the friend to be discreet. Breaking confidences is seen as a particularly serious betrayal, and can lead to friends being 'dumped'.

Acceptance and affirmation are also key elements of the morality of friendship. A friend is someone who accepts you for who you are. Not being judged or disapproved of can be an immensely valued aspect of friendship:

> I mean it's about sort of unconditional acceptance, isn't it, really? Yeah – I mean they get on your nerves, don't they, but you know, it doesn't change the way you feel. You don't wake up one morning and think: 'I don't love them any more.'

Running slightly contrary to this, however, is the view that good friends should be honest and 'tell it how it is.' Indeed, some feel that friends can be more honest with each other than with certain members of their family, because friends do not feel obliged to protect each other to the extent that parents and adult children do. But resolving the tension between affirmation and honesty is not straightforward. Julian, a nonconformist minister in his forties, described the different reactions among his friends when his marriage broke up:

> There were some people who came wading in and told you how to put it right or whatever... then there were others who were sort of, you know:

'Oh, it doesn't matter' and 'Carry on', and you think: 'Well, obviously it matters'. . . There were loads of people to give you advice/judgment/ what God thinks/what the Bible thinks, whatever, but there weren't many people who just wanted to be there.

He recounted his own dilemma when dealing with a friend who was experiencing similar problems:

I said, 'Look, I tell you what, just come and be, just come and, you know, get the bike out, let's go for a ride, just chill. If you wanna talk, talk, if you don't, don't. If you wanna cry, do – whatever, just do it'. . . With one exception. . . there was one day I said: 'Look, I think, because I've tried to be a friend, I probably haven't been a true friend, cos I've thought I can't tell you what I think. . . so I'll just tell you once what I think, and then if it hurts too much and you don't wanna see me again I'll run that risk, but other than that I'm not gonna say it.'

Not wanting to 'hear it how it is' can actually deter people from confiding in friends. For example, a number of men in our study had decided not to tell close friends they were planning to leave their partner: 'I had already made up my mind. I didn't want advice. . . I knew what they'd say.'

Friendships are also supposed to be reciprocal relationships, yet the importance people attach to reciprocity varies enormously. For some it is a major factor and they resent friends who are too demanding but offer little in return. They describe being disenchanted with certain friends who are very needy and only phone when they are trouble. It is not that friends are necessarily keeping a precise tally: 'No one's keeping a record of, "Oh that's twice you've done that to me, and I've only done it back to you once." It's just an ongoing thing.' The sense of reciprocity within friendship is usually much more diffuse, but some people need to feel that in the long run there is some balance in the relationship.[24] For others, reciprocity is less of a central concern. They accept that some friends are less able or less willing to contribute to the relationship, but find that the friendship has other qualities which are valued, for example, shared history and experiences, shared interests, fun. Sometimes it is a case of balancing reciprocity across the friendship repertoire, rather than looking for it in a particular relationship.

Mutuality, the sense that people feel the same way about a relationship, is something people hope for but which they acknowledge may not always be present in friendships. In our own study we found that people are sometimes aware of disparities where they feel they care less or more than their friend, and this was borne out when we interviewed the other party to a friendship and found that in some cases friendships are not equally valued. Where relationships become very unbalanced, the person who is doing all the running may finally decide to let the relationship fade, but the less committed party may not always be able to shake off a friendship. Ending friendships can sometimes be difficult when one party wishes to maintain the relationship, where there are friends in common, or where the relationship is based on a strong sense of obligation.

Another rule of friendship concerns sexual relationships. Some people feel very strongly that you should not have sex with friends because this alters the nature of the friendship and, if and when the sexual relationship ends, may jeopardize the future of the friendship. People vary in the extent to which they feel comfortable having friends of the opposite sex. In heterosexual cross-sex friendships, there may be a sexual element or tension, which has to be sorted out.[25] Patrick described the difficulty of managing friendships with women. When he had first started his medical training, surrounded by nurses, he had felt 'like a boy in a sweet shop'; he found it difficult to

> draw the line, but I'm getting better at it now... I have to make a conscious effort and work at it, because if I like a woman, I like her sexually as well... because usually I go for physically attractive women to make friends with.

Of course, friendships may develop from past love affairs, though exlovers were only occasionally mentioned as friends in our study. For some people, however, there is no conflict between sex and friendship and certainly, for some of the gay men we interviewed, sex with friends is not necessarily out of bounds and may even be a key component of developing a friendship.[26] One aspect of sex and friendship, which is seen as taboo, is sexual relations with the partner or spouse of a friend, because it is a betrayal of trust. However, some gay men in our study felt there were no hard and fast rules about this, arguing that it would depend on the extent to which a sexual relationship was meant to be exclusive.

Because friendship is a chosen relationship, it is based on voluntary commitment rather than formal obligations. Although friends may hope for loyalty, constancy, trustworthiness, acceptance, honesty and reciprocity, they cannot expect these as of right. Friends recognize that 'you shouldn't push friendship too far', 'my theory is that you should not put too much on friends... it's not fair to test them', and this last rule, the idea of setting limits to expectations, seems to encapsulate the essence of commitment within chosen relationships. Not all friendships are based on these qualities, nor do people look for commitment in every friendship. Where friendships are strongly committed, however, they are considered special and highly prized, precisely because the commitment is freely given.

This chapter has given a picture of friendships at a particular point in their history and described the way they can change over time. We now look at friendship over the life-course, exploring how different stages and events provide opportunities and constraints in the friend-making enterprise, and how people vary in the way they make and keep friends at different times in their life.

CHAPTER FOUR

Patterns of Friend-Making

Surely this Sort of Friend. . . having been tryd, & found, kind and officious so long, thro so many accidents and needs of life, is surely Equal to a meer Natural Tye. Indeed tis Nature that makes us Love, but tis Experience that makes us Grateful.

— Pope

Each person's life can be seen as comprising a series of strata, almost like geological layers – early childhood, school, college or university, past or present work, past or present neighbours – some of the companions from which may be retained as he or she ages.

— Willmott

As Willmott suggests, exploring friendships and friendship repertoires at a particular point in people's lives is like taking a snapshot of friendship imprints. But friendship is dynamic and, as we saw in the previous chapter, individual relationships may follow quite different trajectories, becoming deeper or fading in importance over time. Friendship is also dynamic in the sense that people vary in the way they make or lose friends at different stages in their lives. In this second chapter on friendship, our concern is to understand how people come to have a particular set of friends. We find that people have rather different patterns of friend-making, or *friendship modes*, and that, while some make the most of their significant or important friends at a particular stage in the life-course, others are open to making these kinds of friends throughout their lives. We describe four different friendship modes in the latter part of the chapter, illustrating each with a case from our study.

In order to make sense of these friend-making modes or patterns, however, we need to understand the way different life-course stages and events provide a set of contexts in which friendships can be formed and maintained but in which they can also be lost. Of course, friendship and the life-course is a very well-researched and documented area, and those already familiar with this field may decide to skip ahead to the second half of the chapter.[1] Our reason for including a discussion here is not to provide new insights but to provide a context for our review of friendship modes, and to give a basis for our structural analysis of personal communities in chapter 7.

Friendship and the Life-Course

In exploring relationships throughout the life-course we have been influenced by the idea of people having a 'social convoy' or a set of significant others, be they family or friends, which may change over time.[2] In the case of family, it is easy to see how members of a convoy may change as kith and kin are added or lost through birth, marriage, remarriage and death. With friends, however the process is not quite so straightforward since friendships are not usually simply acquired but have to be established and maintained. Each life-course stage and event is an opportunity for friend-making, providing a context in which people discover they have something in common, be it circumstances, interests, lifestyle, values.[3] But the very same situations and life-course stages are also the contexts in which friendships are conducted. As such they may provide opportunities for relationships to strengthen and deepen, but may also be a source of pressures and conflicting commitments, so that some friendships are neglected, and people drift apart. (This process is shown diagrammatically in Figure 4.1.)

For children and adolescents, school is the context of most of their earliest experiences of friendship.[4] Maintaining friendships once people have left school, however, is not always easy and some school friendships do not last, especially where they were simply fun friends or associates. Take the case of Don, for example, a young man of eighteen who left school two years ago. Don is single and looking for work. He was brought up in care but recently moved into a rented flat, where he lives on his own. Even though Don lived with a series of foster parents he always remained in the same neighbourhood and was able to stay at the same secondary school, where he had a wide circle of

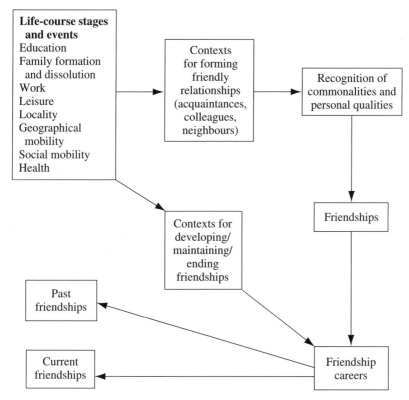

Figure 4.1. Friendship and the life-course.

friends. Two years later, although the friendship group has dispersed and Don has lost touch with seven members of the original 'gang', he is still in contact with some of the group and included nine school friends in his personal community, several of whom he considers helpmates and confidants.

Changing or leaving school can test a relationship because friends have to make an effort to keep in touch. While some school friendships fizzle out simply through lack of regular contact, others fade because leaving school is a major life-course transition. People make a range of different choices, meet a new set of friends, and sometimes discover that their different experiences mean they no longer have much in common. In Don's case, some of the friendships had ended through lack of contact, but others had faded because the friends had followed very different paths, for example, going straight to work, attending local college or going away to university. Don was not surprised, nor did he have regrets about losing touch with some of these friends. He even claimed he knew when he left school which friendships were likely to last and which would probably come to an end within a short space of time:

> These ones, the ones I've not put on the map, were best mates at the time, but they were just part of a group, you know, that went around together at school. But we didn't sort of see each other out of school, it wasn't a special friendship, if you know what I mean.[5]

However, where school friendships survive the early years of adulthood and the competing commitments of work and family formation, they can become life-long relationships.[6] In our own study, we encountered people in their forties, fifties, sixties and even seventies who still had one or two friends from school days. Terry, in his mid sixties, whose friendship with his model boat club associates we described in the previous chapter, is someone who is still in touch with a number of friends he made at school. Five of these – two helpmates and three fun friends – he considers sufficiently important to include in his personal community. All five still live in the same neighbourhood in which they grew up.

College and university are also important contexts in which friendships are made, partly because there are concentrations of people of similar ages and interests, and also because they are very sociable environments. While student friends are often simply fun companions, people can still form strong and intimate ties in a relatively short time.[7] This is particularly true where people are living together away from home, and there is a greater intensity of contact. Emily, single in her late twenties, has recently graduated from Bristol University and is about to move to London to start a new job. Although she has a couple of close longstanding friendships from her teenage years, and some other friends from jobs she did before becoming a student, the majority of the friends listed in her personal community have been fellow students in Bristol. Some of these are light-hearted, essentially fun, friendships, but Emily has also made some very close confiding friendships in the three years she spent away from home. She described the way in which sharing a flat provided an easy environment for intimacy to be established: 'I've spent a lot of time with Suzy, just all day and all night and you know... we can talk about just absolutely everything.' The fact that Suzy was seven years younger than Emily was not an issue, and Emily felt she had more in common with her – because of their shared lifestyle and stage in the life-course – than with friends of her own age who were starting to settle down with long-term partners:

> What I like about her, she's funny, she wants to do things, she wants to travel and stuff like that. . . and also, I think, she's going through different things with boyfriends and friendships, and it's just discussing all those things, again, that people that are older don't talk about anymore.

While college and university are environments that provide many opportunities for making friends, being a student sometimes makes it difficult for people to keep up with other friends. There are the distractions of new friendships, and different experiences can mean that erstwhile friends find they have little in common. We found cases where those who did not go on to higher education felt that their student friends had left them behind. For example, Emily recalled an initial period of adjustment in her relationship with her two best friends, Judy and Rebecca, both of whom opted to start work straight from sixth-form college, and continued to live at home:

> I think we've had up and down periods but I think that we know that. 'Cos when I've been at university, I think there's been a time when, like at the beginning, I was making new friends and they were sort of. . . 'Oh, we're making new friends, we've moved on', or something like that. And then I think it was just a bit of a sort of misunderstanding, misconnection, stuff like that, and then we all sort of. . . well, we're good friends now. Maybe it's just growing up a bit and realizing that you still keep in touch with your old friends anyway.

As with school friends, while some student friendships go on to be long-term relationships, others fade almost straight away. Emily, for example, felt she knew which friendships were well founded and solid and those which were unlikely to survive lengthy separation. Indeed, even over the course of a few months, she had already lost touch with some student friends.

Going out with a boyfriend or girlfriend, settling down with a partner, or getting married all have an immense impact on people's friendships.[8] Being part of a couple provides an opportunity to make new friends. The new couple may adopt some of each other's friends, developing an intimate friendship of their own, or, alternatively forming a simple fun friendship, accepting that the original friends will have the closer relationship. As a couple, people also make new friends together, often with other couples. In our own study we found that while some couples have an almost completely overlapping set of friends, most of whom are other couples, others have a number of friends in common but also retain their own separate set of friends. In a few cases, however, we found couples that did not include any common friends in their personal community.[9]

Where friendships are foursomes there is sometimes, though not always, a particular dynamic, with people being more comfortable with the friend of the same sex. Esther, whose friendships we described in the previous chapter, contrasted evenings spent with one couple where

> you find with a foursome that George and Martin end up talking to each other, and then I end up talking to Claudia... They tend to talk about business and we talk about fashion, and what's next, and the children, and where we can meet again.

By contrast, with her great friends Sarena and Robert the four all talk together rather than with the friend of the same sex.

Being part of a couple can also make it difficult to maintain earlier friendships. The main problems arise because of competing commitments and loyalties. At the beginning of a relationship, the couple spend a great deal of time together and old friends may be neglected. Emily's friend, Judy, recounted how she and Emily felt when their great friend Rebecca became engaged:

> I mean Jack's a really lovely bloke and I've, you know, met him through my brother and ... I mean she couldn't have really met a nicer bloke but it... I think... I'm not sure whether it's because she'll be married that will make the difference. I think it's probably also because we feel that we're sort of having to share her now, and she's got this other person that she can talk to and do things with, whereas before it was always me and Emily, the three of us.

Also, with today's companionate marriage, couples may expect to be good friends and to spend a lot of time in each other's company. Charles, a translator in his mid fifties who was married for twenty-five years before he came out as gay, went so far as to claim that heterosexual marriage placed great pressure on friendship because it was generally too exclusive and possessive:

> I've seen it so often in married relationships, how they actually have very few friends... I think that one of the tragedies of marriage is that so often it is a bar to this outer world of relationships.

Charles himself felt that he had been much freer to invest in friends since his divorce:

I had always gone through life regarding friends as very important, and seeing the husband and wife relationship as a bar to friendship. And I think that my life is measurably richer in many ways because my marriage broke up. It gave me the freedom to live as I want to live, which is surrounded by a large number of friends.

Sometimes one partner makes little effort to get on with, or actively dislikes, some of the other's friends. Unless the friends meet separately and work at maintaining their friendship, they can easily lose touch and the friendship can fade, especially if the partner acts as a kind of gatekeeper, limiting or discouraging contact. Sometimes it is the case that a friend does not like the new partner and the friends may opt to cool the relationship rather than risk upsetting the partnership. Roger, a lone parent in his fifties, whose circle of friends we encountered in the previous chapter, described the rift that occurred when a longstanding friend formed a new attachment:

There used to be three of us, there was Paddy and me and a chap called Dick, and we were friends for thirty-five years... then Dick fell in love with this woman, and she's appalling, she's absolutely the worst person you could ever meet in your life. And now we don't have anything to do with each other... yet Dick and I had been friends for years and years and years.

The first major upheaval takes place in late teens and early adulthood when people start pairing off. Terry's great friend John remembered how a childhood friend resented it when he and Terry began to form attachments with girls:

Len was sneering, you know what I mean, because we'd been buddy-buddies together, and of course I was going with Edith, Terry was going with Doreen. 'You're not going to the pictures? Why, won't the bride let you?' you know, that sort of thing.

Once the pairing off begins, friendship groups of singles and couples can be difficult to maintain, as Harriet, whose friendships we described in chapter 3, explained: 'we had the archetypal friends gang, and then it all went horribly wrong 'cause people started splitting up and seeing each other.' Harriet, who is coming up to forty, is single and living in London. Her circle of friends is changing as her previously single friends settle down with their partners. She recently lost touch with one fun friend since it was mainly a singles relationship that suffered once the friend had 'snared her man'. As we saw in the previous chapter, Harriet has a number of 'high maintenance', intimate friends:

'and it does mean phone calls several times a week, for an hour or whatever, just not hurrying somebody through it.'

She recognizes that this situation is manageable while she is still single but that she may get distracted once she settles with a partner. This concerns her, since she does not want the value of friendships to be undermined. She is well aware of the need to retain supportive friends because of the possible dangers of splitting up with a partner: 'I'd hate to just take that away because who knows what might happen. Things change all the time.' Some women regretted that they had let their relationships with men affect their friendships so much. Jenny, a young woman in her mid twenties who has recently bought a flat with her boyfriend, was aware how much her social life revolved around her partner's circle of friends and how she had neglected fun friends and confidantes from her single days:

> For a while I didn't keep in touch with [my friends] when I started seeing Duncan, and then I thought, 'this is really stupid, I'm surrounding myself with people I know through him... if we split up or anything, then I'm going to be left with absolutely no mates'... I'd make a lot more of an effort there, if I sort of had the chance again.

With the increase in short-term cohabitation, divorce and remarriage, however, the difficulty of maintaining friendships in the face of new partnerships is not confined to a particular stage in the life-course, but may occur throughout adult life. Friendships can wax and wane depending on whether a friend has a new partner. Henrietta, whose broad friendship repertoire we have already described, is in her mid fifties and has a number of women friends whose availability varies according to the status of their romantic attachments: 'she floats in and out of my life... she comes and goes. I mean... she's in the first circle [on the map] when she hasn't got a man.'

When partnerships and marriages end, this again has an impact on friendships.[10] Where people have maintained their own individual friends, then these relationships tend to survive, but the partner's friends and some joint friends may be lost. In some cases, where friends side with the other partner, the split allegiances mean the friendship becomes impossible to sustain; sometimes the friendship becomes tainted: there are just too many unhappy associations, and people want to make a fresh start. Charles, for example, had lost touch with most of his friends from his married days, and even from the town where he and his wife had lived, because of unpleasant memories.

On the other hand, splitting up can also be the making of some friendships when the relationship moves to another level. People spoke of friends helping them to keep their sanity when their relationships were breaking down. For example, Chantal, a teacher in her mid forties, described this kind of relationship with a friend from work who was going through a similar crisis:

> You know we'd do the telephone thing where I'd ring her, and we'd spend two hours on the phone, and then we'd have a wee break, and then we'd go back and she'd ring me. Or we'd cook and I'd take food round for her on a Friday evening. . . or she'd cook and bring stuff over here.

Becoming a parent is another life-course event that has major implications for friendship.[11] Once they become parents, people have little time or energy to spare and find it difficult to give much attention to their friends, especially if they are also trying to maintain work commitments or build a career. While well-established relationships may remain intact, friends who are high maintenance, who do not live locally or who do not have children may be neglected or lost. Roger recalled how hard it had been for him, when he became a lone father, to socialize with fun friends when his daughter was young because none of his friends had children at that stage.

When people become parents, their friends without children can feel neglected and left out. Some greet the news that a friend is expecting a child with mixed feelings as they anticipate, or know from experience, that the friendship will change. If people have not had children themselves, being surrounded by friends with children can be a frustrating, and sometimes painful, experience. Diana is in her forties, has made three complete career changes – from nurse, to music teacher, to careers adviser – and lived in different parts of the country. She has never married or had children, something she regrets but also feels very strongly has affected some of her friendships:

> We used to go out to dinner and go round to each other's houses and have a circle of dinner parties, but in the end they were only talking about their children and their achievements. And in the end I said to Jackie, 'Do you know, tonight, we've talked about nothing but other people's children?' So they dropped me, and I was glad they had, because I just couldn't sit there. We weren't talking politics, we weren't talking anything interesting, they were only talking about their children.

On the other hand, because of the difficulty of keeping up with friends, parents, particularly mothers, often make new friendships in the course of having and caring for their children.[12] A number of women in our study met other mothers through antenatal classes, playgroup, nursery, school and extra-curricular activities. These friendships often involved an exchange of favours and practical help, with friends looking after each other's children, taking and collecting them from school. Where both parents become involved, the couples may form companionable friendships or the two families may become family friends. Sometimes these relationships develop into more intimate confiding ties, and the friendship survives long after the children have left home, but in other cases they remain favour friends and tend not to last. Some women in our study regretted that they had not developed deeper friendships with other mothers. For example, Gill, in her mid fifties, gave up work in an advertising agency to care for her husband's children at a time when none of her own friends had children. Then, in her late thirties, she had children of her own but felt that, by that time, she had 'missed out':

> I was really too old to be friends with the other mums. . . I don't have any friends that I can go off with and have a drink in the pub. I don't have friends like that because I've been with children for twenty-odd years.

Brenda, whose neighbourly friends we described in the previous chapter, also regretted that she had neglected individual friendships:

> When the kids were young that was enough for me, like, you know, you're married, you think your kids come first. There was always somebody about, and I worked a bit in between, you know, so I was quite happy and content with that. . . I've always been one that's had a lot of friends, if you know what I mean, not one in particular but there's always been, like, a gang so if one dropped out you know there was still another gang, but now I've just got nobody at all.

Work is another extremely important context in which friendships can be made. Where people spend a lot of time with workmates and colleagues, there is an opportunity to get to know each other fairly well. Judy, for example, who commutes to London and works as a pensions administrator, has made many of her friends through her job, and most of her weekday socializing is spent with past and present colleagues. Working in a common professional field, and sharing a common interest or set of beliefs, can also be a powerful basis for friendship. Robert, a psychotherapist, whose great friendship with his soulmate Christopher we have already described, felt that their relationship was partly based on the fact that 'we are [both] concerned tremendously about human beings and their care'.

But people do not make friends indiscriminately at work, and tend to be quite selective, befriending only some of the people they work with. They are aware of a number of strains in work-based friendships. There can be competition between status equals, and status differentials can inhibit the formation of friendships as people are wary of letting down their guard with those in different positions within the hierarchy.[13] Work environments also vary a great deal in terms of their friendship potential.[14] For example, Harriet contrasted her experience at a computer games company – where most of the workforce came from similar backgrounds, were of a similar age and at the same level within the organization – where she numbered fun friends and confidants among her colleagues, with her current employment in a medical charity – where the workforce was more stratified and heterogeneous – where she had made fewer, mainly sociable, friends.

Some work friendships are very much of the moment and do not endure once people have moved to another job or retire. This is particularly true where the friendships were context dependent and based on easy sociability. On the other hand, some work friendships are lasting and, rather like school and college friends, if they survive the initial separation may continue and deepen over many years.

While work can be a rich source of friends, work commitments also take their toll on other friendships. People entering the world of 'serious work' commented on the impact of new routines on their social life. Jenny's partner Duncan, an art teacher in his early thirties, explained:

> I don't sit up till two or three in the morning like I used to. We used to stay up late, late, on a regular basis, drinking and chatting. But that's all changed. That's the big difference, that we don't see each other as much as we used to, you know, we used to see each other every night.

Long hours, shift work, travelling on business, commuting and relocating for work mean that it can be very difficult to keep up with friends from other contexts.

Despite work and family commitments, people also make friends through their leisure time pursuits. People in our study had made friends through a range of activities and memberships, such as playing golf, tennis, bowls and bridge, drinking in a particular pub, dancing, going on holiday, through church, an athletics club, a model boat club, the trades union movement, through gay and lesbian groups. While many of these relationships are fun friends or associates, some have developed into more intimate ties. Clearly, different stages in the life-course afford different opportunities for leisure. As we saw with Harriet, when people are single or childless, socializing with friends is a major leisure time activity. Ben, a chemistry teacher living in Manchester, spends a lot of his leisure time with friends he has met through the clubbing scene in Manchester. Although Ben is in his late thirties, he is still living a young singles lifestyle, which he is aware is rather different from the more settled and sedate way of life of some of his friends:

> Bruce seems to have put his slippers on early. A lot of these people are quite old yet they're still out there, clubbing, doing these things, that's the difference, but Bruce is putting on his slippers.

Later, children leaving home and retirement can lead to a real renaissance in friendship. People have time to re-establish contact with fossil friends, nurture established 'pick up where you left off friends' and, if they take up new hobbies and activities, make entirely new friendships. Edith is a particularly striking example of someone who has enjoyed a new flowering of friendships in later life. In her early seventies, Edith lives with her husband John in a large Victorian house on the outskirts of Manchester. Both she and John are now retired after careers which took them from skilled manual to white collar administrative work. The couple have one daughter and four grandchildren. Since retiring, Edith has started visiting art galleries with an ex-colleague, but has also made a whole new set of friends through playing bridge and golf. She and John have joined a golf club and both spend a lot of time socializing with their new golfing friends. On the other hand, of course, for some people retirement can mean a retraction of their social circle, especially where they do not drive and have limited access to public transport.

Locality can also be very important in terms of meeting and maintaining friendships. But just as working environments vary in their friendship potential, so do local communities.[15] In our own study we found that where people made friends with a lot of their neighbours, they lived in small communities, such as villages, or socially homogeneous neighbourhoods, such as established working-class districts, middle-class enclaves, or college campuses. Brenda, for example, who is friendly with many of her neighbours, lives in a long-established working-class neighbourhood in Stockport. Similarly, Muriel, a retired financial adviser and her husband Donald, a retired computer systems engineer, have a pattern of making friends with their neighbours, and, in their case, some of these relationships have developed from neighbourly or favour friendships into very close ties. The two have lived in several different parts of the country, relocating to further Donald's career, but they have always chosen to live on middle-class, executive housing estates. Now they have retired, they have moved again to live near Muriel's twin sister and have bought a house on a brand new gated estate. Within the space of a few months they have already made friends among their new neighbours. In larger or less homogeneous environments, it seems that people make local friends through intermediary channels, such as working locally, having children at a local school, playing a sport, joining a local club, or through other local friends, rather than simply through being in the same neighbourhood.

Physical proximity is particularly relevant at the beginning of a relationship when regularity of contact enables people to discover whether or not they have things in common and like each other. It is also important at certain life-course stages. Local friends are a boon when people are tied to their neighbourhood, for example, when they have young children or are in poor health.[16] Being able to meet up locally is important for people when they are young, or single, when socializing is a central part of their life. For example, Duncan explained:

> If we're going to go out, if we're gonna go down to Pizza Express for our dinner, we'll just phone them up to see if they're free. And if they're gonna just go somewhere, you know, cheap and cheerful, then they'll ring up here, or we'll ring them up.

Harriet also stressed the importance of easy access to sociable friends:

> I mean if it's not taxiable or driveable or just round the corner or whatever. . . I mean actually most of the socializing is all done locally. I don't have to travel to socialize. It's either here [through work] or a walk down the road to the bar and we find a bar that's central to all of us.

Geographical mobility is clearly a major life-course event as far as friendships are concerned.[17] It is much easier to retain friends if people remain in the same local area, and people in our study who lived all their lives in the same village, town or neighbourhood maintained friendships for many years with friends who continued to live locally. Moving away from an area often leads to the loss of at least some friends, and we found that many more friendships faded because people lost touch than because they fell out with each other. On the other

hand, moving gives people a chance to make new friends and to revital-
ize their friendship repertoire. Geographical mobility also provides a
testing ground for existing relationships, and some people found that
physical separation actually strengthened some of their friendships.
And, where a move involves living away from any immediate family,
this can also reinforce people's commitment to making and sustaining
their friendships. The impact of geographical mobility and the 'freight
of distance'[18], however, also depend on people's resources: whereas a
distance of a few miles means some people lose touch with friends if
there is poor public transport, they do not drive or have no access to the
internet, others are able to maintain friendships which span a number
of different continents. For example, Sarena and Esther, whose close
friendship we reported in chapter 3, and Esther's husband, George,
sustain relationships in America, the Caribbean and Africa. Sarena
recounted how the first person she contacted when she received some
distressing news was her confidante Sarah in Trinidad, even though
this meant disturbing her in the middle of the night, Trinidad time:

> When my mother was diagnosed with cancer – and that's some years
> ago, six years ago, I think it was, yeah – Sarah was the person that I rang
> at four o'clock one morning, 'cos I just knew, I knew it was OK to do that,
> you know. And it was, it wasn't a problem at all.

Social as well as geographical mobility can also affect people's friendships. Friends often come from similar social backgrounds, and this is
one of the reasons they feel at ease with each other.[19] When friends'
lifestyles diverge they can feel uncomfortable in each other's company
and there can be jealousies and resentments. People spoke of 'lying
low' when their own lives were 'not going so well', waiting to contact
friends until their life was 'back in order again – you don't want anyone
to pity you'. Henrietta, who comes from an aristocratic family, was particularly aware of the impact of class differences. While she thought
that these had not been at all important at art school, she had found
they became more obvious and disconcerting later on when friends
started to lead quite different non-student lifestyles. She felt that her
greatest friends now came from similar backgrounds, or at least had
similar lifestyles, living in the same kind of houses: 'I think that if you
come from exactly the same background you're more at ease aren't
you, not having to pretend anything or whatever?'

Edith's husband John described the difficulties which arose with his
two oldest friends when he moved from a skilled manual to a non-
manual occupation – from running a shoe repair business to working

as a sales representative and later as a debt negotiator for a large engineering company:

> Jack kind of resented that I had a company car a bit and, of course, Len sneered at me going into an office – 'bloody white collar business' and all that. So, although I've put them down as friends, you can see there's, you know, that friction between us.

Finally, friendships can be affected when serious health problems arise. Some friendships deepen because of the level of support provided, and people spoke of friends visiting in hospital, helping with household chores, offering comfort and support. For example, Edith's close friend Doreen recounted the way Edith had helped when she had a bad accident that kept her immobile for almost a year. During this time Edith had done all the ironing and most of the shopping because Doreen's husband was working full-time and her daughter, a lone parent, was caring for a young child. In other cases, however, friends – even supposedly close friends – shied away, as though they were 'frightened off' by serious illness. Edith's husband, John, recalled bitterly that very few friends had been to see him when he was ill in hospital, and, as we saw in chapter 3, David, whose partner died of AIDS, found that during his partner's illness,

> many friends came and went. . . some people who had been very much part of our lives kind of disappeared. . . they couldn't hack it, they couldn't handle it.

Where illness affects people's ability to interact or communicate, this can prove the toughest test.[20] For example, some of the people in our study suffered mental health problems and had lost a number of friends over the years because the friends were unable to understand or cope with the situation. Amy, in her early forties, works for a mental health charity and has suffered episodes of clinical depression herself. Many of her current friendships have been made through her work as she finds people working in the field of mental health more supportive and understanding. Henrietta, two of whose friends suffer from mental health problems, described the strain this put on their friendship, and the way the relationships had deteriorated:

> Charlotte I've known for years and I love her, but she has very bad, sort of, nervous breakdowns on and off so, I mean, I love her, but, I mean, she's too sort of unstable. Gemma's another great friend, I adore her too. . . but she's been in and out of St Josephine's [psychiatric hospital]. When they've been ill, so ill on and off, they're not really a part of my life anymore.

Derek, a retired journalist whose personal community we describe in chapter 6, suffers from aphasia following a stroke, and has problems with language and speech functions. This has meant that it is difficult for Derek to socialize with friends and he relies mainly on his long-term lover and his support worker, both of whom know how to communicate with him.

FRIENDSHIP MODES

Of course, the eventfulness of people's lives varies enormously. Some people appear to have very stable lives, journeying through life with few crises or hiccups. They may stay in the same neighbourhood, close to their family and friends, study locally or work for only one or two organizations, remain with the same partner, and avoid serious illness or tragedy. Others, by contrast, lead much more turbulent lives. They may be adopted or taken into care, move many times and be uprooted from friends and family, or have chequered work histories or many partners, they may have a serious accident or suffer bouts of serious illness. But people also respond to these life events differently in terms of the way they make, maintain and lose significant friends at different stages in their life.

We refer to these different patterns of making and losing friends as *friendship modes* and identified four distinct variations within our study: *bounded, serial, evolving* and *ruptured*.[21] Each mode differs in the way friends are made, kept or lost at major life-course transitions, and we illustrate each mode with one or two examples.

Bounded Friendship Mode

In a bounded friendship mode, people have made most of their important friends (those they include in their personal community) in a particular context or at a particular stage in the life-course, very often during late teens and early twenties when they are single and friendships revolve around 'going out', or a bit later, when they settle with partners, and friends are formed around children and family life. While some friendships made at this time subsequently fade, few, if any, important friends are added later on. It is as though, after a burst of friend-making, people rely on their existing friendship repertoire, and put their remaining energy into family life or work. New ties remain casual friends or acquaintances. People with this kind of friendship mode may have lived in the same area for a long time.

An example of someone with a bounded friendship mode is Winston. In his early forties, Winston was born in Tobago, and as a young child was brought up by his maternal grandmother. As a teenager Winston came to join his parents and older brother who were already living in London, and he has remained in London ever since. After attending technical college, he took up a trade as a painter and decorator. Winston has seven children, ranging in age from one to eighteen. The three oldest are by his first partner, the fourth from a short-term relationship, and the three youngest by his current partner. Winston keeps in touch with all the mothers of his children, and is very close to all his siblings, considering them friends as well as family. He also feel he has a friendship with his eldest daughter.

Nearly all Winston's current friends were made within the first two years of arriving in Britain, and, apart from one friend from college, Winston met many of his friends through his older brother. The friends all know each other, live nearby, and several are related, as brothers or cousins. As well as socializing, some of the friends have also worked together, setting up a painting and decorating business for a while. Apart from one very close friend, Richard, whom Winston describes as a brother, the others are strictly fun friends. Winston's social life revolves around his friends and his family; he goes out drinking with his brothers and sisters as well as with friends, and has parties to which all his children and their mothers are also invited. Although Winston has a lot of people with whom he is 'friendly', he does not include them within his repertoire of significant relationships, and has not added to that repertoire in the last fifteen years.

Michelle is another person with a bounded friendship mode, as is her husband Mervin. As we described in chapter 3, Michelle is in her mid thirties, married with two teenage sons, and has lived all her life in the same area. After working as a secretary, she took time off when her children were young but now works in a friend's dress shop. Michelle is fond of her sisters and cousins, and considers her parents-in-law almost as close as her own. She made most of her friends in her late teens and early twenties from among 'a local crowd', many of whom her husband also knows. Although some of these early friendships have now been lost as people moved away, Michelle has not added new friends to her personal community in the last few years, despite having made acquaintances through her children's school. One or two early friendships have become much closer over the years, but Michelle sees herself as a mainly family-oriented person.

Serial Friendship Mode

By contrast, in a serial friendship mode there is a totally different pattern of friend-making. People's friendship repertoires are almost completely replaced at each new life-course stage or event; there is little continuity and friends from earlier stages fade while new friendships are made to replace them. So, for example, people make a new set of friends when they leave school, go to college, start work, change jobs, get married, get divorced, and particularly when they move to another part of the country. People in our study with this kind of friendship mode were highly geographically mobile, and had sometimes experienced a number of crises.

Colleen is an example of someone with a serial friendship mode. Now in her fifties, Colleen, who is the oldest of seven children, was born in Ireland but moved to London when she was twelve. Colleen went straight to work after leaving school and was employed as an office junior until she married at the age of eighteen. After their marriage she and her husband went to live in India, where they had three children, the first of which died. Twenty years ago, Colleen and her husband returned to Britain and she now lives in East London, close to all her family. Since her return she has worked part-time in a number of different fields, including telesales, but is now a childminder looking after one of her sisters' children.

Before she went to India, Colleen had a number of friends in London but lost touch with them during the fourteen years she was away. Although it took her a while to meet people in India, and she had no close friends at the time of her baby's death, she did eventually make a new set of friends during her time there. When she returned to Britain, however, she lost contact with her Indian friends and had to start all over again. Colleen now has a new group of friends: two are extremely close and she has known them since she came back to live in Britain; the remaining three are new friends whom she has met at the school gates when collecting her nephew and niece. These more recent friends are much younger than she is, and the relationship is centred on the children.

Colleen is aware that, in the past, she has tended to put family first, though now she is closer to her greatest friend Elsa than to some of her own brothers and sisters. She sees her life as a series of separate compartments, each with its own set of friends:

I put my life into little boxes and I. . . sort of open up the box and I've got sort of special memories from there and different friends are in there. . . But my friends now are in this current box.

Evolving Friendship Mode

An evolving friendship mode, on the other hand, includes elements of both bounded and serial patterns. New friends are added to the personal community at key life-course transitions, but some friendships are also retained from earlier stages. So, while there is some changeover in membership there is also a degree of continuity in the friendship repertoire. In an evolving mode friends are drawn from a range of different contexts, and current friendship repertoires may include friends from childhood, college, different work environments and locales. People with this pattern of friend-making are open to forming significant attachments to new friends, but also have a sense of loyalty to existing ties. However, at particular stages in their lives they sometimes feel their repertoire is 'full up', and they can't take on any more friends until others 'fall off the map'.[22]

For example, Ben and Edith both have an evolving friendship mode. Ben is in his late thirties and was born and brought up in London. He started a university degree but did not enjoy the course and dropped out. After working as a film technician for a few years, Ben went to university in Kent and then five years ago moved to Manchester to do a teaching qualification, staying on after the course to teach chemistry in a large secondary school. Ben's parents, brother and sister still live in the south of England, but Ben has an aunt and uncle in Lancashire.

Ben has a large number of friends and included many more friends than family in his personal community. Although he has lost touch with some of his earlier friends because of the geographical distance, he still has a friend from sixth-form college whom he has known for twenty years, some friends from his film technician days, and from his first university. These university friends had been extremely important to him because they supported him through the breakup of his first serious relationship. Ben has also made new friends since moving to Manchester. Some of these are fellow students from his teaching course, some he has made through work, some through local friends, and, more recently, he has met another circle through clubs and parties. Ben distinguishes between different kinds of friends, some of whom are strictly for fun while others act as confidants and offer various kinds of support. Friends are extremely important to Ben, and one of the reasons he has decided to stay in Manchester is because he wants to enjoy the friendships he has made.

Edith, on the other hand, is in her seventies and has lived all her life in the Greater Manchester area. She is married with one daughter and four grandchildren, all of whom live within twenty miles. Her parents and step-brothers are now dead, but she has a brother and sister living fifty miles away. After leaving school at fourteen Edith initially worked as a switchboard operator and a knitting machinist, but then moved into clerical work and was employed as an administrative assistant at the local university. As we discussed earlier, in her retirement Edith has taken up bridge and golf and is an active committee member at the golf club.

Edith has a wide range of friends, including soulmates, confidants, helpmates and associates. Although she has lost touch with primary school friends, she still has important friends from her teenage years, some of whom she met through her husband, and whom she has known for fifty years. Other friends were made through work, and she has one particularly close friend who is an ex-colleague from the university. Since retiring she has made new friends through charity work and the golf club, though the golfing friends are largely sociable rather than intimate or supportive relationships. Edith considers herself very family-minded but, in practice, friends rather than family play a bigger role in her day-to-day life.

Ruptured Friendship Mode

Finally, in a ruptured friendship mode there is an almost complete replacement of the friendship repertoire following a dramatic change in circumstances. Prior to the crisis, people might have had a bounded or evolving friendship mode, retaining friendships from earlier stages of their life, but afterwards nearly all these earlier friendships are lost. In our study, these crises included serious illness, marital scandal, difficult divorce, and coming out as gay.

Ronald is an example of someone with a ruptured friendship mode. In his late fifties, Ronald was born in the Midlands, is married and has three children and five grandchildren. Both parents and one sister are dead, he is estranged from another sister but is still in touch with his two brothers. After leaving school Ronald worked in a local factory before joining the army where he trained as a fitter. While in the army, Ronald moved to a number of different bases in Britain and

Germany, and gained some academic qualifications. After leaving the forces, he and his wife settled in Cheshire, where they lived for nearly twenty years and Ronald worked for a local health authority. Six years ago, Ronald took early retirement, moved to a different town, joined a different church, and now does voluntary work two days a week.

Although Ronald is still in touch with a few work colleagues, he has lost contact with nearly all the friends he and his wife made through their previous church. Because of his affair with a woman in the parish, Ronald and his wife decided not to stay within the same community. They moved several miles away and now have a new set of friends through the local church. Before this marital crisis, Ronald's pattern of making and retaining friends was essentially evolving, and friends are an important part of his life. Significantly, when he and his wife were thinking of moving to their present home, the availability of potential new friends was a crucial determining factor. They were both strongly committed to the church and so came and worshipped locally to 'get to know a few people before we actually made the move. If we didn't make friends there, then we probably would have looked elsewhere.'

Of course, friendship modes are constructed retrospectively, at a particular point in people's lives, and it is difficult to know how friend-making patterns might develop in the future. Nevertheless, even by their mid twenties, people in our study were already exhibiting different patterns. For example, while Wayne, whose friendship repertoire we described in chapter 3, had made all of his friends as a teenager, either from the local school or neighbourhood, Judy had retained friends from secondary school, but had also made new significant friendships in Essex and London, through sixth-form college, a Saturday job, and her full-time employment.

So far we have been describing different forms of friendship, and the way friends are made at various stages in the life-course, as though friends are a particular and bounded kind of social relationship. In the following chapter we broaden our focus, looking at ways in which friendship can be a component of many different categories of relationship. In particular, we compare friends and family, and explore the extent to which they represent distinct or overlapping ties.

CHAPTER FIVE

Friends and Family: The Case for Suffusion

I have another family who are my friends... I don't really subscribe to the definition of family as people that you're related to by blood or by marriage.

— Charles

Over a long life I have had friends... from numerous... spheres of interest. These have included kin-friends, a real category to be distinguished from simple kin.

— Firth

Companionate marriage... this is marriage of a late modern type, organised in terms of a model of friendship.

— Giddens

Up to now we have been talking about friends as distinct kinds of relationships, separate from family, partners, husbands and wives. In this chapter we explore the idea that friendship may be part of these other relationships and that 'family' and 'friend' are not necessarily mutually exclusive categories. As we saw in chapter 2, these terms have had different meanings in different periods and cultures, so we begin by looking at some current stereotypes about 'friends' and 'family'. When we compare real-life relationships with these stereotypes, however, we discover that family ties may have friend-like qualities and, conversely, that friends may feel like family. Not only can there be a blurring of boundaries, but this process of suffusion is sometimes acknowledged in the way people talk about these relationships, for example, calling a cousin a friend, or a friend a sister. In the case of partners and spouses, the situation is even more complex; with the increase in companionate marriage and cohabitation, partners are an intriguing blend of family and friend. We describe different kinds suffusion, illustrating each with the story of relationships we encountered in our study.

Contrary to predictions that increasing individualism and choice are necessarily leading to a world of casual, fleeting ties, we argue that suffusion can sometimes lead to stronger rather than weaker social bonds. Of course, not all friendships and family relationships are suffused and, for some people, the roles played by friends and family remain highly specialized. These different *patterns of suffusion or specialization* are discussed at the end of the chapter.

Chosen and Given Ties

The question of choice seems central to definitions of friendship and family. The adage 'you can choose your friends but you can't choose your family' is a theme that lies at the heart of popular perceptions of family and friends.[1] Family relationships are characterized as those ascribed through blood or marriage and, as we have already shown, many anthropological studies have constructed elaborate kinship systems according to the principle of ascription.[2] The given-ness of family ties, it is argued, means that there is an automatic relationship, linking not just immediate family members but also more distant kin, regardless of whether or not there is any contact. Friendship, on the other hand, has to be established; indeed, friends are often seen as archetypal chosen relationships.

In practice, however, the distinction between given and chosen is not always very clearly drawn and the idea that there is an automatic relationship with family members does not help us understand the diversity of family ties. While there is no doubt that some people have a very strong sense of family, feeling a connection to both immediate and extended family members, others accept that, while they cannot choose who is related to them, they can choose to have affectionate and active relationships with some relatives but not others. Some relatives are family in name only and there is tremendous variation in the extent to which family members maintain contact.[3] So, while some people in our study felt close to aunts and cousins, to step-brothers and sisters, travelling around the world to keep in touch, others had little if any contact.

> At one stage I had sort of twenty-three cousins which was great for
> presents at Christmas but, I mean, most of them bore me rigid. My par-
> ents try to have a family party every year in the summer and... now the
> cousins have got children, and they arrive and we all play cricket and
> stuff. But, I mean, I see them once a year, I'm not close. And their chil-
> dren – I can't even remember their names.

As we saw in chapter 2, relatives may not be listed as part of a personal
community because they are not considered important now and, while
these tend to be extended family or step-relations, we also found some
cases where brothers and sisters, parents and even children were off
the map. Even the notion that family necessarily refers to relationships
based on biological relatedness or marriage is now being challenged
by anthropologists who are keen to explore the meaning of kinship in
different cultures and contexts, allowing for the possibility that people
may be designated kin for other reasons or qualities.[4]

Similarly, while friendships are characterized as chosen relationships, sometimes friends come as part of a package and feel more
of a given tie. In some cases, the friend is part of a wider friendship
group, in others the connection is through a partner, but in either case
dropping the friendship would be difficult:

> It's, like, a permanent fixture, you know, it's just one of those things,
> you're stuck with it. It's, like, family members that you don't want... It's
> a terrible thing to say really... but it's true.

Clearly, the notion that friends are chosen and family are given needs
further exploration. What assumptions do we make about the nature of
given and chosen relationships, of family ties as distinct from friendship? One key assumption is that duty and obligation are essential
components of family relationships.[5] Even if family members are estranged, they may still feel obliged toward each other, or at least still
acknowledge each other as family. With friendship, on the other hand,
there is no automatic expectation that friends will feel any sense of
obligation, though, as we have seen in chapter 3, some may prove
extremely committed and loyal.

Further assumptions concern the degree of importance we attach to
different relationships. In the case of friends, importance supposedly
depends on the quality of the relationship itself, whereas, with family,
there may be strong normative expectations that family ties are the
most important, that 'blood is thicker than water'.

> Your family come first... because it's your blood, your family, you know,
> who better can you trust more than your family? ... Those friends that

I've written down there, believe it or not, I could trust those friends with my life... but they've still got to be out there [third ring on map]. And I think if they were to be standing here tonight they would be happy to be there because they know they're not the immediate family and the cousins, they know they're in the next line, which is friends.

We seem to expect family relationships to continue indefinitely. These relationships give a structure, a sense of who you are and where you come from: 'it's one of the foundations of my life that my family are there.' Even if there are rows and family members fall out with each other, they are still 'family'.

Family relationships seem to be almost carved in stone... I don't question them, I don't nurture them... nor do I withdraw from them as such. It's almost like I expect, because they're family, that they will be ongoing. I don't expect to fall out with family, or particularly fall in with them.

By contrast, friendships are not necessarily expected to endure and, in practice, some are rather short-lived, but others have much greater permanence, lasting almost a lifetime.

Apparently, we also seem to believe that family and friends will feel different kinds of affection for each other. We assume that people will love their family – particularly members of their immediate family, such as children, parents and sometimes siblings – because they are family, even if people don't like them.[6] Friends, on the other hand are expected to like each other, with love reserved for special friends who have grown closer through shared history and experience.

Family members, especially immediate family, are supposed to help and support each other. Seemingly, you can rely on family 'no matter what'. You can just turn up on their doorstep and they will stand by you in a crisis. Of course, friends may also help each other, but there is a feeling that you can have higher expectations of family than of friends, that you 'take them more for granted, that they're going to be there when you need them, but friends, I mean, they do it, you know, out of kindness'.

On the other hand when it comes to being able to talk to someone about personal concerns or problems, apparently it is close friends rather than family who are assumed to be the main players, because they may have been in a similar situation or can at least relate to it. Friends are also seen as less likely than family to worry about and dwell on the problem: 'you can shut the door on friend crap', and this frees up the possibility of mentioning passing concerns without risking a sustained interrogation. By contrast, with family, especially young children and older parents, there are concerns about not wanting to worry or upset them. Parents might be shocked or upset, for example, about sexual behaviour, marital problems, debt or drugs:

> We were brought up with a certain code, and if I were to say that I'd stepped outside that code, they would feel like they had failed... and I just don't think it's necessary to hurt them in that way.

As well as wanting to avoid upsetting family members, people are also keen to avoid being lectured or judged.[7] There was a feeling that family can be quite critical. People can also be wary of confiding in their family because they want to preserve their privacy. A major problem is that family members are not always discrete, especially siblings: 'you tell one something and before you know it the loud speakers are already on and the whole rest of them know it.'

Finally, we seem to expect friends to enjoy each other's company, sharing interests or sense of humour. Family, on the other hand, are 'not necessarily the people I relate to best'; 'my brother is important inasmuch as he is family... but from a social point of view he's pretty well non-existent'; 'I'm just thinking, one's sisters are not much fun'.

A Blurring of Boundaries

Of course, real-life relationships do not always match these cultural stereotypes. For example, people may confide in or have more fun with family than with friends; friends may feel a strong sense of responsibility for each other and be more important than family ties; family relationships may break down while friendships last almost a lifetime. In chapter 2 we suggested that the division of relationships into those which are given and those which are chosen may fail to capture their complexity, and we put forward the notion of given-as-chosen and chosen-as-given ties. In the case of family and friends this blurring of boundaries, or process of suffusion, can happen in many different ways, as Figure 5.1 shows. Family relationships can become friend-like when people choose to spend time with their relatives rather than feeling obliged to do so, where they feel they have things in common, enjoy each other's company, or can trust the other as discrete and non-judgemental confidants. Conversely, friends can become family-like where there is a strong sense of obligation, where the relationship is of central importance, long lasting and surviving a number of ups and downs. Where friends love as well as like each other, where they are utterly dependable and reliable, supporting each other no matter what, then they take on a family-like quality.

In some cases it is simply that friends and family have similar qualities or play similar roles. In other cases, however, suffusion is explicitly recognized so that people actually refer to family as friends and friends as family. But what does it mean to call a sister a friend, for example, or a friend a brother? It is very important to stress that, in our own study, people were not suggesting that there had actually been a change of status, that a friend had actually turned into a brother, but that a particular relationship had taken on certain attributes, becoming more like a friend or more like a member of the family.

Family as Friends: Given-as-Chosen Ties

Where people recognize someone in their family as a friend, this tends to be someone of their own generation, such as a special brother, sister or cousin. Roger, for example, feels he has a friendship with his older brother Michael. As we saw in chapter 3, Roger is a lone parent in his early fifties. His brother Michael is very much family in that 'we help each other out, you know, if he needs some gardening done or something lifted', and Roger knows he can always rely on his brother for support, something which was very important to him when his daughter was young: 'I mean if something nasty had happened to me, then my brother might have had to look after her.' What makes Michael a friend, however, is that the two men share some common interests, enjoy each other's company, and choose to spend time together.

> [Although we're] completely different in temperament and occupation. . .
> I'm really good friends with my brother. And we sail together, we're racing
> a boat together on Saturday.

Jackie is another person who has a friendship with someone in her family, calling her older sister Gloria her best friend. As we saw in chapter 3, Jackie is in her thirties and lives with her partner and three young children. She became particularly close to Gloria when she ran away from home as a teenager:

> I was sixteen and had had enough of my Dad's laws, so I ran to my sister's.
> She didn't pressure me to go home, she let me stay there, and so I had,
> like, all my troublesome years there.

Jackie feels she has a friendship with her sister because the two spend a lot of time together out of choice rather than a sense of duty:

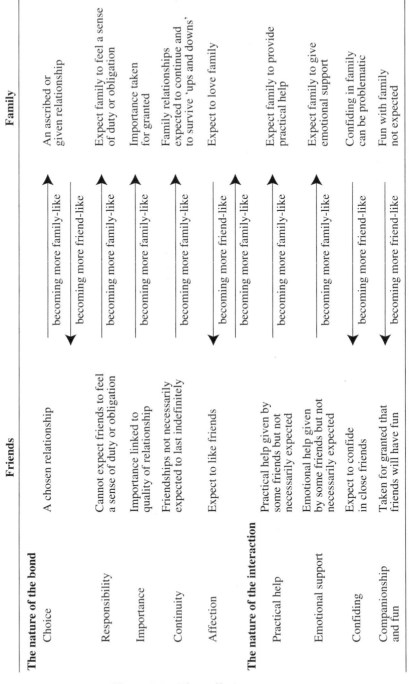

Friends | | **Family**

The nature of the bond

| Choice | A chosen relationship | becoming more family-like →
← becoming more friend-like | An ascribed or given relationship |

| Responsibility | Cannot expect friends to feel a sense of duty or obligation | becoming more family-like → | Expect family to feel a sense of duty or obligation |

| Importance | Importance linked to quality of relationship | becoming more family-like → | Importance taken for granted |

| Continuity | Friendships not necessarily expected to last indefinitely | becoming more family-like → | Family relationships expected to continue and to survive 'ups and downs' |

| Affection | Expect to like friends | ← becoming more friend-like
becoming more family-like → | Expect to love family |

The nature of the interaction

| Practical help | Practical help given by some friends but not necessarily expected | becoming more family-like → | Expect family to provide practical help |

| Emotional support | Emotional help given by some friends but not necessarily expected | becoming more family-like → | Expect family to give emotional support |

| Confiding | Expect to confide in close friends | ← becoming more friend-like | Confiding in family can be problematic |

| Companionship and fun | Taken for granted that friends will have fun | ← becoming more friend-like | Fun with family not expected |

Figure 5.1. The suffusion process.

We go out to parties and to the sauna sometimes, or I'm often down her house and she's always cooking something nice and my kids move up there in the holidays. So we do quite a lot of stuff together... I don't sort of see her because I think, 'Oh, I'd better go and see her.' It's usually like we've rung each other up or whatever and, especially in the summer holidays, her kids and my kids, we'll plan day trips together somewhere. She was here yesterday; we cooked a lovely meal for everyone.

But Jackie also describes Gloria as a friend because she can confide in her and trusts her to be discreet. After her best friend gossiped behind her back, Jackie no longer confides in friends.

While some cousins may be off the map, special cousins who really like each other are often described as friends.[8] Patrick, a hospital consultant in his forties whose friendship with his old professor we described in chapter 3, described one of his cousins, Jim, as 'my closest friend... I have known him for so long, all my life, that I would consider him as probably the guy that I was closest to.' The two played together as children.

My older brother quickly realized that I was... a problem... I was always a liability to him, because he was matched with me, and everywhere he went I was kind of tagged on. So, I think he spent his whole time trying to ditch me... But these two guys [Jim and a mutual friend] were my age, and therefore we sort of grew up together, we were much more at ease.

As adults, Patrick and his cousin still keep in regular contact and enjoy each other's company. It seems the lack of competition between cousins as compared with siblings can sometimes make it easier for friendships to develop.[9] Colleen, the oldest of seven, described the legacy of childhood jealousies:

When you're younger you sort of get this rivalry and I think that carries on in a certain way... I mean sometimes it did get into, like, fisty-cuffs and you sort of fight for space or your own things, and then, as you get older, I think we all find it very hard to share.

Robert, whose relationship with his great friend with Christopher we described in chapter 3, felt he had a friendship with his cousin Lance:

I think it's because it's not only about obligations, it's not only about blood relations, it's about other things that we have in common, that we could do, that we could talk about... you know, the warmth that we feel in each other's company.

Friendships with family can also reach across generations, for example, with an adult son or daughter, with a parent, or a favourite niece or nephew. Jackie's sister Gloria, for example, feels she has a friend-ship with her two older daughters. In her early forties Gloria was born in Jamaica, but moved to East London when she was four years old. She is the oldest of six children, all of whom live within a few miles. Recently widowed, Gloria has been married twice and has four grown-up children from her first marriage, a nine-year-old daughter from her second marriage, and four grandchildren. She has worked as a cleaner in a number of hospitals, though she is currently at home looking after her youngest daughter. She and her older daughters speak almost every day and regularly go out socially. Recently, they have been look-ing for work together. Gloria considers her daughters friends, not only because she enjoys their company, but because 'I can talk to my two girls about *anything really*'. She even confided in them about prob-lems she had been having with her late partner in a way she could not confide in the rest of her family, with the exception of her sister Jackie whom she can tell anything and whom she also considers a friend.

Being able to confide is also the reason that Edith considers her favourite niece a friend. Edith, whose pattern of making friends we described in chapter 4, is particularly close to her husband's niece Janet, who lived with Edith and her husband John when her parents divorced. Edith finds her niece a better listener than her daughter:

> I think daughters can brush you off, can't they? Yeah you know, she can get impatient with you... but your friends don't somehow... Funnily enough, I could tell things to Janet that I couldn't tell to Jean [daughter]... I couldn't tell Jean if I'd got a complaint against her dad, but I could tell Janet, 'cos her mother, which was John's sister – I mean John would deny it heartily – but they're very much alike, they can be really awkward customers, and Janet understands that.

Sometimes people feel they have a friendship with their parents, as in the case of Diana, for example. As we saw in the previous chap-ter, Diana lives in Suffolk, is single and in her forties. She has worked in a number of different fields, as a nurse, a music teacher, and now as a careers adviser. She is extremely close to her father and mother, enjoying their company and confiding in them. Initially she described them as her best friends, something she later changed to 'good friends, not best friends' because there were limits on what she could confide: 'they're still in a parental relationship with me, and so they're not the sort of friends that you would tell everything.' One of the things Diana

cannot talk about with her parents is how she feels about not having had children, because she knows how distressed this would make
them:

> They would do anything, they would sell their souls to make it better for
> me, but... they can't, and so if I get upset, they get upset on my behalf
> because they love me, but it doesn't solve anything.

Because of issues of authority and responsibility, however, some people feel that friendship between parents and children is difficult, or
only possible when the children are well-established adults.[10] Duncan, an art teacher in his early thirties, was adamant his parents were
not his friends:

> They are just my parents and I get on with them really well. I've never felt
> this need to call them friends. I don't see the need to make a big display
> of it... It's like going to a gig with your parents, you know, when you're
> fifteen. I mean you sometimes see kids with their parents... and, I mean,
> I just think popular music is about rebellion. You detest everything your
> parents stand for. That's the whole point... I really hope, if I ever have
> kids, I hope that by teenage years, I hope that they absolutely loathe
> everything I like, and that I absolutely loathe everything that they like.
> That's how you learn to respect each other. I mean that's how I learned
> to respect my parents. So my parents are *not* my friends.

FRIENDS AS FAMILY: CHOSEN-AS-GIVEN TIES

Not only can family members be friends, but friends may also take on
a family-like quality. Winston, for example, described his great friend
Richard as a brother. As we saw in chapter 4, Winston, a painter and
decorator in his early forties, was born in Tobago and came to live in
Britain when he was seventeen. His parents and older brother were
already living in London and Winston made a number of friends,
including Richard, through his brother. Winston and Richard have
known each other for more than twenty years, and became firm friends
almost immediately because they share the same sense of humour.
Richard is heavily involved in Winston's family, included in 'nights out'
and invited to all family parties. When they were younger the two men
shared a bed when they stayed at each other's family home.

> Richard is... part of the family... He calls Mum, Mum. Mum is Mummy,
> Daddy's Daddy.

Richard is also like family because of the length and strength of the
relationship, which has survived a number of ups and downs. Richard,

'a real stirrer', has caused trouble between Winston and his partner, but the two men have made sure that their friendship remains intact.

Sarena and Esther consider each other sisters. As we saw in chapter 3, the two women are soulmates; they have lot of fun together, confide in each other, and are godparents to each other's children. Sarena feels that the relationship is family-like because of the sense of commitment both women feel, and because they love as well as like each other. Like the friendship between Winston and Richard, their relationship has survived occasional conflicts:

> Esther and I are like sisters... you have your ups and downs and your disagreements and your fallouts, but it doesn't mean it's the end of the friendship. So the other week there was a problem between myself and Esther and I needed... to go and see her. And I was very upset that I'd upset Esther, I was very hurt that I'd hurt her, and so I needed to go and sort that out, 'cos I wasn't prepared just to let it go.

Where people call a friend a brother or sister they sometimes have an idealized notion of brotherly or sisterly love.[11] In some cases in our study, friends are loved as siblings in an almost compensatory way, where relationships with a real sibling are distant or the person does not have any brothers and sisters at all. For example, Robert loves his great friend Christopher like a brother but has drifted apart from his natural brother. Sarena considers Esther her only sister, although she has two half-sisters whom she hardly knows.

Sometimes a friend is seen as a cousin, as in the case of Gloria, who not only describes her daughters as friends, but also thinks of her two closest friends as 'more like sort of cousins, if you know what I mean... It's like somebody you've been brought up with, like family.' The women's parents had also been friends and the girls had stayed at each other's houses and slept in each other's beds as children. Like Sarena and Esther, they have worked to make sure the relationship survived:

> We've never fallen out. We've had our little disagreements but, you know, nothing too drastic sort of thing. When we had a disagreement – me and Dawn had a disagreement through our two daughters – she got on the phone and she made it clear to me that she wasn't prepared to lose her friendship with me because of the kids, you know, and I agreed with her, you know, and I said to her, 'the only solution is keep them away from each other so that we can keep our friendship still going', you know what I mean?

Sometimes it is an older friend who is considered family, as a mother or father figure, an aunt or uncle. In some cases a family friend has played a crucial role in the person's childhood.[12] Both Patrick and Sarena's husband Robert referred to women who had acted as second mothers to them when they were children. In Patrick's case,

> Mrs Rivers is a sort of interesting individual, because she formed a kind of surrogate mother relationship with us... When I was growing up my mother was depressed, chronically depressed... and a lot of the time she was kind of... the term they use is 'emotionally unavailable'. And it's only in retrospect I realize now what was going on, but Mrs Rivers lived in the same house, it was a big Georgian house, in Belfast, and she used to come up and, effectively, I suppose, was a helping hand. But I now realize that she was actually more than that, she was actually quite a permanent and... a very important figure in our lives.

Esther describes a friend and ex-neighbour as a kind of mother figure, calling her Auntie Sophie. Esther felt as though she had slotted into the older woman's extended family.

> She's sixty, and her children are about the same age as me... [When] I moved... she'd lived there for many years, and she lived a kind of life that was very similar to mine, very close to her family. She had a big house... and she lived with her own mother, and there were, like, four generations in this one big house, and it was nice to see. And for instance, I'm sat... in my dressing gown and she would be in her dressing gown, and she'd ask me if I'd want a cup of tea in the kitchen, side-by-side... She always remembered birthdays, she always remembered my children, she always had ice-pops in the fridge. She taught me a lot about children.

From the cases we have described it seems that calling friends family, and family friends, often implies a strengthening rather than a weakening of the tie, as though the relationship has taken on extra or special qualities. For example, when people use a family analogy they are recognizing the strength of commitment within a friendship. The only time 'friend as family' implies 'less' rather than 'more' is when a relationship is maintained entirely out of a sense of duty. Harriet, whose friendships we described in chapter 4, has this kind of relationship with an old university friend:

> I don't actually feel that we have much in common at all and I think under any other circumstances we probably would have lost touch. But she's an incredibly loyal friend. She went a completely different path to me. As soon as she left university she was married... she's got three kids, she lives in suburbia, she married an accountant, she doesn't listen to

the radio or anything – I mean she watches soaps. Completely different lifestyle... And we often sit together and say we've got absolutely nothing in common... I was her maid of honour at her wedding and I'm also the godmother of her first child, so in that sense it's become like family. And I think if those ties weren't in place... I probably would have removed myself. But now I feel obligated and I would keep it going now because of the godparent issue.

Similarly, where family members are likened to friends this often implies a particularly affectionate relationship since the relatives choose to spend time with each other. Of course, the introduction of choice into family relationships also means that people can decide to ignore their kin and this may lie at the heart of current concerns about the transience of social ties. Perhaps those who draw pessimistic conclusions from changing family patterns are thinking more in terms of marriage and relations between partners when they bemoan the breakdown of family life, basing their conclusions on rising levels of divorce and cohabitation. But where do marriage and cohabitation fit in terms of given and chosen ties? Are they based on a family or a friendship model?[13]

PARTNERS AS FAMILY AND FRIEND: GIVEN AND CHOSEN TIES

Partners are usually, but not always, treated as family, especially when the relationship is formalized through marriage or the couple have children.[14] In chapter 2 we saw that current partners are given a central place on personal community maps, sometimes regardless of the quality of the tie, which puts them firmly in the category of family. Relationships with partners are also perceived to be based on love, help and support, qualities associated with family ties. Yet spouses, partners and lovers can also be seen as friends. People usually choose their partners,[15] and talk about their partner as someone they like and with whom they share companionship, interests and fun, someone in whom they can confide, all qualities linked with friendship.[16] It seems in many ways that partners are the archetypal suffused relationship. As Figure 5.2 shows, partners are family-like to the extent that the relationship is based on love, is considered important, involves responsibilities, is lasting and provides support. They are friend-like to the extent that the relationship is chosen, involves liking, is based on companionship and confiding, but can also break down.

Expectations of a partner	Family or friend-like trait
A chosen relationship	Friend-like
Based on	
Love	Family-like
Liking	Friend-like
Of central importance	Family-like
With mutual responsibilities	Family-like
Expected to last	Family-like
But the relationship can break down	Friend-like
Providing	
Support	Family-like
Companionship	Friend-like
Confiding	Friend-like

Figure 5.2.   Partner as family and friend.

Not only is friendship found between partners, but people may openly refer to their partner as a friend, sometimes their best or greatest friend. Rupert, for example, feels he has a friendship with his wife Jane. In his forties, Rupert was born in the Cotswolds and brought up in Hertfordshire, attending boarding school from the age of eight. After school he went to study and work in London, where he met Jane. The couple moved to the country when their youngest child, who is now aged nine, was one year old. While Rupert commutes to London, where he works as a solicitor, his wife works locally as a part-time teaching assistant. Rupert considers Jane a friend because of their sense of companionship but also because of the way they share decisions and work together as a team, as 'equal partners' in running the household.

> We sort out the children and we figure out how we're going to pay the bills, and we figure out what we're going to do. . . Actually it's a good, it's a very good, I hate to say. . . working relationship, but it is to an extent, and running a household is a working relationship and you have to figure out how you're going to get the gutter fixed or whatever. I mean that's all part of it.

Ian also refers to his wife as his friend, in fact, he considers her his best and only 'real' friend. Now in his late thirties, Ian was born in Libya, and he and his older brother spent their childhood in different parts of Germany and Britain as their father was in the army. While

Ian was at boarding school in England, his parents divorced, and both parents are now dead. After school, Ian went to college and now works as a medical technician, supplementing his income with bar work at the weekends. He is married with two young children, and lives in Essex. As an 'army child', Ian moved countries and schools many times which made it difficult for him to make friends, but he has formed a close friendship with his wife, indeed he considers her his best friend. Ian calls her a friend because of the way they can confide and talk about problems:

> My wife is my friend. OK, she's my wife, but she's still my best friend, maybe not financially, but emotionally... We talk about problems and this, that and the other – we have our ups and downs, but at the end of the day we go to bed and whatever and we go to sleep and it's still the same, we're still the same... she's the one I turn to every time.

For Esther, having a friendship with her husband means feeling like equals and being free to tell him anything:

> Sometimes you can – like a lot of relationships that I've seen when I go out with my friends as a couple, you know, if I go out with husband and wife, or I go out with my acquaintance – I can see that their relationship very much is based on the husband and wife and the children, and there's a kind of... it's a kind of formal thing, I'm the man, you're the woman... and I don't see a friendship... And the friendship is the ease of – I never worry about what I have to say to George, I never worry that there is a financial problem and I can't discuss it. I think a lot of people say: 'I don't know how I'm gonna tell my husband.' I don't have a problem with that, but I see that they have a problem because they haven't made their husband their friend.

In some cases, partners are seen as friends because there is a special sense of connection and companionship. This special quality is described by Ron, whose friendships we described in chapter 3. In his fifties, Ron is divorced and living with a new partner. He describes this new relationship as

> like your left arm, your left hand... your biggest buddy in the world... You can talk about anything... You're sharing life together – that's what it's about, you're sharing life.

Where partners are perceived as friends this seems to imply a bonus, a sense that the relationship has extra qualities. Of course, not everyone speaks of a partner as a friend, but where people comment on the lack of friendship they seem to do so with regret, as Henrietta explained:

I would be his friend, but he's not good at making friends, I mean he doesn't need people, he's a loner. I mean if I was run over by a double-decker bus, I'm perfectly sure he'd find somebody who's just as close... He doesn't get very close to people... I don't really confide in him. He's not that interested, otherwise I would. I mean certain of one's great friends are interested... they actually enjoy hearing every drama in your life.

One husband joked that men sometimes draw back from friendship with their wife because they are more comfortable having their wives and children 'on in the background, rather like Radio 4'.

Alternatively, lack of friendship is sometimes seen as a sign that a relationship is in trouble. Jackie said of her relationship with her partner Winston:

Now I think we just sort of have responsibilities together, and that's being blatantly honest. I think our friendship broke down... We didn't... find time to talk about problems, we just let it bottle up until we'd end up screaming at each other and... Oh we have times when things are going really well, but I wouldn't say it's a friendship really.

The idea that a partner is both friend and family is sometimes openly recognized. For example, Sarena felt that her relationship with her second husband worked

on many different levels really... He's my friend, he's my husband, some-times he's my father... he's not afraid to stand up to me and tell me what he really thinks if he thinks I'm wrong... he's my confidant as well, and he's my lover, and he's, he's a bit of everything really, and I really like that.

The fact that some relationships contain both family-like and friend-like qualities does not, of course, mean that all relationships are suffused. Casual friendships are not likely to qualify as family. Similarly, distant 'duty' relations, estranged parents and children, or jealous siblings are unlikely to be seen as friends.

PATTERNS OF SPECIALIZATION AND SUFFUSION

As well as looking at the degree of suffusion within individual relationships, we also need to know the extent to which friends and family play separate or overlapping roles within people's personal communities as a whole. Figure 5.3 shows different degrees of suffusion and specialization.

Where friends and family play overlapping roles, many different people may act as sociable companions, helpers or confidants. Rupert's wife Jane, for example, is someone whose personal community

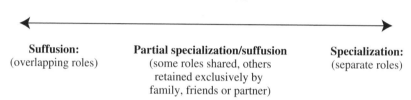

Figure 5.3. Patterns of suffusion within a personal community.

is highly suffused. A teaching assistant in her mid forties, married with young children, Jane can confide in her husband, her brother, her sister-in-law and half a dozen friends. Both friends and family provide practical and emotional support, and, while Jane's main companions are her husband and her friends, she also has fun with her brother, sister and sisters-in-law. Jane actually describes her brother and one of her sisters-in-law as friends. In other cases, however, suffusion is linked to just two or three pivotal relationships, such as a partner, key family member or close friend. In Winston's case, for example, the key players are his soulmate Richard, who is like a brother, and his siblings, whom he sees as friends.

Sometimes personal communities are partially suffused, with some roles shared, but with family, partner or friends retaining a specialized function. Huw, a retired Welsh farmer in his mid seventies, is an example of someone with this kind of personal community. Widowed and living alone, Huw relies entirely on his family, particularly his adult daughters and brother-in-law, for help and support, and these are his only confidants. On the other hand, Huw enjoys companionship and fun with both family and friends. Another example is Mervin, a loans and mortgage adviser, who is deeply embedded in his Jewish community and has lived all his life on the borders of northeast London and Essex. He has known his wife, Michelle, since they were both fourteen (they are now thirty-six). The couple have been married for nearly twenty years, have two sons aged eighteen and sixteen, and live in a comfortable semi-detached house built in the 1950s. Mervin relies exclusively on his wife and favourite cousin for emotional support, but confides in and has fun with partner, family and friends. In Ian's case, his wife, whom we have already discovered is his best friend, is also his only confidante, but Ian can ask for practical help and have fun with friends, family and partner. Harriet, on the other hand, turns exclusively to friends for emotional support, confiding and fun, but her parents, sister and friends will all lend a helping hand. Finally, Sarena shares confidences and has fun with her husband and very close friends, but not with members of her family. On the other hand, she can rely on her mother and brothers as well as friends and partner for practical help and support.

In other personal communities, however, we find a high degree of specialization so that people interact with friends and family in very different ways. An example of someone with this kind of personal community is Wayne. As we saw in chapter 3, Wayne is in his twenties, lives at home with his parents, and works in a local garage. He has lived all his life in the same town and has a number of local friends with whom he goes out drinking and clubbing. When he needs help of any kind Wayne looks to members of his immediate family, to his parents and sister, rather than to friends; on the other hand, for companionship and fun, it is friends rather than family who come to the fore. Where roles are highly specialized in this way, relationships tend to conform to popular stereotypes of family and friend, with family members playing a supportive role while friends act as companions and confidants. Perhaps unsurprisingly, none of those with specialized personal communities referred to family as friends, or to friends as family.

GIVEN AND CHOSEN TIES REVISITED

Those who view friends and family as being some kind of polar opposites fail to appreciate the subtlety and complexity of people's microsocial worlds. Not only can friends and family play overlapping roles, but kin and non-kin can occupy similar positions in terms of the degree of choice and commitment the relationship entails. As we argue above, however, where people acknowledge a process of suffusion, it is not the case that they believe that family members have actually become friends, or friends have become family, but that there has been some blurring of boundaries. The evidence from our study suggests that, contrary to gloomy forecasts predicting the erosion of personal responsibility, the process of suffusion – with given-as-chosen or chosen-as-given ties – may involve a high degree of commitment and does not necessarily imply a loosening of social bonds. We take up this theme again in chapter 8.

The extent to which trusting and intimate relationships are confined to family members and partner, the degree to which family of origin is supplanted by the family of creation, or the degree to which these relationships have been chosen in a new world of non-kin is a central issue, and one of the key components of the classification of personal communities presented in the next chapter. Even the most family-focused people may have some ties they refer to as friends. Similarly, even the most committed members of 'families of choice' based on friends and acquaintances have probably not cut off all links with parents or children or siblings. Although extreme cases can and do exist – some people *can* be bound solely by natal families or have no links beyond a small circle of friends – in practice, personal communities appear to reflect a range of different kinds of tie and diverse patterns of commitment.

As we saw in chapter 1, debates about the extent of social change have a long history, and seem likely to rage for decades to come. The role of the family is a particularly contentious issue, as is evident from arguments about the extent or scale of expansion of companionate marriage, the so-called 'transformation of intimacy', or the return of a three-generational matrilineal family in the face of the defection of multiple male partners from daughters or grand-daughters. Some may wish to interpret our discussion of suffusion as evidence of the decline of the so-called traditional family, and the spread of friend-like values as people choose their salient family relationships, or, alternatively, as evidence of the growing strength of familial values penetrating chosen ties. But, in practice, our finding that people engage in relationships based on distinctive mixes of choice and commitment does not fit easily with the expectations of those who seek unambiguous markers of social change.

Of course, it may be that significant social changes are taking place, but we cannot address this kind of question through our study. We simply cannot assume that our qualitative study of people's micro-social worlds at the turn of the century in England can give any firm guide to the degree or direction of social change; for that we would need longitudinal studies, or a careful replication of our study at some time in the future. In any case, the suffusion we have described is not a process of change precisely related to some previous base level; rather, it is simply a way of describing the patterns we found empirically, based on the roles people play and the language and terminology they themselves use.

We recognize that this chapter may be the most problematic and controversial in our book if this point is misunderstood. In some respects we would bow to those critics who might accuse us of focusing more thoroughly on analysing the complexities of friendship than exploring, say, the nuances of changing conceptions of cohabitation, partnership and marriage. We do not deny that there are many possible currents of change flowing simultaneously in contemporary society. However, even if contemporary society is highly complex, or in constant flux, that does not mean that one cannot study just a part of it, nor that every such study must contribute to some meta-theory of social change. We are reporting on a process of suffusion between friends and family: this process may or may not have been more powerful in Ancient Rome, during the Civil Wars in England or America, or in the 1960s; we simply do not know. However, studies are now becoming available which describe in considerable detail the relationships between friends and family in former times, exploring with great subtlety both the process of suffusion and the comparability of the terms and relationships used then with those we use now.[17] Our research is a contribution to this ongoing field of exploration.

But we have expressed caveats enough; it is time to describe the rich diversity of personal communities we found in our study, building on the analytical ideas developed in this and earlier chapters.

CHAPTER SIX

Personal Communities Today

My subject is a familiar chaos. Nothing is more familiar to men than their ordinary, everyday behaviour; and should a sociologist make any generalization about it, he runs the risk that his readers will find him wrong at the first word and cut him off without a hearing. They have been at home with the evidence since childhood and have every right to an opinion. A physicist runs no such risk that the particles, whose... behaviour in the atom he describes, will talk back... Social experience is apt to come at us too fast to leave us time to grasp it as a whole. Nevertheless the purpose... is to bring out of the familiar chaos some intellectual order.

— Homans

Having explored the nature of friendship, the way friendships are made or lost at different stages in the life-course, and the relationship between friends and family, we return in this chapter to our broader interest in the nature of people's micro-social worlds. We have already described the way personal communities vary in their overall size and composition. For example, the smallest personal community in our study contained just five people, the largest more than forty; the number of family members ranged from two to thirty-one, and friends from one to twenty-four. In some cases family outnumbered friends by a ratio of four to one, in others there were ten times as many friends as family. Some people included a lot of neighbours, others included none. But what do these variations mean? How can we make sense of this diversity?

At first sight each personal community seems different and, of course, to the individual his or her own is unique. But, with further analysis, recurrent patterns can be found amidst the seemingly end-less variation. In this chapter we show how different kinds of per-sonal community can be identified through their particular profile or cluster of features. A series of different modal types is presented and then described and illustrated in detail. The way personal commu-nities develop over the life-course, and the way they may be shaped by factors such as age, sex, social class and geographical mobility, are addressed in the following chapter. In the final chapter, we consider the implications of our findings for debates about community, social capital and friendship as a neglected form of social glue.

It is important to stress that these modal types are not meant to be used as a set of simplistic labels which diminish the richness of people's lives. We are not labelling for the sake of it, nor are we putting people in boxes. The classification is intended as an analytical device to help us understand the nature of micro-social worlds and, by being analyt-ically explicit about how we developed this classification, we enable readers to construct and compare their own personal community, if they wish.

The dimensions which underpin our classification have emerged from the detailed analysis of our findings discussed in earlier chapters. Each type of personal community displays a different combination of features and has a particular profile in terms of:

the criteria for inclusion, and whether ties are included in a personal community because of the intrinsic nature of the relationship or for largely normative reasons (chapter 2);

the relative numbers of different kinds of tie and in particular the ratio of family members to friends (chapter 2);

the relative importance of different kinds of relationship on people's maps and who is in the centre (chapter 2);

the range of different kinds of friends included and whether people have a broad, focal, intense or basic friendship repertoire (chap-ter 3);

the way in which people make and retain friends throughout the life-course and whether they have a bounded, evolving, serial or ruptured friendship mode (chapter 4);

the breadth of roles played by friends, family or partner and the extent to which roles are suffused or highly specialized (chapter 5).

Taking these six different dimensions we could have constructed a set of theoretical types based on all the possible different combinations or, alternatively, on the dominance of particular features. So, for example, there could be personal communities where all ties are given or, alternatively, ones where only chosen criteria operate. We might have proposed a type of personal community where all relationships are weak, casual or transient, so that friendship repertoires are narrow, friendship modes are serial, family play highly specialized, narrow roles, and partnerships are frequently dissolved. This would seem to fit the kind of postmodern, individualistic social world based on 'liquid love' as described in chapter 1. Alternatively, there could be personal communities where all ties are strong, with intense friendship repertoires and close family relationships. Instead, however, we have chosen to construct our types empirically, describing only the kinds of personal communities we encountered in our study.[1] However, the distinctive feature of this approach is that, while our typology is firmly grounded in our findings, the analytical components allow us to recognize other kinds of community when we find them. Not everyone's personal community will necessarily fit our types very neatly and we discuss some personal communities that we ourselves found difficult to classify. But the types we describe here are the best fit in relation to our data, bearing in mind that these relate to a particular time and place. The range of personal communities we have identified may develop in the future, new types may need to be added, especially if the study were to be carried out in other contexts.

PERSONAL COMMUNITIES TODAY

The following kinds of personal community were evident in our study:

friend-based (including *friend-like* and *friend-enveloped*);

family-based (including *family-like* and *family-enveloped*);

neighbour-based;

partner-based;

professional-based.

Each of these is composed of distinctive combinations of given and chosen ties, and each has a different profile in terms of the roles played by family and friends (Figure 6.1). Whereas in *friend-based* personal communities chosen ties predominate and people have formed

Type of personal community	Criteria for inclusion	Balance between different kinds of tie	Centrality of ties	Friendship repertoire	Friendship mode	Pattern of suffusion or specialization
FRIEND-BASED Friend-like	Mainly chosen	Friends outnumber family	Friends in centre of map with close family	Broad OR Focal	Evolving	Friends (or friends and partner) specialize in certain roles or a suffused pattern
Friend-enveloped	Mainly chosen, some given	Friends outnumber family or equal numbers	Family only in the first ring	Broad OR Focal	Evolving OR Ruptured	Friends (or friends and partner) specialize in certain roles or a suffused pattern
FAMILY-BASED Family-like	Mainly given, some chosen	Family outnumber friends	Family only in the first, and sometimes second ring	Focal OR Intense	Evolving OR Ruptured Bounded Serial	No clear pattern of suffusion or specialization
Family-enveloped	Mainly given	Family outnumber friends	Family only in the first, and sometimes second ring	Narrow	Bounded	Family (or family and partner) specialize in certain roles or complete separation of roles between family and friends
NEIGHBOUR-BASED	Mainly given	Neighbours equal or outnumber family and friends	Neighbours in central ring	Focal OR Narrow	Bounded OR Serial	Neighbours and friends specialize, separation of roles between friends and family
PARTNER-BASED	Chosen and given	No clear pattern in balance of friends and family	Partner or partner and family in the first ring	Narrow	Bounded OR Serial	Partner specializes in certain roles, complete separation of roles between family and friends
PROFESSIONAL-BASED	Mainly given	No clear pattern in balance of friends and family	Professional supporters in first or second ring	Narrow	Serial OR Ruptured	Professionals specialize in certain roles, complete separation of roles between family and friends

Figure 6.1. Profile of personal communities.

intimate and supportive relationships outside the family circle, *family-based* personal communities contain more given than chosen ties, and intimate and supportive relationships are largely or exclusively confined to kin. In *partner-based* and *professional-based* personal communities, friends and family play rather restricted roles. Finally, *neighbour-based* personal communities are largely given but support is sought and provided from outside the family.

These personal communities also vary in the breadth of their supportive base. *Friend-like, friend-enveloped, family-like* and *neighbour-based* personal communities are all broadly based in the sense that support is provided by several people within the social world; by contrast, partner-based and professional-based personal communities are usually narrowly based with only a few members playing a key role.

Each type is described in detail below and illustrated with one or two case studies. A key to the abbreviations used on the personal community maps is given on p. 155 at the end of the chapter.

Friend-Based Personal Communities

Friend-based personal communities are very much chosen communities where people are mainly included because of the intrinsic quality of the relationships, rather than for normative or cultural reasons. Friends outnumber family and chosen ties or ties with some chosen-like qualities predominate, so that friends, friends who are like family, and family who are like friends are in the majority. Nevertheless, some immediate family, such as parents and siblings are sometimes included out of a sense of loyalty, even if the relationship is somewhat ambivalent, but extended family are only included if there is a close bond.

These communities are characterized by the wide range of roles played by friends, and friends provide the mainstay of social support. People with friend-based personal communities have broad friendship repertoires including soulmates, confidants, helpmates, fun friends and associates, or a core of close friends and a larger group of more casual friendships. Some friendships are longstanding and have been maintained for many years, others are more recent, but new friends have been added at each life-course stage. Friends, or friends and partner, may be the sole providers of certain kinds of support, for example, sharing confidences or having fun, while other roles, such as providing practical help, are shared with family members; alternatively, there is a high degree of suffusion with friends and family providing similar kinds of support and companionship. In these personal communities, spouses and partners are usually considered friends.

Within friend-based personal communities, however, there are two slightly different sub-types – *friend-like* and *friend-enveloped* – which differ from each other in the way the importance of friends and family is recognized. The distinctive feature of *friend-like personal communities* is the strong emphasis on choice so that the quality of different ties is reflected in the mapping process. Close chosen relationships, such as long-term, multifaceted friendships, are considered so important that they are placed in the central ring while simpler more light-hearted friendships are further from the centre. Similarly, only close immediate family are given a central place; other family members are placed further out or excluded altogether. These communities most closely resemble the 'families of choice' described by Jeffrey Weeks.[2] Indeed, some close family members are considered friends.

To illustrate a friend-like personal community in more detail, we take the case of Sarena. As we saw in chapter 3, Sarena is in her forties, from a black Caribbean background, and has lived all her life in Greater Manchester, where she is employed as a social worker. Her mother and two brothers live close by, but her late father returned to live in Barbados, where he remarried and had another family. Sarena is married to Robert, who was born in Dominica and came to live in Britain in his late twenties. She and Robert have a four-year-old son, and Sarena has an eighteen-year-old daughter from her first marriage. Robert has two sons in their twenties.

Sarena's personal community includes fifteen friends, seven members of her family – her husband, children, step-children, mother and brothers – and two next-door neighbours (Figure 6.2). However, she decided to exclude her half-brothers and half-sisters, who live in Barbados, because she hardly knows them.

With a broad friendship repertoire, Sarena's personal community encompasses soulmates, confidants, helpmates and fun friends. Five women friends – Chantal, Felice, Patricia, Sarah and Esther – are particularly close. Esther is considered almost a sister and Esther's husband George is also a friend in his own right, although the friendship is not as close as between the two women. Sarah is a well-established confidante, so that although the two women rarely see each other – Sarah

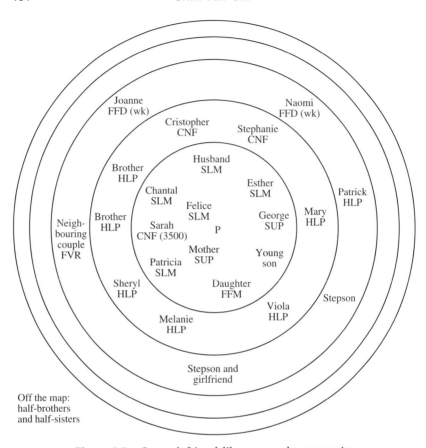

Figure 6.2. Sarena's friend-like personal community.

now lives in Trinidad – theirs is a 'pick up where you left off' friendship, and, as we saw in chapter 4, it was Sarah whom Sarena called in the middle of the night for support when her mother was diagnosed with cancer. Felice is an especially trusted friend who, in addition to being a confidante, is someone on whom Sarena can rely to take care of her children:

> I know when I was a single parent bringing up my daughter, she was the one person that I had down that in the event of anything happening to me – and my mother wouldn't be able to look after her – she would have been the person that I would have made the legal guardian. . . 'Cos, knowing my daughter's father's family, I knew that she would stand up to them and ensure that my. . . wishes were carried out. . . and that she wouldn't be afraid to take that on and do it. And I just believe that she

would, you know, execute the things that I've asked her to, would want her to do. And likewise with my son – 'cos Mum, you know, is definitely out of the equation now really in the event of anything happening to us, for instance, really, she's just too old, isn't she, really – but Felice, she's actually his godmother, but she would take on the role of his legal guardian in the event of anything happening to us. And interestingly enough, while we were away for the two weeks [he was staying with her], I knew that he wouldn't understand the concept of the time, 'cos it's a hard thing for them to get to grips with really, but he said to her, 'I want my mummy and daddy to come back, but if they don't come back,' he says, 'I think I'll call you Mummy then.' So I think for him as well there's something that connects him with Auntie Felice.

Sarena is also close to her husband's friend Christopher, and Christopher's wife Stephanie. The four have been on holiday together and know from first-hand experience some of the tensions in each other's marriage. The two women have also found some common ground:

Christopher and Stephanie are people that again I'm growing to love more, but. . . I've only known them as long as I've known Robert because they were actually Robert's friends before they were ever mine. So I still feel as though. . . my own relationship is finding its own path with them, and that's why they're here somewhere [second ring], but I do have a lot of time and a lot of regard for them. And Christopher and Robert in many senses are very. . . similar in lots of ways, and Stephanie and I spend a lot of time laughing at the two of them, because of the things that they do, and we howl some days because there's so many sort of odd things about them.

Other friends can be relied on for help and support, for example, Mary, Viola, Sheryl, Esther's mother Melanie, and Chantal's partner Patrick. The two remaining friends, Naomi and Joanne, are colleagues with whom Sarena has fun and with whom she shares a number of professional interests. As well as having many different kinds of friends, Sarena has made friends in a range of different contexts and at different stages in her life. Some of her friendships have lasted more than thirty years, others are more recent. For example, Sarena has known Chantal since they were teenagers and belonged to the same youth club but only became friends with Chantal's partner Patrick three years ago; Naomi and Sarena were friends at school more than thirty-five years ago, and then re-established their friendship when their paths crossed again through work. Felice, Patricia, Mary and Viola are 'church friends' whom Sarena has known for nearly twenty years;

Esther and Sarena met through their husbands and became friends eleven years ago.

Sarena's relationships with the family she included on her map are mainly close. She describes her husband as a best friend, and has the beginnings of a friendship with her eighteen-year-old daughter. She has a strong attachment to her mother but does not treat her as a confidante. Her two brothers can be relied on for help, and one brother often collects her children from school. In some respects Sarena's friends and family play overlapping roles, for example, both friends and family provide practical help and support, but for sharing confidences and having fun, Sarena turns to her husband and friends rather than to family members.

Finally, Sarena's personal community is largely choice-based, and her map reflects the quality of her diverse relationships. Six close friends are placed in the central ring alongside her husband, teenage daughter and four-year-old son; fun friends, neighbours and stepsons are further out; on the other hand, her half-brothers and half-sisters in Barbados are not included.

In *friend-enveloped* personal communities, on the other hand, the intimacy and support enjoyed with friends is not directly reflected in the way people perceive the importance of their personal relationships. In friend-enveloped personal communities, no friends, no purely chosen ties, not even closest soulmates and intimates, are placed in the central ring, despite their pivotal role. This position is reserved exclusively for immediate family, usually a partner and children, sometimes parents or key siblings, though, interestingly, some of these may be given-as-chosen ties where the family member is also seen as a friend. The key feature of friend-enveloped personal communities is that core friends play a more supportive and day-to-day role yet immediate family members are perceived as the centre of people's lives. Indeed, in some cases, so central are spouses and children that people did not initially list them, taking it for granted that these are the most important people and seeing them as 'part of me' – part of the centre of the map. Nevertheless, we call these communities friend-enveloped because people with this kind of personal community include more friends than family, valuing and relying on close friends to a great extent, even though these relationships are not necessarily recognized as the most central.

Charles, whose views on friendship and marriage we described in chapter 4, is an example of someone with a friend-enveloped personal

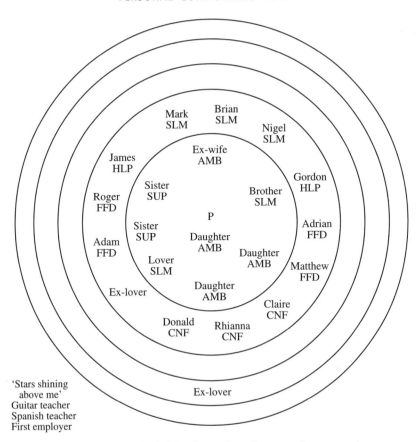

Figure 6.3. Charles's friend-enveloped personal community.

community. In his fifties, Charles works as a translator, and, having moved home a number of times in the United Kingdom and abroad, now lives on the border of England and Wales. Both Charles's parents are dead, but he has two sisters who are a hundred miles away and a brother in New Zealand. Charles was married for nearly twenty-five years and has three daughters, aged eighteen, twenty-one and twenty-three. About seven years ago Charles's marriage broke up and he came out as gay.

Charles's personal community (Figure 6.3) contains twelve friends, one current and two ex-lovers, and seven members of his family: his sisters and brother, his three daughters and his ex-wife. Charles also included three people who are deceased, but who were extremely influential in his life: his guitar teacher, his Spanish teacher and the person who had first given him translation work and helped him in his career.

Like Sarena, Charles includes more friends than family in his personal community, and has a broad friendship repertoire. Among the twelve friends listed on his map, three are soulmates: Nigel, Brian and Mark, all of whom are gay and have become friends since Charles decided to come out. Then there are three confidants, Donald, Claire and her daughter Rhianna, who knew Charles at the time of his divorce and helped him through a very difficult time. Claire, in particular, had been a close confidante who also offered a lot of emotional support:

> When my marriage broke up, I went to live in a house which turned out to be next door but one to her, so that's how I met her – she's seventy-five, she's been through a lot of trouble in her life, through marriages to abusive husbands – and she was very understanding. She became my mentor – my friend and mentor – and we spent a lot of time laughing and giggling, and then we'd cry on each other's shoulders.

Two other friends, James and Gordon, offer practical help and support, and the four remaining friends – Roger, Adam, Adrian and Matthew – are strictly fun friends. Charles's pattern of friend making has been affected enormously by his divorce and open acknowledgement of his sexual orientation. In this respect, he has a ruptured friendship mode, as, apart from Claire, Rhianna and Donald, most of his current friends have been made since these major life events took place. Charles described the way he lost touch with earlier friends because they took sides, or because they were a painful reminder of a very difficult period in his life.

Many of Charles's current friends are gay and met him through parties and gay organizations such as dining, walking and dancing societies. In addition to the friends included in his personal community, Charles has 'literally hundreds' of gay acquaintances, but he did not consider these important enough to include on his map.

Charles is also extremely close to his brother and sisters, 'without whom I think life would be impossible to imagine', and describes his current lover as a soulmate. He can confide in all these people and also sees them as good companions. Because of these close relationships, there is a certain degree of suffusion in Charles's personal community, with partner, friends and siblings playing overlapping roles. His relationship with his daughters and ex-wife, however, is rather difficult: while he feels an immensely strong bond with them, they are estranged from him and blame him for the divorce.

But Charles's personal community differs from Sarena's in one major respect: the quality and diversity of Charles' relationships with friends is not reflected in his map. No friends appear in the central ring, despite the key roles they play and the fact that Charles describes them as his 'other family'. All his friends are placed in the second ring, regardless of whether they are soulmates or fun friends. The centre of Charles's map is reserved for his current lover, his ex-wife and his blood family: his three daughters, his sisters and brother. If his parents were still alive, they would have been placed in the centre as well. Yet, although all these family members are very important to Charles, not all are as intimate or give him as much companionship and support as his friends. Typically for those with friend-enveloped personal communities, Charles relies mainly on friends but still perceives immediate family relationships as the closest bonds.

Family-Based Personal Communities

Family-based personal communities, by contrast, are largely given. Family members outnumber friends and given and given-as-chosen ties predominate, so that family members are in the majority. Family members play a wide range of roles and there is a strong emphasis on the importance of family in general, not just on the nucleus of parents and their children. This importance is reflected in the fact that family members only occupy the first and sometimes the first and second ring on people's maps. Within family-based personal communities, however, are two rather different types, family-like and family-enveloped, which vary in the extent to which they contain close friends and in the roles played by friends and family, respectively.

Family-like personal communities, despite their focus on given relationships, do contain a few key chosen ties. But, just as in friend-enveloped personal communities, the pivotal role played by close friends is not reflected on people's maps: only family members occupy the central ring, and sometimes the first two rings; friends are placed further out, and close friendships may be in the same ring as more casual ties. People with this kind of personal community have a strong normative or cultural belief that family must come first, and it is this belief which prompts them to give priority to kin, even where they have formed strong attachments to friends.

We call these communities *family-like* because they are based on a family model. Given ties, regardless of the quality of the relationship, are seen as the most important, and where friends become close they are often acknowledged as 'honorary' family. In this way chosen become chosen-as-given ties, but these close friendships do not qualify as 'real' or 'blood family' and are not placed in the inner circle of the map.

Esther is an example of someone with a family-like personal community who, by her own admission, is 'very family-minded. I was brought up with this thing, the old fashioned way, that this is your family and your extended family – full stop.' Now in her late thirties, Esther is the daughter of a Nigerian father and a Ghanaian/Syrian mother, and was brought up in Nigeria, Ghana and the United Kingdom. She has been working in Manchester for nearly twenty years and manages a dental practice. Esther is married to George, a doctor who was born in Ghana, with whom she has three young children. Her mother, two sisters and a half-brother live just two miles away, another sister is based in London. Two half-brothers and five cousins live thousands of miles away in America, Ghana and Nigeria.

Esther's personal community (Figure 6.4) includes sixteen family members – her husband, children, siblings and cousins, as these are the most important to her – but Esther felt she could have added at least a hundred extended family members. Initially, Esther listed only four friends, but during the interview she decided to add a childhood friend, an ex-neighbour and her daughter, and a number of couples with whom she and her husband regularly socialize.

Among the friends Esther eventually included on her map is a core of close confidantes and then a larger group of sociable friends, some of whom Esther described as more like acquaintances. In the core are Claudia and Sarena and their husbands, Martin and Robert. Both women are considered soulmates, and Esther sees Sarena as a sister. Their husbands, on the other hand, are good friends but not close confidants.

Another good friend is Leila, a family friend from childhood, to whom Esther feels a strong sense of attachment and responsibility:

> I've always known her since we were little... We lost touch, then we kept in touch, then lost touch – we were, like, you know, kids growing up really, we've always had that relationship... I wouldn't like to lose touch 'cos it reminds me of my childhood, and reminds me of my father, and reminds me of her father – we both lost our father... Leila is a very wealthy woman who has a lot of extended family around her, and her husband left her with... a very big burden with tax problems and things like that, and she couldn't leave her home, and her business was from

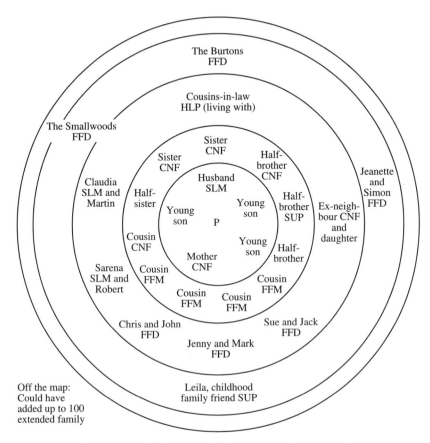

Figure 6.4. Esther's family-like personal community.

home. So she had to face that, so it was not easy for her to come out, but she sometimes, sort of, puts on her nightie, gets in her car and drives to my house, just to breathe. That's the relationship we have.

Apart from these friendships, Esther's other friends are mainly couples she and her husband have met locally, through business contacts or their children's school. The friends go out for meals together, and attend various charity events, but Esther does not turn to them for help or support. Apart from Leila, Esther has lost contact with friends from earlier stages of her life and most of her friendships have been made within the last few years.

Esther is close to all the family included on her map and considers some of them friends. For example, she regards her sisters and two of her cousins as pals because she chooses to spend time with them and because she can talk to them like friends, relaxing and exchanging confidences. Esther also feels she has a friendship with her husband, because 'I never worry that... there is a problem I can't discuss'. In fact, Esther has a highly suffused personal community, with family, partner and friends playing overlapping roles. Despite her close ties to family, however, Esther acknowledges that friends can play a unique restorative role:

> I think it's probably the special times... when you can relax. When you're in the family... you're... tending to sort things out, do things, the pressure is on... it's like you've got to run your family home, you've got to be in charge, whereas with friends... I can be in a more relaxed mode. It's like you've pushed the family aside and with my friends... there's no responsibility, you know what I'm trying to say?... You don't owe them anything, your friends, so you don't have to try, like you do with your family, to keep [them] happy.

Esther's map largely reflects the quality and importance of family ties, with family occupying the first two rings, but does not capture the degree of intimacy and support she enjoys with her close friends. Soulmates, one of whom she considered a sister, are placed in the third ring alongside more casual relationships, and her childhood friend, Leila, is in the fourth.

Not all family-like personal communities, however, involve quite such close family relationships as those enjoyed by Esther. In some cases, people included family members about whom they felt ambivalent or even indifferent, yet attached more significance to these relationships because they were family than they did to intimate and supportive friendships. They had been brought up to believe that family ties were the most important regardless of the degree of affection or intimacy involved.

By contrast, *family-enveloped* personal communities lack any close friendships. People with this kind of personal community have a narrow friendship repertoire in which friends play only a limited role as associates or sociable companions, and most friendships have been made during one key period in people's lives, in adolescence or early adulthood. Family members, on the other hand, play a wide range of roles and are the mainstay of social support. The reason we call these personal communities *family-enveloped* is that the family provides a kind of taken-for-granted context and structure to people's lives. However, the fact that family ties are considered the most important, does not necessarily mean that all family relationships are close, and

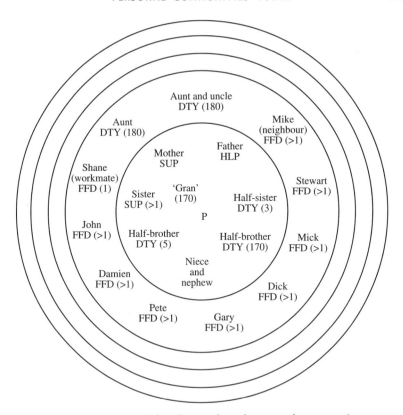

Figure 6.5. Wayne's family-enveloped personal community.

a feature of family-enveloped communities is that they may contain a number of duty relations.

To illustrate this kind of personal community, we take the case of Wayne. Single and in his mid twenties, Wayne has spent all his life in the same town in Cheshire, where he lives at home with his parents. He went to the local school up to the age of sixteen, took a training course in car finishing, and now works for a garage in his home town. He has a full sister, and two half-sisters and a half-brother from his father's first marriage.

Wayne's personal community (Figure 6.5) contains twelve family members: his parents, sister, half-sister and half-brothers, his grand-mother, two aunts and an uncle, and his nephew and niece. Apart from his aunts and uncle, his grandmother and one brother, the rest of his family live within two miles of each other. Also included are eight friends, a neighbour and a workmate.

Typical of someone with this kind of personal community, Wayne's friendship repertoire is narrow; all eight friends are strictly fun friends with whom Wayne goes clubbing or drinking at the pub. He describes all his friendships as

> pretty much the same really. I see some of them more often than others. . . I suppose some of them are more of a laugh.

He has a similar matey relationship with his neighbour Mike and work-mate Shane. He is 'friendly with' others at work but Shane is the only one he socializes with outside a work context. Apart from Damien all of Wayne's friendships were made more than ten years ago when he was at school.

Wayne is close to some of the family members included on his map, such as his mother and father, his full sister Lucy, and Wayne turns to his parents and sister for help and support. The importance of these family ties is reflected by their central position on the map, whereas friends only appear in the second ring. Interestingly, however, Wayne's half-sister and half-brothers are also placed in the centre even though Wayne admitted he hardly ever sees them 'but they're my brother and sister aren't they – so they've gotta be pretty close haven't they?' Wayne's personal community is highly specialized with family and friends playing very different roles.

Neighbour-Based Personal Communities

As we might expect, *neighbour-based* personal communities contain as many (if not more) neighbours as friends or family, neighbours play a wide range of roles with some being considered good friends, and the importance of neighbours is reflected in their central position on people's maps. Other friendships are more casual and tend to have been made at one particular time in people's lives or replaced at each new life-course stage. Family relationships are not necessarily close. This kind of personal community is largely given in the sense that neighbours and family together are in the majority, but also contains given-as-chosen elements where neighbours become good friends.

Brenda is an example of someone with a neighbour-based per-sonal community. In her sixties, Brenda has two brothers, a sister, four grown-up children and five grandchildren. Twice divorced and now widowed, Brenda has moved around the country several times and two of her children and all her grandchildren live several hundred

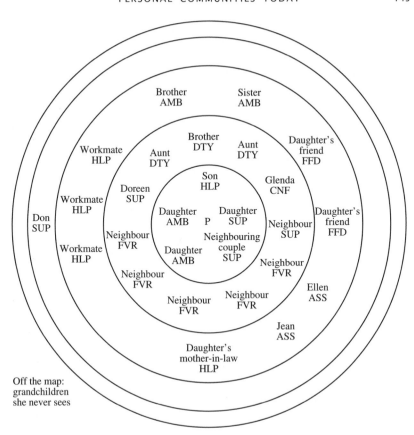

Figure 6.6. Brenda's neighbour-based personal community.

miles away. About fifteen years ago Brenda returned to live near Manchester, where she grew up and where she now works as a part-time cleaner and barmaid.

In her personal community (Figure 6.6) Brenda includes eight neighbours, seven friends, two of whom are actually her daughter's friends, three workmates, and ten family members: her children, her brothers and sister, two aunts, and her daughter's mother-in-law. She excluded her grandchildren because she rarely sees them.

Although Brenda has one supportive friend, Doreen, and one friend in whom she can confide 'a little bit', most of her friendships are casual, and revolve around catalogue parties at which she sells clothes and alcohol:

I've got – what should I say – I've got loads of acquaintances and people that I've known, and people that call and come, but I wouldn't, you know, call them best friends.

She does not have a soulmate and feels that there is no one 'really special', no one of her own age. As we saw in chapter 4, at this stage in her life Brenda regrets that she did not put more energy into friendships when she was bringing up her children.

All Brenda's friends live locally, and, apart from Doreen, she has hardly any friends from earlier stages of her life. Brenda's relationships with her family are quite complex. She is estranged from her sister and one of her brothers, and only included her other brother out of a sense of duty. She has an ambivalent relationship with two of her grown-up children, feeling that they often let her down, and she cannot rely on them for support. On the other hand, Brenda is very well-supported by several of her neighbours, and places neighbours more centrally on her map than several members of her family. Some of these people are 'just neighbours – they're near if I need them or anything, they do odd jobs for me and that', but they do not visit each other's houses socially; others, however, are also considered friends:

> With Marge and Harry, they help me out like the others but I go to their house, you know, and they come here and we're more like friends... If they have parties I get invited, if I have parties I invite them here. She calls in two or three times a week, they buy things off me and I buy off her – she does Avon... And Harry helped me out once in something that happened and I owe him one there, you know.

In addition to neighbours, some of Brenda's work colleagues also provide support, inviting her to go bowling or for a pub meal. They have also been sympathetic about her poor health and will rearrange her shifts so that she does not lose money.

Brenda's social world is very place-based and largely given, in that neighbours, family and workmates make up two-thirds of her personal community. Her case fits the neighbour-based profile most closely though other people in our study included a large number of 'neighbours as friends'.

Partner-Based Personal Communities

As the name *partner-based* implies, in this kind of personal community the partner is the focal point of the person's social world, acting as confidant, provider of emotional and practical support, and constant companion. One might assume that, for people with partners, this would be the most likely type of personal community anyway, but this is not the case. What defines partner-based personal communities is not that partners play a key role – they do this in other kinds of personal community as well, but that they do so exclusively because other sources of support are missing. Although partner-based personal communities contain some friends and family, family relationships are not usually very close, apart from those with young children, and friendship repertoires are narrow, consisting of fun friends, favour friends or associates. Friends tend to have been made at a particular time, or lost and replaced at different stages in the life-course. In this sense, these personal communities are very specialized, with friends and family playing separate and limited roles. Partners occupy the central ring on people's maps, sometimes on their own, sometimes with members of the immediate family. Partner-based personal communities are an interesting hybrid in terms of given and chosen ties, with chosen-as-given being the central tie.

Ian is an example of someone with a partner-based personal community. As we saw in chapter 5, Ian is in his late thirties, married with two young children, and works as a medical technician, acting as a part-time barman at the weekend. In his personal community (Figure 6.7), Ian included his wife, six other members of his family – his son and daughter, brother, parents-in-law and wife's grandfather – and two friends whom he sees as more like acquaintances. Later in the interview Ian decided to include a friend from the pub.

Ian has few friends and his friendship repertoire is very narrow. Sally and Mark are friends of his wife and the main friendship is between the two women, although the four of them socialize together from time to time. His other friend Tom drinks at the pub where Ian works, and, although Ian does not consider him a close friend, Tom has offered to lend Ian money to start his own business, an offer Ian declined because he feels that friends and money don't mix. Ian has no friends from earlier stages in his life, and attributes his lack of friends to an army childhood:

> you make friends, but you don't let them get that close – you know what I mean? . . . Because you know you're gonna get uprooted – you can be friends, you can be muckers and this, that and the other, but you know you're gonna get uprooted, so what's the point in making friends – deep friends – you know what I mean? And that's why my wife is my best friend. OK, we have our ups and downs, and this, that and the other, but she's been my only one and permanent friend.

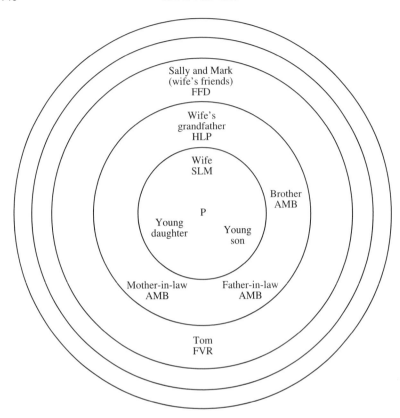

Figure 6.7. Ian's partner-based personal community.

Ian's personal community is very specialized. As we have seen, his wife plays a pivotal role, providing emotional and practical support, and acting as his sole confidante. Ian is fond of his wife's grandfather, who lends them money from time to time, but has a very difficult relationship with his parents-in-law, who are critical of him, siding with his wife in domestic arguments. His relationship with his brother, who threw him out of the family home when their mother died, is deeply ambivalent. Unsurprisingly, the only people in the centre of Ian's map are his wife and two young children.

Professional-Based Personal Communities

Finally, *professional-based* personal communities are characterized by their heavy reliance on professional sources of support, from such as counsellors, therapists or social workers, rather than friends or family. Not only this, the importance of professional help is recognized by the central position given to these professionals on people's maps. Although professional-based communities sometimes contain friends, the friendship repertoire is narrow and friends are strictly for fun. Some family members may also be included, but relationships are not close or the relatives are unable to play an active part. These personal communities are essentially given, though given-as-chosen ties may be included where professionals are also considered friends.

Shelley is a case of someone who is extremely dependent on professional help. At the age of thirteen Shelley was taken into care and, after living in a series of care homes, was brought up by foster parents. These moves involved changing schools several times and Shelley lost touch with all her friends. After school, Shelley worked in a number of unskilled jobs but is currently unemployed. Now nearly twenty-one, she is living on her own, but regularly attends a centre for young adults who have recently left residential care.

In her personal community (Figure 6.8), Shelley included her grandfather, her foster parents, three youth workers, a social worker, a support worker, a counsellor and two friends. Shelley's parents were excluded as was her natural sister. Four friends were also left off the map because they 'get me into trouble', involving her in criminal activities.

Shelley has a small and narrow friendship repertoire. Just two friends are considered important enough to be part of her personal community, and they are strictly fun friends. Shelley does not confide in them or look to them for any kind of practical help or support. All her friends, including those she deliberately excluded, have been made through the day centre and all were brought up in care.

Relationships with immediate family are difficult. Shelley is estranged from her natural parents and has lost touch with her younger sister, who remained in the family home. On the other hand, Shelley's foster parents still keep in touch and she loves her grandfather, visiting him occasionally when she can organize transport, but at eighty-two he is unable to offer her much help or support. As a result of her experiences, Shelley lacks confidence and relies heavily on a range of staff attached to the day centre she attends. It is to these professional workers that Shelley turns, confiding in them, looking to them for emotional and practical support, and seeing them as friends. Shelley's personal community is very specialized, with most key roles played by social workers, youth workers and counsellors. When Shelley becomes

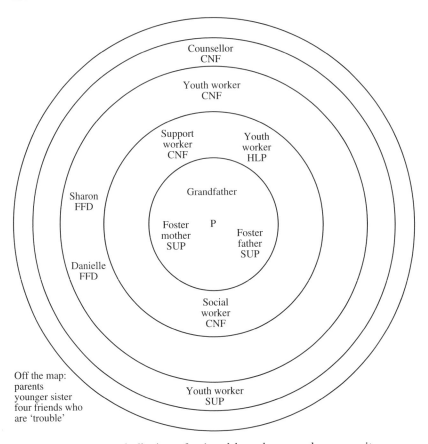

Figure 6.8.   Shelley's professional-based personal community.

twenty-one, however, she will no longer be eligible to use the day cen-tre or entitled to call on the services of its staff. The importance of these professionals in her life is reflected by their relatively central position on her map, although the central ring is reserved for her grandfather and foster parents.

Although Shelley is the most professionally dependent person in our study, Derek's personal community, discussed below, has a number of professional-based features.

THE LIMITS OF CLASSIFICATION

As we suggested earlier, not all the personal communities explored in our study fit neatly into these modal types, although the seven pre-sented above are the best fit for most of our data. As is clear from

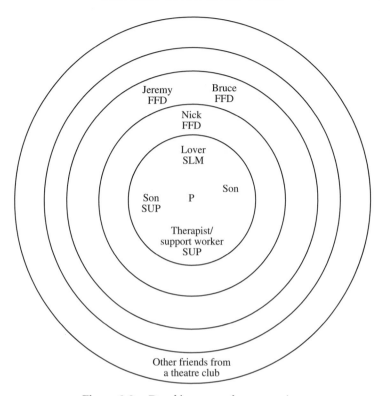

Figure 6.9. Derek's personal community.

the cases described below, classification becomes particularly difficult when personal communities are very small.

One such case is Derek, a retired editor in his sixties, who has two
adult sons, is divorced, but has a longstanding lover, who is still married and lives with her husband. Following a stroke, Derek suffers from
aphasia, which affects his language and communication facilities. In
his personal community (Figure 6.9), Derek includes his lover, two
sons, a support worker from the Aphasia Society, and three friends.
The friends, however, are strictly sociable companions, as are a number of other acquaintances from a theatre club whose names Derek
was unable to articulate, but Derek claims that, even before his stroke,
he had no close friends because of the pressures of his job. Although
he is fond of one of his sons, it is to his lover and his support worker,
both of whom he considers to be friends, that Derek turns for companionship and for emotional and practical support, and it is these
people who have learned how to communicate with him. What makes

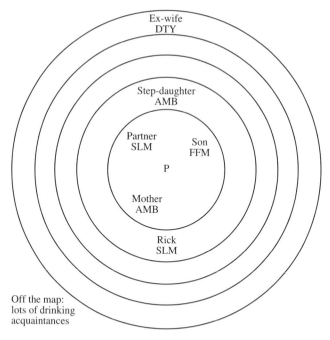

Figure 6.10.   Ron's personal community.

Derek's case difficult to classify is that there are both partner-based and professional-based elements in his personal community.

Ron's personal community is also difficult to classify. In his early fifties, divorced with one adult son, Ron is currently living with a new partner. He works as a fitter for a small engineering company in Essex. Ron's personal community is very small, containing his partner, mother, son, step-daughter, ex-wife and just one friend (Figure 6.10). Ron has an intense friendship repertoire, including only his best friend Rick with whom he can talk about 'anything and everything'. The two men have known each other for more than thirty years and supported each through the breakup of their first marriages. Although Ron has a wider social circle, as we saw in chapter 3, he decided not to include other friends and acquaintances on his map.

Apart from his son, with whom he has a friendly relationship, Ron is not close to the other members of his family, and does not look to family for any kind of assistance. Instead, his sole confidants and supporters are his partner and his best friend Rick. In many respects, Ron's personal community is partner-based except for the key role played by Rick.

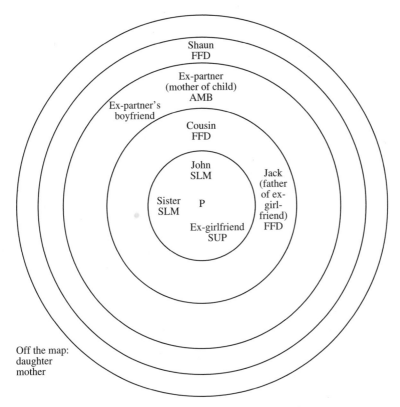

Figure 6.11. Gary's personal community.

Finally, there is Gary, who, at thirty-seven, has separated from the mother of his ten-year-old daughter, is unemployed but looking for casual gardening work, and currently living with his mother in London. In his personal community Gary included a sister, a cousin, three friends, his ex-partner and mother of his child, his ex-partner's new boyfriend, his first girlfriend, another ex-girlfriend and her father, whom Gary also considers a friend (Figure 6.11). Gary did not include his daughter or mother, claiming that it did not occur to him to list them, yet he did not add them later during the interview and became upset when discussing them. He also decided not to include his brother and three of his sisters because the relationships are not at all close. On the other hand Gary is very fond of an older sister, whom he describes as a kind of mother figure and whom he placed in the centre of his map. He is also very close to his best friend John, whom he placed in the central ring alongside his sister. The two men have known each other since childhood and John supported him through many drink and drugs escapades in the past.

> He's always there, you know... puts up with, like, the bullshit and every-thing. You know it's quite upsetting to talk about it actually, yeah... 'cause I've been through a lot of shit you know... But he, he was the one, he was good.

Also in the inner ring is his first girlfriend, with whom Gary has recently established a supportive relationship after a twenty-year gap,

> Emma's my original girlfriend from years and years ago. Anyway, we lost touch and I met up with her again about four years ago, it's really weird, at a party. And she lives down at the coast, down in Poole in Dorset. I went and stayed there with her, like. She'd been married twice, got, like, five kids, but she's just, like, a soulmate... like a good friend, you know... there's nothing sexual between us, we're just very close friends... She's, like, the person I should've married but it just didn't happen, you know, it's weird... She will always be my friend, like, stable friend, not always there but always there, if you know what I mean, not around me close but I know she's always there.

Apart from John and Emma, Gary is not close to his other friends, who are purely drinking companions. Gary does not make friends eas-ily and admits that he has a drug problem, which has caused rifts with friends in the past. Although Gary still keeps contact with the mother of his child, this is volatile relationship.

Gary's personal community is difficult to classify because, although he has one very close soulmate, his community is not friend-like; although he is close to his sister, his community is not family-like or family-enveloped. It seems that Gary has been quite dependent on partners in the past, and ex-girlfriends feature strongly on his map.

Recognizing Diversity

Our exploration and illustration of personal communities in this chap-ter demonstrates the sheer diversity of people's micro-social worlds today. While some people look to family or partner for intimacy and support, treating friends as purely sociable companions, others look to friends as their closest confidants and supporters, considering family simply as a reliable backstop. Yet others have highly suffused personal communities where friends and family play varied and overlapping roles. In the light of this, it make little sense to claim that people nowadays have abandoned traditional 'families of fate' for 'families of choice' based on friends, since the truth, perhaps unsurprisingly, is far more complex.

As we shall see in the final chapter of this book, it is this multiplicity of personal communities, and the range of relationships people have with their friends and family, which can help us address some of the debates about community and social capital today. Of course, we are not claiming that our typology of personal communities is exhaustive. There may well be additional types, which we have not been able to identify because of the nature of our sample, but identifying further types would only serve to strengthen our argument.

Key to the Maps

For ease of recognition, we have adopted the following conventions in the personal community maps:

'P' in the centre of the map refers to the participant.

Friends are given a first name while family members are designated by the particular relationship.
The following abbreviations are used to signify the content and basis of different kinds of relationship as discussed in chapters 3 and 5:

ASS: associate (friendship confined to a single activity/context)

FFD: fun/sociable friend

FFM: fun family

FVR: favour/neighbourly friend

HLP: helpmate or helpful family (practical help)

SUP: supportive friend or family (emotional support)

CNF: confidant or intimate

SLM: soulmate

AMB: ambivalent or 'heart-sink' relationship with friend or family

DTY: relationship based mainly on normative expectations/sense of duty

CHAPTER SEVEN

Micro-Social Worlds in the Making

Notions like class, age, and gender are treated simply as traits that a person has in some form, rather than being regarded as features of a social landscape that facilitate or discourage, to differing degrees, in interaction with other aspects of social topography, the emergence of particular social patterns.

— Allan

At the beginning of this book we argued that although friends as paired relationships have been studied extensively, the role of friendship as a form of social glue has largely been ignored. Consequently, we set our study of friendship in the context of debates about the quality of social life at the end of the twentieth century, and fears about the weakening of social ties. Chapters 3–5 explored the nature and dynamics of friendship and the relationships between friends and family. We described a series of analytical ideas – friendship repertoires, friendship modes and patterns of suffusion – which, in turn, formed the basis of the typology of personal communities presented in chapter 6. The lens of personal communities enabled us to look at the extent to which people feel surrounded by important or significant others who offer companionship, intimacy or support. We found that whereas some people, as adults, still rely heavily on kin and keep their friendships at a lighter more casual level, others develop intimate and supportive relationships outside the family, and, indeed, in some cases, look to friends rather than family in times of need.

In order not to distract from the logic of the book, we have not paused along the way to discuss how different patterns of friendship and types of personal community might come about. It is time now, however, to consider whether, and how, factors – such as age, life-course stage, gender, social class, social mobility, race, ethnicity and so on – might shape the formation of different kinds of friendship or the development of different micro-social worlds. In discussions with others, we have met with contradictory responses. On the one hand, there are those who are curious to discover, for example, whether women have a distinctive approach to their personal social worlds not typically shared by men, or whether distinctive patterns of geographical or social mobility affect the balance in importance between friends and family. Even those who do not often use the language of class may be prompted to ask whether the middle class is more likely to have a different kind of pattern from the working class (whatever they may mean by these terms).

On the other hand, however, there are those who are deeply suspicious of what they perceive to be deterministic labelling. If, personally, they are among those who consider that they have established their own personal community, they may be resentful of the idea that their choices are, say, strongly shaped by their occupation or their experience of social and geographical mobility. Their resentment is likely to be most powerfully focused on a factor such as class, particularly if this is seen to be originally determined by their parents' position in the occupational structure. The implication then seems to be that people are not free to make the kind of life that is right for them personally. Yet even those most hostile to 'putting people into boxes' will quite readily concede that, for example, young people are likely to have a different pattern of friendships from the one they are likely to have when they are living with a partner and young children, or when they are retired.

In this penultimate chapter we turn to the question of how different kinds of personal community come about. What leads some people to have all their supportive and intimate relationships with given family ties while others develop these kinds of relationships with chosen ties, with people who are not automatically connected or obligated to them? Essentially, we are searching for patterns of association: what kinds of people have which kind of friendship repertoire, or personal community, and why? In practice, this turns out to be extremely difficult to disentangle. How can we explain our finding, for example, that people with family-like personal communities include Mary, a retired packer in a local factory, who was born and brought up in a small village in Essex, and George, a Nigerian doctor, who attended schools in

Nigeria and Ghana, studied medicine at Birmingham University, works in Manchester, and maintains links with family and friends around the world?

When we search for patterns of association we are not in the business of identifying statistical relationships between variables, for example, establishing that particular age groups or social classes are correlated with particular kinds of personal community. We do not have a statistically representative or large enough sample. Nor can we establish causal links of the type that state that X causes Y. Nor would we wish to, since the nature of analysis and explanation in qualitative research are different kinds of enterprise. Rather than trying to specify 'isolated variables that are mechanically linked together'[1], our approach is to evaluate the interplay of a number of factors and influences.[2] Our aim, therefore, is to try and unpack some of these complexities and consider the influence of factors such as gender, age, occupational background and history, degree of social and geographical mobility, cultural and ethnic background as *structural locations* and *contexts* that shape people's choices. Our approach recognizes that informal social relationships are socially patterned but also reflect individual preferences and decisions.

We begin by checking the location of personal communities, establishing the extent to which they are embedded within a local neighbourhood or transcend geographical boundaries. We then explore the socio-demographic profiles of people with each type of personal community, searching for any overall patterns. These patterns, however, are treated as clusters of factors that may have contributed to the development of different kinds of micro-social world, rather than as links between variables.[3]

The discussion then moves from description to interpretation and we explore possible explanations for the profiles we have found. Drawing initially on the conclusions of other studies, we examine the possible influence of structural contexts in the shaping of people's micro-social worlds. We then turn to our own data, comparing the role of different influences and choices in more detail, and considering what people themselves tell us about how and why they have developed particular patterns of reliance on family or friends.

THE LOCAL EMBEDDEDNESS OF PERSONAL COMMUNITIES

We found tremendous variation in the extent to which personal communities are embedded within a particular locale and include local sources of companionship, help and support, or are more geographically dispersed. By 'local' we mean that members of a personal community can visit each other and return home, should they wish to, within less than half a day, or during the course of an evening.[4]

Theorists and social commentators tell us that globalization processes have radically altered our sense of attachment to place, and that we live in a transient and transnational world[5], so it is striking to discover that personal communities still appear to have a considerable local element. The extent of this localness, however, varies between different kinds of personal community. Unsurprisingly, perhaps, given greater levels of geographical mobility, friend-based personal communities are the least local, yet they still tend to include more local than dispersed ties. By contrast, family-enveloped personal communities are the most locally based, with members living in the same neighbourhood, or at least within half a day's return visit. Nevertheless, we did encounter some personal communities which contained almost no local ties at all. This occurred where people had recently moved to a new location and had not yet established new roots, where their work involved them in a great deal of travelling, or where they were part of an affluent or cosmopolitan elite.[6]

However, it is not simply the overall balance between local and non-local ties that matters, but the extent to which people are surrounded by sources of support, which kinds of support are more easily, or can only be, provided on a local basis, and whether such supportive ties are with family or friends. Furthermore, with family it is not just a question of how many live locally, but whether they are in a position to offer help as in the case of siblings, active parents or adult children. In our study we found that friend-like and partner-based personal communities were rather distinctive: fewer potentially supportive family lived locally than was the case in other kinds of personal community. Having local non-dependent kin, however, does not guarantee that support is offered, requested or given. As will become clear when we explore people's own accounts in more detail, the content and quality of relationships is key: people do not always get on with or receive support from members of their immediate local family, and local friends vary in the extent to which they offer companionship, intimacy and support.

SOCIO-DEMOGRAPHIC PROFILES

Looking at the socio-demographic characteristics of people with different kinds of personal community, some interesting profiles emerge.

The men and women in our study with friend-like personal communities range in age from eighteen to sixty-eight and include teachers, social workers, health administrators, a student, a pensions officer, an accounts assistant, an academic, a solicitor, the aristocratic wife of a city financier, a retired receptionist, a retired childminder, and a retired corporate debt collector. Those with friend-enveloped personal communities include small business proprietors, teachers, a nonconformist minister, a translator, a psychotherapist, a museum buyer, a pensions administrator, a shop assistant, a retired taxi driver, and a retired insurance adviser. Ranging in age from twenty-six to sixty-three, these people have a slightly older profile. By contrast, people with family-enveloped personal communities are aged between twenty-six and seventy-nine and include a cleaner, a part-time debt collector, a car finisher, a full-time housewife, and a retired farmer. People with family-like personal communities, on the other hand, comprise a childminder, a painter and decorator, a ground crew supervisor at an airport, a hairdresser, an electronics technician, a retired packer, a retired assembly line worker, shop assistants, but also include a mortgage adviser, the manager of a dental practice, and a doctor. With an age range of thirty-five to seventy, this group has the oldest age profile. Finally, people with partner-based personal communities include a medical technician, a hospital consultant, a computer engineer, and a retired systems analyst. They range in age from thirty-nine to sixty-seven, and all are men.†

In traditional variable analysis, where, as Allan says, 'notions like class, age, and gender are treated simply as traits that a person has in some form',[7] and where the aim is to account for most rather than all of the variance,[8] we might be tempted to conclude from the patterns we have identified that friend-like and friend-enveloped personal communities represent the micro-social worlds of highly educated, middle-class, geographically mobile people, while family-enveloped personal communities are a working-class, non-mobile pattern. Family-like personal communities, on the other hand, would be seen as a more puzzling phenomenon. Furthermore, the overall finding that friend-like and partner-based personal communities are the least locally embedded might be taken as providing further support for the conclusion that certain kinds of personal communities are a geographically

---

† We have not given profiles of people with professional-based, neighbour-based or unclassified personal communities since the numbers of people with each type of personal community were very small.

mobile phenomenon. After all, this would only confirm what others have already concluded:

> The patterns of informal sociability of the working class are more likely than those of the middle class to revolve around close contacts with kin and a small set of friends all of whom are relatively closely connected with each other. On the whole, these are likely to be friends of longstanding, often old school friends. By contrast, the social networks of the middle class tend to be much more extensive and diverse. They are likely to see twice as many colleagues from work fairly regularly outside the workplace; they draw their friends from a more diverse range of sources and those friends are not often closely connected to each other... Finally, those in the middle class seem less likely to limit their interaction with friends to a particular sphere of activity in favour of engaging them in multiple kinds of endeavours.[9]

Alternatively, if we were interested in gender differences, we might conclude that women were more likely than men to develop friend-like and family-like personal communities, while men were more likely than women to have personal communities that were partner-based or very small. And, finally, if our focus were sexual orientation, we might take the fact that all the non-heterosexual people we interviewed had a friend-based personal community as evidence that 'families of choice' are the norm among gay men and lesbians.[10]

But these conclusions would require statistically significant correlations, something a qualitative study cannot generate, and, in any case, such conclusions would be misleadingly simplistic. For example, recent research by Mike Savage and colleagues at Manchester University has helped us to recognize the fluidities and nuances of a factor such as class, and the need for sophisticated analysis. Their approach has revealed the importance of structures, processes and change, showing how people move through the life-course in particular trajectories or careers, and that single-variable analysis misses much of the complexity of people's distinctive life-worlds.

Indeed, in our own study, a detailed look at socio-demographic profiles suggests an intricate interplay of factors. For example, among those with friend-like and friend-enveloped personal communities, despite a clustering of people who have received further or higher education, lived in a number of different places and who work in professional, managerial or service occupations, there are also others who come from working-class backgrounds and have lived all their lives in the same neighbourhood. Similarly, although family-enveloped personal communities appear to be associated with manual occupations and residential stability, some people with this kind of personal community have experienced further education and have moved around the country. With family-like personal communities, there is an even more complex mix of class backgrounds and experiences of mobility. Interestingly, among those with this kind of personal community there is a clustering of people from minority ethnic backgrounds, some of whom came to Britain as children or teenagers, some of whom were born and brought up in the United Kingdom, and some of whom have lived in a number of different countries and whose personal communities span several continents.

If we are to avoid deterministic thinking, how can we make sense of these multifaceted and often overlapping patterns? Taking clusters of factors as structural contexts, we need to explore, for example, *how* geographical mobility, educational experience and occupation can have an influence, and *how* gender role socialization, stage in the life-course and the presence or absence of children can shape people's choices. Clearly, ethnic and cultural backgrounds are also very important, as is evident among those with family-like personal communities, but how do cultural factors help mould people's pattern of reliance on family or friends. As outlined above, we begin by exploring findings from previous research and then, in the case studies at the end of the chapter, consider the way such factors provide a context in which different kinds of personal community may develop over time.

FINDINGS FROM PREVIOUS STUDIES

Gender

Whether or not men and women have different kinds of micro-social worlds, different patterns of reliance on family or friends, or even different kinds of friendship, has been the subject of a great many studies. While surveys of personal networks, for example, have found no overall difference in the size of men's and women's networks, there is some debate about their composition, in particular, the relative numbers of kin and non-kin. Some studies have shown that women include more kin and men include more non-kin, while others have found no significant differences between the sexes.[11] Even with non-kin ties, there are also conflicting findings about the proportion of friends included in personal networks. Some studies report, for example, that women of all ages consistently include more friends and men include more colleagues; others purport to show that, among people in white-collar occupations, men have more friends, but that there are no differences between men and women in blue-collar occupations.[12] It has been argued that any differences in the numbers of friends reported by men and women reflect the fact that men and women are in very different friend-making situations, so that men have more opportunity to make friends through their work, whereas women are more tied to the home through their domestic and maternal responsibilities.[13] With the increasing number of women in the labour market, however, these arguments may no longer be very persuasive. Where women work part time, they may have opportunities to make friends through both their work and their home life.[14]

Perhaps the greatest debate centres on the question of whether men and women have different styles of friendship. Some studies, for example, have shown that although men may have more friends than women, women have more intimate friends.[15] It has been argued that women have more complex, multifaceted friendships, that women like relating to a friend in many different ways, whereas men have more specialized friendships to meet different needs.[16] At the heart of the imputed difference between men's and women's friendships is the degree of self-disclosure involved. There is evidence to suggest that women talk with friends about personal issues and difficulties to a greater extent than men: 'talk is the substance of women's friendships'[17], whereas men's friendships are more activity based:[18] 'what (men) do may differ by age and class, but that they tend to do rather than be is undeniable.'[19] Women's friendships have been described as 'face-to-face', men's as 'side-by-side'.[20]

Of course, men also talk with friends as well as sharing activities, but the topics of conversation are different. In same-sex friendships, men are more likely to talk about shared hobbies, sport, work or experiences, and less likely to confide or to express emotional vulnerability, whereas women talk about feelings, problems and relationships.[21] Some studies have shown that women are more likely to have a friend in whom they can confide, while men often lack a confidant among their friends, but may turn to a female relative.[22] Both men and women are more likely to confide in a woman than in a man.[23] It has been argued that women receive more emotional support from friends than men do.[24]

Differences between male and female friendships are explained in terms of gender socialization and become apparent by adolescence; for example, boys play in bigger groups, which suit sporting activities; girls spend more time in friendship pairs, which facilitate intimate talking; girls spend more time talking than boys.[25] Men and women are taught different friendship styles: girls are socialized to pay attention to relationships, men to demonstrate competence rather than vulnerability, and, it is argued, unless society stops having different expectations of mothers and fathers, then women and men will continue to have different kinds of friends.[26] Some writers have suggested that the socialization of men to be independent and self-sufficient, and consequently to limit intimacy in relationships, is not universal but a particular feature of Protestant moral culture, with its individualistic vision.[27]

Nevertheless, despite the seemingly overwhelming evidence that men and women appear to have different friendship patterns, there have been a number of challenges to this orthodoxy.[28] Some critics maintain that differences reported in surveys reflect cultural stereotypes and refer to the way men and women talk about friendship in general rather than how they actually behave with their friends; some women, especially those in professional or managerial occupations do not necessarily talk openly about their feelings with friends, and some men in manual jobs do.[29] In a similar vein, it has been claimed that apparent differences between men's and women's friendships arise from differences in the way men and women describe relationships and the language they use, so that men do not use the word 'intimate' to describe friendships, even ones which are very important to them. Some even argue that women's friendships appear to be more intimate than men's because the language of friendship has been feminized: taking self-disclosure as an indicator of intimacy is a gendered measure, biased towards women's friendships. Shared activities or adventures can also lead to intimacy, which is not only achieved through self-disclosure.[30]

The idea that women's friendships are based on talk while men's are based on activities has been criticized as overstated: men do more talking than is recognized and women friends also share activities.[31] Most of what both men and women talk about is topical rather than personal, covering daily activities, civic or local affairs and family events; women only occasionally talk about personal issues.[32] Some argue that differences in intimacy are just a question of degree: men are intimate with their friends, just not as intimate as women; similarly, men may not receive as much emotional support from friends as women do but they still receive some.[33] Alternatively, some authors claim that men reserve intimacy for their closest friends, and that differences between the sexes become less pronounced the longer a friendship has lasted.[34] It has been claimed that men express affection and intimacy in a different way: for example, through joking rather than hugging; alternatively, men have a more active rather than verbal style of conveying intimacy because they have internalized cultural restraints on the expression of emotion.[35] Yet again, some argue that men are capable of intimacy but simply do not want intimacy with male friends.[36]

Finally, and perhaps most tellingly from our point of view, some critics have pointed out that any statistical differences in the numbers of men and women with particular kinds of personal networks, or friendships, are actually very small. 'The differences reflect widely overlapping distributions. They refer to global, men-on-the-average versus women-on-the-average differences.'[37] So, for example, although women in Britain and America may be more likely than men to have intimate friendships, establishing confiding, or emotionally supportive relationships outside their families, not all women do so, and some men do form close bonds with friends, something certainly borne out in our study. What these large-scale, 'global' statistics do not seem to tell us is *what kinds* of women and men have particular kinds of relationships or offer any clue as to *why*.

Despite these caveats, however, the research evidence on gender, personal networks and friendship does give us some insight into the way gender can influence the development of different kinds of personal community, and different patterns of reliance on friends or family. It can also help us understand why, in our study, more women than men had friend-like personal communities. One of the analytical building blocks of personal communities is the breadth of the friendship repertoire and whether or not it includes confidants and emotionally supportive friends, as well as helpmates and sociable, fun friends. If statistical studies show that, even to a small degree, women are more likely than men to establish confiding and emotionally supportive friendships, then this could help explain the stronger pattern of broad repertoires among women in our own study.

Indeed, some of the women we interviewed commented on differences between men's and women's friendships. This is evident, for example, when they compare their relationships with male and female friends. Harriet, whose friendships we described in chapter 3, spoke of her friendship with some male friends as 'very boyish', one that involved a lot of drinking and watching 'boy movies'. Although she is very fond of some of these male friends, none is as emotionally close or intimate as her greatest women friends. The special quality of close female friendships was described by other women in terms of the way women are interested in the minutiae of each other's lives. As we saw in chapter 5, for example, Henrietta can confide in women friends in a way that is not possible with her husband, because, unlike her husband, 'one's great friends are interested. . . they actually enjoy hearing every drama in your life'.

Statistical evidence that men are less likely than women to form intimate relationships outside the family, and theories of gender socialization, can also give us some insight into the exclusive reliance by men on their partners in partner-based personal communities. Patrick, for example, a hospital consultant whose friendships we described in chapter 3, is aware that he does not 'nurture' friendships and acknowledges his girlfriend's encouragement for him to be more emotionally open in his relationships. He feels that there 'was never a culture among our family of discussing personal problems, or personal difficulties, particularly emotional difficulties. . . there was no emotional language.' This lack of emotional communication may go some way towards explaining Patrick's present pattern of social relationships. Donald, a retired computer systems engineer, describes himself as 'not the kind of person who talks about personal things' and as someone who prefers to 'sort things out' himself. Interestingly, three of the four men with partner-based personal communities have been to private boarding schools, and perhaps this has contributed to their proverbially 'stiff upper lip' approach. By contrast, none of the gay men in our study has partner-based personal communities, though some have long-term partners. On the contrary, they all have friend-based personal communities and broad friendship repertoires. Each of them talked quite openly about the way they confide in friends and rely on them for emotional support.[38]

This brings us to the problem of how to explain the personal communities and friendships of those who do not fit the 'men-on-the-average' or 'women-on-the-average' mould. Of course, since these statistical averages often represent only small differences between men and women, the considerable overlap can help us to account for the fact that some men do develop intimate friendships and broad friendship repertoires, and that some women restrict intimate relationships to family ties. But broad theories of gender socialization alone cannot help us understand why these different patterns occur. So, although gender is clearly an important influence, there are also other factors at work, and in order to understand these different patterns, we need to explore other aspects and contexts of people's lives, for example, their social class, stage in the life-course, experience of geographical mobility and cultural background.

Class and Status

Up until the 1970s, numerous studies painted a vivid picture of working-class life and various theories were put forward to account for differences between working-class and middle-class culture: for example, the idea that the classes differed in their communication patterns, sociolinguistic codes and social skills; in their educational attainment; and in their lifestyles.[39] Working-class and middle-class patterns of sociability with kin and non-kin were also thought to vary considerably. For example, community studies, carried out in Britain between the 1950s and 1970s portrayed the working-class as relying heavily on family while the middle-class turned more to friends.[40] Moreover, differences of this kind have also been found in America, France and Australia, as well as in Britain.[41]

More recently, surveys have demonstrated a relationship between social class and the size and composition of people's personal networks. In general, middle-class networks are larger with proportionately fewer kin; working-class networks are smaller with proportionately more kin. This pattern holds when social class is defined in terms of a person's occupational classification, and also when other class indicators, such as income and level of educational attainment, are used.[42] It seems that middle-class people include more friends and more colleagues than do their working-class counterparts.[43] However, these conclusions are majority findings, and, as we saw with gender, do not tend to account for the degree of overlap or attempt to explain the outliers, the cases that buck the general trend.

But, if class, in the sense of people's position in the division of labour, influences the development of personal communities, how does this happen? As Elizabeth Bott maintained almost half a century ago, it is not a question of simple determinism. For example, she argued that the density or connectedness of social networks were not simply the result of the husband's occupational or class status considered as single determinants. Connectedness depends on a whole complex of forces – economic ties among members of the network, type of local area, opportunities to make new social contact, physical and social mobility, etc. – generated by the occupational and economic systems, but those forces do not always work in the same direction and they may affect different families in different ways.[44]

Some writers have suggested that patterns of sociability and reliance vary by class because people are in very different material and economic circumstances.[45] Members of the working-class have not necessarily got the financial resources to develop friendships that transcend particular contexts, preferring instead to keep friends context-specific. A friend from work or from the pub remains just that, as this makes it easier to contain expectations and financial commitments. Only family are invited into the home. In the same way, family are relied on for help and support because this does not set up a cycle of expectations or concerns about reciprocity, which might be the case with friends. Members of the middle class, on the other hand, tend to extend the frame of reference of a friendship. They can afford to meet friends in other contexts, perhaps going out for a meal or to a cultural event, and have the kind of houses with sufficient space and privacy to be able to invite each other round to dinner. They may also have more resources to offer help. As Allan concludes:

> the structural conditions of middle-class social existence lead to an emphasis on the deliberate *making* of friends; on the transformation of contextually specific relationships into ones whose parameters are less narrow, through purposeful involvement in aspects of life otherwise kept separate. Hence, middle-class sociability typically depends on establishing sociable contacts. . . and then developing these in a fashion that clearly celebrates personal commitment above circumstances.[46]

However, portrayals of traditional working-class sociability confined to the public rather than the private sphere are now being challenged. They may have fitted particular working-class neighbourhoods and council estates in the middle of the last century, but do not take account of increasing levels of affluence.[47] With more money, better housing and more home ownership among the working-class, friendships may be less tied to specific contexts.[48] The class dichotomy is perhaps overdrawn.

Another reason that working-class people appear, in surveys at least, to have fewer friends may be do with terminology. It is argued that middle-class people have more friends because they use the word 'friend' more liberally, including a range of different relationships under the banner of friendship, whereas the working class may use the term 'mate' rather more readily than friend.[49] There is certainly some evidence in our own study that people from middle-class backgrounds not only include more friends in their personal community, but also have a broader friendship repertoire, calling a wider range of relationships friends, and considering these different kinds of relationships sufficiently important to include on their map. In the same way that critics have suggested there may be a gender bias in definitions of close friendship which stress personal disclosure, it has also been suggested that there may be a class bias in definitions of friendship when the term is used to imply relationships that are chosen and based on an appreciation of the special qualities of the friend,

> because... working-class constructions of sociable relationships down played the significance of the abstracted relationships in favour of context, the terminology of friendship often seemed to be inappropriate. Culturally, friendship involves an emphasis on the particularity of the relationships over specific contexts of action. As this ran counter to much working-class practice, there was a hesitancy about describing these relationships as 'friendship'.[50]

An interesting example of this kind of 'hesitancy' can be found in our study. As we saw in chapter 6, Ron, who would be classified as working class because of his skilled manual occupation, lists only one friend in his personal community, although Rick is not the only person who might be called a friend.

> Well, I suppose there was others... but, I mean, they're just – I wouldn't call them close friends... I meet lots and lots of people, but... you'd call them just friends, or acquaintances really, I suppose.

It may be that by asking about 'people who are important to you now', we deterred Ron from including more context-specific friendships. But what is significant here is that Ron does not consider these other relationships sufficiently important to be included, rather than that he is not sure whether to call them friends or acquaintances. On the other hand, it is interesting that Ron, out of a sense of duty, does include several family members about whom he feels deeply ambivalent.

Instead of defining class solely as a person's position in the division of labour, some writers think of class in ways more closely allied to notions of status, or social standing. For example, class is sometimes defined in terms of people's sense of where they belong, their 'habitus' or social identity, which is not just a question of attitudes and beliefs but an identity embodied in social practice and behaviour. Differences between the middle and the working classes, it is argued, are reflected in the way people apprehend and express this sense of position and potential.[51] Class is therefore shorthand for a range of opportunities and experiences to which people in different positions in society are exposed. For example, different family backgrounds, educational experiences, working milieux, and residential locations provide people with different kinds of cultural capital as well as different material resources which translate into different kinds of lifestyle.[52] They also give people different experiences of choice. As we saw in chapter 4, going away to university, for example, or relocating for work, means that people have to form new non-kin attachments, and this gives them an opportunity to experience different kinds of relationships.

In our own study, people seemed to recognize the importance of cultural capital, as well as material resources, in the formation and maintenance of friendships. People were aware of status similarities and differences, and tended to feel more comfortable with others who had similar values, interests and lifestyles. For example, one woman, who works as a ground crew supervisor at an airport, described class differences among her colleagues that affected friendships at work:

> we don't come from the same – alright, even if you get rid of this class factor – we don't come from the same background, we don't have the same interests, they were brought up totally differently... It's your upbringing, your family life... it is to do with education, it's also to do with the way that you, your family is, you know, you're actually brought up at home, because I think your home life is very, very important. It's not about money, though having money helps... but, I mean, you can get people, millionaires, and they're ignorant pigs and you wouldn't be friendly with them.

As we saw in chapter 4, Henrietta, who comes from an aristocratic background, became very aware of class differences once she left art school and found that fellow ex-students from working-class backgrounds were not comfortable when they came to her house. She realizes that most of her current friends come from similar upper-class backgrounds, and have similar ways of life. Terry and Doreen, whose friendships we described in chapter 3, live in a traditional working-class neighbourhood near Stockport in Greater Manchester. Twelve years ago, on a package holiday, they met and made friends with another couple with whom they felt an immediate sense of recognition, a sense of being 'on the same wavelength'. On returning home, however, they became aware of differences between their own and their new friends' circumstances. Over the course of the friendship the four have evolved a way of meeting each other that feels comfortable:

> When they've been going away, when they've been flying from Manchester airport they've drove down here, Alan has took them to the airport and they've left their car here. They've never actually stayed here overnight but when we go up to Scotland we usually stay a week with them... They have plenty of room, they've got a very big house with plenty of room, and plenty of ground space as well, you know, so it's a lot more convenient. Jim is a bloke that likes you there rather than him here.

So class may help to shape the development of different kinds of personal community, in terms of providing different material resources, and encouraging different patterns of sociability and reliance. Different cultural resources, and the recognition of different statuses and lifestyles may act as a filter in the formation of friendships. But class clearly is not the only factor involved, since a number of people we interviewed, who in terms of their occupations would be classified as working class, have nevertheless developed friend-like and friend-enveloped personal communities, including more friends than family, developing a range of different types of friend, and looking to friends as well as, or instead of, family for intimacy and support.

Age and Stage in the Life-Course

As we saw in chapter 4, different ages and life-course stages offer both opportunities and barriers to the development and maintenance of non-kin relationships. They also, of course, bring different kinds of responsibility for and reliance on kin. Certainly, the kind of kin included in people's personal networks changes over the life-course,[53] and there is evidence that older people tend to include more kin, particularly adult sons and daughters.[54]

In the case of friends, many studies have looked at friendship and ageing and there is some debate about the importance of friends at different stages in the life-course.[55] Some writers argue that young adulthood is a time when friends may be lost because people are starting their career, forming a relationship, getting married, all of which may involve geographical mobility so that friends lose touch.[56] Other studies show that friends are more important in young adulthood and in older age, and less important in middle age when the responsibilities of a career, marriage and children leave little time or energy for friendship.[57] However, it is difficult to evaluate the evidence about the importance of friends unless we know how importance is interpreted. If frequency of contact is taken as a proxy measure for closeness, which is the case in some surveys, then it is easy to see that a decline in contact might be taken to mean a decline in the importance of friends. People in our study certainly found it difficult to make much time for friends when they were very busy with children and a career. But if by importance we mean how people feel about relationships, or the extent to which they can rely on friends, then our study suggests that, in friend-based personal communities at least, friends are extremely important during these middle years. Friends confide in and support each other even if the frequency of contact declines. This is the time when people value established relationships, the 'pick up where you left off friends', where constant maintenance is not required for the relationship to survive. Although people with friend-based personal communities have lost touch with some friends because of pressures of time, they have also retained some long-established relationships as well as making new friends with others at a similar stage in their lives.[58] By contrast, people with family-enveloped personal communities have simply lost touch with many friends through pressures of work and child rearing.

Interestingly, some writers have tried to link life-course factors with class, suggesting that middle-class people have different perceptions and experiences of particular life-course stages from their working-class counterparts. For example, although there is little empirical evidence to confirm it, one thesis suggests that while young adulthood is a time for settling down and having a family for the working class, for the middle class, it is a time for exploration and the discovery of identity. The years between thirty and forty represent a time for getting quieter and wiser for the working class, whereas, for the middle class, this period represents a time for accomplishment and establishing oneself. On the other hand, the middle class sees middle age as the prime of life, but for the working-class this is a time of decline. Lastly, old age is a richly earned holiday for the middle class but a wretched time for 'making do' among the working class.[59] Based on this argument, one might conclude that links between life-course stage and patterns of friend making should vary according to class.

However, the relationship between age and life-course stage, and the implications of this for patterns of sociability and reliance, has become immensely more complicated with changing social trends in cohabitation, marriage, childbirth and divorce.[60] More people are living in single-person households, not just because of widowhood, but because they choose to remain single or because they find themselves single after a relationship has broken down. Some couples are opting not to have children. Some women are having their first child in their late thirties or early forties; new partnerships and remarriages may involve older people becoming parents or step-parents to young dependent children. With the breakdown of marriages, grandparents may become involved in an active caring role for young children.[61] In our own study there were men in their fifties who had young second families when other men of the same age had adult children who had left home. Some people were still living a young, singles, 'going out' lifestyle in their late thirties and were aware that friends had become less available because of changes in their responsibilities and commitments. As we saw in chapter 4, Harriet recounted the way one of her friends was no longer keen on socializing, but had become focused on her new relationship once she had 'snared her man', and Ben commented that one of his closest friends had 'put his slippers on early', preferring DIY to clubbing.

Clearly, there are differences in the frequency and nature of socializing at different stages in people's lives, and in the roles played by family and friends.[62] Some studies have shown, for example, that older people have more complex, multifaceted friendships than younger people, partly as a function of the duration of the relationship.[63] But it is difficult to establish a clear link between types of personal community and age or stage in the life-course, since it seems to be more a matter of how people respond to different life-course events, as we saw in chapter 4.[64] Nevertheless, a closer look at patterns of friend-making reveals that in an evolving friendship mode (associated with friend-based personal communities) people may lose friends but they also manage to sustain friendships and make new ones at each life-course transition. By contrast, with a bounded friendship mode (associated with family-enveloped personal communities) people tend not to add significant new friendships beyond their teens and twenties. For them, life-course transitions may signify the loss of friends but without their subsequent replacement. People with serial or ruptured friendship modes are most influenced by life-course transitions, however, since they replace friends at each stage or have to start again after some kind of crisis. In order to understand these life-course influences, however, it is important to disentangle the extent to which events have involved people moving away from familiar neighbourhoods, milieux and sources of support.

Geographical Mobility and Local Embeddedness

It seems that people vary enormously in the extent to which important kin and friends live locally, and in the extent to which personal communities are embedded within a particular place.[65] Clearly, geographical mobility is an important factor in helping to explain these different patterns. The more people have moved, it is argued, the less likely they are to be surrounded by their family and to have local friends. Furthermore, there is evidence to suggest that patterns of geographical mobility and local embeddedness are linked to social class, with the middle class being more geographically mobile and less tied to a local community than their working-class counterparts. Middle-class jobs may involve relocating to another part of the country and, as owner-occupiers, middle-class people have more freedom to choose where they live since they can afford to travel to work.[66] But some studies suggest that the picture is rather more complex. Not all middle-class people are 'cosmopolitans', moving around the country with little attachment to place; some remain within the same neighbourhood for most of their adult lives, retaining a strong sense of local identity, and some have a strong regional connection.[67] Similarly, with greater affluence, and higher levels of home ownership, the residential stability of the working class may now be overstated.[68]

Geographical mobility, it is assumed, involves a disruption of ties, whereby people are uprooted from family and friends. However, in practice, the extent of disruption varies. In the case of working-class mobility, for example, a gradual process of migration may mean that extended families are not completely separated from each other, because those making an initial move are subsequently followed by other family members.[69] This pattern of 'chain' or 'stepwise' migration is evident among people in our study who have moved from the Caribbean to live near relatives in Britain. White middle-class migration, on the other hand, may well involve a move away from parents, siblings or adult children.

The disruption to friendships also varies. While geographical mobility is given as one of the main reasons for friendships fading as people gradually lose touch with each other, some friendships do survive and become stronger as a result of separation. Of course, whether friendships are lost is partly linked to the type of relationship. We find that confiding and emotionally supportive friendships can be sustained at a distance, whereas those based entirely on practical help or sociability need to be more local, leading to the loss and replacement of some of these ties with each move, or their development into more complex forms of friendship.[70] Another factor is the extent to which a friendship is context-specific. As we discussed earlier, some friendships are tied to a particular setting so that friends only interact within that environment, while others transcend the context in which they were originally formed. It seems that context-free friendships are less likely to be disrupted or lost through geographical mobility than context-specific relationships. Finally, there is the issue of material resources, and the extent to which people can afford to visit each other, as well as to keep in touch through telephone or email.[71]

However, geographical mobility does not just involve the disruption of existing ties but, as we saw in chapter 4, also provides an opportunity for establishing new relationships. Again, the extent to which people make friends in a new area depends on a number of different factors. Firstly, there is the question of whether supportive kin live near by and whether people actually feel the need to establish a new set of non-kin ties. Then there is the issue of whether people are able to keep up existing friendships and consider their friendship repertoire is already 'full up' or whether they are interested in forming any new friendships.[72]

So, it is not just a question of geographical mobility per se, but of how the experience of migration has impacted on relationships with family and friends. For example, working-class migrants may be following or be followed by other members of their family, so that they are not too far away from kin even in a new neighbourhood. Consequently, they may feel less need to establish new friendships. On the other hand, they may also be less likely to sustain existing friendships when they move, either because of financial constraints or because the friendships have been tied to a particular context. Middle-class migrants, on the other hand, are less likely to have kin close by, so there is a greater incentive to form new friendships. On the other hand, because their friendships are less tightly framed, some existing friendships may

survive geographical separation leaving limited room for new relationships.

It seems that unpicking different experiences of geographical mobility can throw some light on the way personal communities vary in their
local embeddedness, and in their reliance on family and friends. However, it is important to distinguish between different kinds of localness: for example, some personal communities are local because ties
have never been disrupted by geographical mobility, others are local
because people have forged new ties when they move to a different
area.

Nevertheless, different patterns of migration cannot help explain
cases where people have not moved, where immediate family – such
as siblings, active parents or adult children – live close by, but where
people turn to friends rather than family for companionship, intimacy
and support. Similarly, they cannot explain cases where people have
moved away from family, to another area, even another country, yet
still remain heavily dependent on kin. To understand this we need to
know more about family relationships, in principle and in practice.

Cultural Influences: The Importance of Family and Friends

Many societies today are richly multicultural, and the place and role of
family ties vary considerably among different racial and ethnic groups.
In Britain, for example, the black ethnic population has increased as
a result of several waves of immigration from the Caribbean and from
parts of Asia.[73] For new arrivals family members play a vital role in
providing practical help, but they also offer important cultural bear-
ings and moral support.[74] There are different customs in relation to
the selection of marriage partners, child-rearing practices, the care
of older relatives, and the perceived importance of extended families. Among people of Caribbean origin, for example, families tend
to be matrifocal, centring around maternal rather than paternal kin,
whereas for people from parts of the Indian subcontinent a wife's
sociability revolves more around her husband's kin than her own.[75] Of
course, patterns and practices change and there is considerable debate
among Britain's ethnic communities about the extent to which particular groups should retain their distinctive customs or adopt those of
the majority culture.

Friendship patterns also appear to vary between different ethnic
groups. For example, studies in Canada have found that French Cana-
dians have fewer friends and more family members in their personal

networks than people from British or other European origins[76]; American women from European backgrounds appear to place more emphasis on emotionally supportive friendships than do African-American women, though these differences may also be linked to social class.[77] Some writers have argued that Americans develop friendships more quickly than Europeans do but that Europeans form deeper friendships.[78] As we saw in chapter 1, some have even gone so far as to claim that American society fosters an adolescent view of friendship, which stops short of intimacy and commitment.[79] However, given the ethnic and cultural diversity within America, such generalizations seem far too sweeping.

In addition to acknowledging different cultural messages and practices, it is also important to explore the way in which people respond to these and the importance they attach to kin and non-kin relationships. As we saw in chapter 6, people with family-based personal communities place a great deal of emphasis on the importance of family and family responsibilities, endorsing the maxim that 'blood is thicker than water'. In some cases, this sense of importance is expressed in the quality of relationships with kin, so that family members look after each other and enjoy each other's company; friends, by contrast, are less important, providing companionship and fun but without a sense of deep attachment or mutual responsibility. Sometimes, however, family relationships are more complex: people may have internalized a set of cultural expectations about the primacy of kin but have found that, in practice, the quality of family relationships does not necessarily match expectations. There may be strong but ambivalent relationships with parents and siblings, for example, with friends playing equally or more supportive and intimate roles. A feature of family-based personal communities, however, is that where there is a disparity between expected and actual relationships this is not overtly recognized in the way people define their significant ties. In friend-based personal communities, on the other hand, particularly those which are friend-like, people acknowledge the cultural messages they have received about family, but tend to evaluate relationships with family and friends in terms of their experienced qualities.

Because relationships with family are a key component in understanding personal communities, a few examples from our study may help to illustrate the different ways in which people acknowledge and respond to cultural messages about kin, and the way they approach and value friendship. Huw, for example, a retired farmer and widower in his mid seventies, whose relationships with family and friends we reported in chapter 5, has lived all his life in the same rural community in Wales. His family-enveloped personal community comprises his two adult daughters, three sisters and their families, but also his wife's brother, Dai Davies, who lives next door, whom he describes as 'part family, part friend'. Huw relies exclusively on his family for practical help and emotional support, enjoying their company at numerous family get-togethers. It is as though Huw unquestioningly accepts the importance of family, taking it for granted that these are the most significant relationships in this life.

By contrast, when it comes to friends, Huw did not initially nominate any for inclusion in his personal community. During the course of the interview, however, he added a number of friends to his map, many of whom had been at school with him in the village. For example, one friend, another retired farmer whom he has known for almost sixty years, is a frequent companion at local auctions, where the two men go to view the livestock, gossip, compare prices and so on. Other friends he knows in connection with a range of village activities. But all these friendships are almost part of the scenery, a taken-for-granted aspect of village life, and Huw is not comfortable with the idea of comparing friendships in terms of their closeness or importance:

> Well it's a funny thing. It's a job to think of who you are really closer to than others because I'm not really sure you see. I've lived here all my life and as you can guess I know everybody – well I don't know half who's in the village now because there's so many new houses come – but the old ones, I know them all just the same.

A rather different example of someone who remains very family-oriented is George. Born in Nigeria, brought up and educated in Nigeria, Ghana and the United Kingdom, George is now in his early forties, married with three young children and working as a doctor in Manchester. George's parents, two brothers and two sisters live in America, other brothers and sisters live in Nigeria. Some of his wife's family live in Ghana and America. Despite the close relationship George has with some of his friends locally, and the physical distance that separates him from most of his family, George still considers his family the most important people in his life. His wife Esther, who has a mixed race heritage, agrees that both she and her husband are very family-minded because of their cultural background, maintaining that a very strong sense of family is 'a Ghanaian, Nigerian and a Syrian thing'. In George's case, even though his closest family live many thousands of miles away, he has the resources to keep in touch and can rely on his family for help and support. For example, he does not hesitate to pick up the phone to his brothers in America, and the family have get-togethers there rather than in Britain or Africa because it is 'more convenient'.

Interestingly, some people with friend-based personal communities also come from very family-oriented backgrounds, but this does not prevent them from acknowledging differing degrees of closeness with kin, nor does it deter some of them from placing close friends as centrally as members of their family. Harriet, who comes from a mixed-race (Caribbean–German) background, was brought up with a keen sense of kinship – 'family values are quite a strong thing in this family' – and still feels a sense of obligation to her parents, sister and cousins. Nevertheless, she goes on to say,

> it doesn't actually necessarily mean that we interact in the best possible way... I certainly don't tell my parents everything... In fact I'm quite careful in the way I present things to them because they're quite critical.

Harriet's experience of university, of work, and of flat sharing means that she has met and made friends with people whom she finds are more in tune with what is going on in her life, who understand and empathize with her dilemmas, and in whom she finds it easier to confide. She is aware that a number of her friends are in a similar situation:

> We all need a lot of support – everyone's got the relationship stuff, the work – and it would appear that people aren't necessarily going to their families for it. So we're all going to each other for it.

In Harriet's friend-like personal community, close friends and confidants are placed in the central ring of her map, alongside her parents and sister.

Similarly, Robert, a psychotherapist whose friendships we described in chapters 3 and 4, comes from a black Caribbean background in which the importance of family is paramount. Over the past few years, however, Robert has come to re-evaluate the meaning of 'family':

> Well, I think there is a strong sense of importance of the family and that they should take priority in whatever one does. And I guess I'm learning that families are not just blood families. But before, it was blood. You know if you had spoken to me maybe ten years ago, all my family would have been in [the centre], because you know, it's the bond, you stay together. I felt... there should be... an obligation. Now I'm much more able to work on what I really feel in terms of my own emotions about people.

For Robert, this recognition that family can include non-kin has come about since he joined a local church and since he formed some very close friendships with like-minded professionals through his work. The process of working out how he really feels about members of his family is reflected in Robert's map. Typically for someone with a friend-enveloped personal community, the centre of the map contains only family – in Robert's case his wife, children and maternal kin (mother, grandmother and great aunt), but close friends, some of whom he feels closer to than his brother, are placed in the second ring, more centrally than other members of his family.

It seems that cultural messages about family, and people's experiences of family life, can be a powerful influence in shaping their approach to friendship and the importance of friends.

The Principle of Homophily

Finally, a strong theme in the literature about friendship and personal networks is the notion of homophily, which maintains that people are attracted to and make friends with others who are similar in some respect. This may be a case of 'status homophily', where people are of the same sex, of similar ages, from a similar occupational or class position, of similar educational level, or from similar racial, ethnic or religious backgrounds. Alternatively, it may be a case of 'value homophily', where people share the same attitudes, values and beliefs.[80] Numerous studies have demonstrated differing degrees of both status and value homophily, though status homophily has received more attention.[81] However, a careful analysis of the evidence suggests that in order to understand particular patterns of friendship similarity it is important to explore the range of contexts in which different people are located, and the nature of the social worlds they inhabit, rather than just assuming that people of different gender, race, ethnicity, age or class background have distinctive qualities by virtue of their category membership. So for example, friendship formation is likely to be the result of a complex interaction of factors, including where people live, where they went to school or college, where they work, what other organizations they belong to, and contacts made through family and marriage.[82] As we argued in chapter 4, people's backgrounds and experiences provide a set of opportunities and incentives for meeting, recognizing and forming relationships with similar others outside their family circle, and influence the extent to which these relationships are purely sociable or involve practical help, emotional support or the exchange of confidences.

EXPLORING COMPLEXITY

From our review of other studies it seems clear that factors such as gender, social class, age and stage in the life-course, geographical mobility, and cultural background all represent contexts which play a part in influencing the development of personal communities and the way people perceive the importance of friends and family. Gender socialization, for example, may encourage women in particular to form intimate and supportive friends outside the family group. People's social class – their position in the labour market, their material resources, and the cultural capital they acquire from their social backgrounds – provides different opportunities and constraints, acting as a filter on the formation of close non-kin relationships. People's age and stage in the life-course, and experience of geographical mobility, present different challenges in the way they disrupt or facilitate informal personal ties. Different cultural, ethnic and religious backgrounds place differing degrees of emphasis on the importance of kin as against non-kin relationships.

Sometimes these influences seem to work in the same direction, so that, given what we know from other studies, it is perhaps not surprising to find that women and men, from middle-class backgrounds, working in professional jobs, who have been geographically mobile, have formed close friendships outside the family and have friend-based personal communities. An example of someone who fits this mould is Ben, a single teacher in his late thirties. Born and brought up in the south of England, Ben took a degree in chemistry and then moved to Manchester to gain a teaching qualification, staying on after the course to teach in a large secondary school. In his friend-based personal community, Ben includes his mother, brother, sister, their partners, a cousin, two aunts and two uncles, together with more than twenty friends, including some from sixth-form college and university courses, and new friends made in Manchester. Ben's education and career have taken him away from his family and now that he has settled in Manchester all his family, apart from an aunt and uncle, live more than three hundred miles away. Consequently, there has been a strong incentive for Ben to make both sociable and supportive friendships wherever he has moved. In fact, Ben openly admits that he chose to move away from his family's sphere of influence:

> I think, growing up both with my mum and father... I did have quite a
> difficult time relating to them because they were old... I felt I was held
> back quite a lot. I've always had a bit of a chip on my shoulder... And
> I think that's possibly one of the reasons why I did move away quite
> readily and quite easily, and I find it very easy now to sort of be living in
> Manchester and have a completely different set of friends that aren't so
> much in contact with the family.

Ben's decisions about education and work, and in particular his decision to set up home in another part of the country, have meant that
he has met a wide range of people. Among these contacts he has discovered a number of different reference points and made friendships
based on shared interests in music and clubbing, a common vocation
in teaching, or similar life-course commitments such as doing up a
house. Ben has found people with whom he has a great deal in common, whom he finds more in tune with his lifestyle than his family, and
in whom he can confide. In other words, he has had the opportunity,
the resources and an element of choice, which have enabled him to
develop a broad friendship repertoire and close relationships outside
the family.

Similarly, it is not difficult to appreciate how people from working-
class backgrounds who have no experience of further or higher education, have not been geographically mobile, whose family still live
close by, and who come from particular cultural or ethnic backgrounds
that place strong emphasis on the importance of family come to have
family-enveloped personal communities and a more restricted repertoire of friends. Huw, whose circumstances we described earlier in this
chapter, is a case in point. Interestingly, so is Wayne, yet the two men
could hardly be more different in terms of their age and stage in the
life-course. Whereas Huw is in his seventies, widowed with grown-up
children and grandchildren, Wayne is in his twenties, single and still
living at home with his parents.

Neither Wayne nor Huw has made any intimate friends, and their
friends are rather context-specific. In Wayne's case, his friends are part
of the local scene, people who go to the pub or clubs, but they are not
people he invites to his home or with whom he goes on holiday, for
example. In Huw's case, one friend, David, is a fellow retired farmer
with whom he still goes to auctions, maintaining the same pattern of
friendship the two men had when they were working, although Huw
occasionally goes to lunch with David and his wife. Huw might talk
to David about village concerns, but he would not confide anything

personal outside the family; other friends are mainly known in the context of village affairs, and sit on the same committees. It seems that these two men, with their close family ties but narrowly framed, context-specific friendships that are just part of the local landscape, most closely fit the traditional working-class mould discussed in the literature.

More interesting and challenging, however, are outliers, cases that confound expectations and deviate from the supposed norm. Take the case of Terry and his wife Doreen, both of whom have friend-based personal communities yet come from solid working-class backgrounds. Both Terry and Doreen include a lot of local friends in their personal communities, from school days, from the neighbourhood and from their work. Although most of their friendships are purely sociable, they also have four extremely close friends in whom they confide, who provide emotional and practical support, and whom they consider more important than some members of their family.

In fact, in Terry and Doreen's case, it seems that relationships with family provide a key to understanding their personal community. Neither Terry nor Doreen comes from a big family and they are not close to their siblings. Terry has one sister, who is much older than he is and with whom he has never been close. He did not attend her wedding and, in the past few years, relationships have become more strained since she inherited all the family money. Doreen also has just one sister and the two have never got on well. As a child, Doreen was a bit of a tomboy and always felt that her sister was their father's favourite. As adults, although they only live three miles apart, the two rarely see each other.

> She's very difficult to describe my sister, she's very, very selfish. She is a person that is only her in her little world type of thing, you know, she doesn't – very seldom – include you in anything. In the forty-odd years she's been married we've never had a meal at their house, we've never been invited up.

Despite this estrangement, her sister did occasionally shop for food when Doreen was laid up for a year after a serious accident, and the two became a little closer for a while, but Doreen would never confide in her, or lean on her for emotional support. On the other hand, Doreen's great friend Edith immediately offered her help and for the entire year shopped, cooked meals and did all the family's washing and ironing.

> I mean Edith is a person to me that I pick up the phone and I say 'can you?'
> and she says 'yes' before she knows what it is. . . she will put anything off
> if I ask her to do something or if I'm stuck. I do the same for her.

So, although Terry and Doreen have not had opportunities of further
or higher education, or the experience of moving to another area
where they had to establish new relationships, the lack of rapport
with and support from their immediate family may have led them to
forge intimate and supportive relationships with key friends, which,
in turn, enabled them to extend their friendship repertoire. Interestingly, Doreen and Terry's close friends Edith and her husband John
come from exactly the same working-class background and also have
friend-based personal communities. In their case, however, both have
been upwardly socially mobile, moving from manual to non-manual
occupations and meeting a different set of people. John made friends
with colleagues through his work as a debt negotiator for an engineering company, and Edith through her administrative job at the university. In retirement, both have joined a golf club and made yet another
group of friends.

   Cultural messages about and relations with family also appear to be
an important influence in other cases where education or class background, or experience of social mobility, might lead us to expect the
development of a different kind of personal community. Take Mervin
and Gloria, for example: both have family-like personal communities,
yet we might have assumed Mervin's would be more friend-based, Gloria's more family-enveloped. Mervin, as we saw in chapter 5, is Jewish
and deeply embedded in his local Jewish community on the border
of northeast London and Essex. Included in Mervin's personal community are five very good friends whom he met at school, through his
family and through business contacts, all of whom he has known for
between twenty and thirty years. One friend, Josh, whom he met years
ago through his uncle, is described as a 'wheeler-dealer who would
trade in anything' yet Mervin trusts him completely. Other friends in
East London are all prosperous entrepreneurs, in the diamond business, ladies fashions or 'the retail/wholesale business'. Mervin's friends
are a solid social convoy who all know each other and have been
through similar life-course transitions:

> As years have gone by you've all gone your separate ways in your lives –
> what business you're in or whoever you're working for. You know – you've
> got married at the same stage nearby each other. You've all brought

houses within the same year or so of each other. We've all had kids within the same year or so of each other and we've all been away on holiday at some time together.

This solid continuity of common experience makes it well-nigh impossible for Mervin to acquire new friends, as they would find difficulty in fitting in to such a long-established circle. Not only do his friends know each other and support and confide in each other, but they also know Mervin's and Michelle's family. Mervin claimed he could trust these friends with his life.

Nevertheless, despite the strength of these friendships, family relationships take precedence over all non-kin ties. Mervin's personal community has sixteen members of his family in the first two circles: his sons, his parents and parents-in-law, his elderly grandmother and a host of nephews, nieces and cousins are all there. Family come first because they are blood: as Mervin remarked, you 'can't have everybody in the front of the queue. Someone's got to take a little back step – so it can be the friends'. What is more, he believes his friends would all recognize the appropriateness of this and they, in their turn, would have their own family members in the centre. There are many occasions in Jewish culture where the whole family gathers and all the cousins, aunts and uncles, nephews and nieces, who don't see each other from one year to the next, come together for their 'kiss and cuddles'. On these strongly family occasions friends are not included and would not expect to be: 'they know they're not immediate family and the cousins, they know they're the next in line, which is friends'. Mervin seems to be an almost archetypal case of someone with a personal community which is bound together by a common culture, and a common set of norms and values about the importance of family ties above those with friends.

By contrast, Gloria comes from a less prosperous background. Now in her forties, Gloria moved to Britain from the Caribbean when she was nearly five years old, and has remained in East London since then. As we saw in chapter 5, she is the oldest of six children, and all the family live within three miles. Recently widowed, Gloria has three adult daughters and a son from her first marriage, four grandchildren, and a nine-year-old daughter from her second marriage. Since leaving school, Gloria has done many different part-time unskilled manual jobs, usually finding work through employment agencies. On Gloria's map are fourteen members of her immediate family, her children, grandchildren, parents and siblings, all of whom are placed in the first two rings of her map. Gloria is extremely close to all her children and grandchildren and has a friendship with her three adult daughters, in whom she can confide about certain problems. She is also extremely fond of one of her sisters, Jackie, who lived with her for a while as a teenager, and with whom she in turn stayed when her husband died. The two are confidantes and also enjoy each other's company.

Gloria also includes three friends in her personal community. One is a current neighbour whom Gloria has come to trust; the two women have only known each other for four years but they help each other out with childcare, 'crack a joke', and share problems together. Her two other friends are from childhood and used to live in the same street. Gloria considers them 'more like sort of cousins, if you know what I mean... It's like somebody you've been brought up with, like family'. The girls used to visit and sometimes stay the night at each other's houses. Despite the fact that these friends are only placed in the third ring of her map, Gloria feels very close to them and is even more comfortable confiding in them than in her daughters and her sister Jackie:

> there's stuff about myself that I would not tell my family but I would tell my friends. With my family I don't trust them not to tell other family members... Friends won't go and tell your family... I'd sooner tell my friends something secret than I would my family.

Clearly, Gloria is very family-minded, and comes from a cultural background that stresses the importance of family. Not only that, all her immediate family live within three miles, and she can turn to them for help and support. Nevertheless she has discovered that friends can sometimes prove more trusted than family as confidants and has a family-like rather than family-enveloped personal community.

For some people, it is a life-course event that appears to alter the shape of their personal community, as in the case of Mary, whose family-like personal community had been firmly family-enveloped in the past. Now in her sixties, Mary was born and brought up in a village in Essex in the southeast of England. After leaving school, Mary worked in a number of unskilled jobs before she married Jack, an assembly line worker, and had two daughters who are now married with children of their own, and who still live in the village. When her daughters were at school, Mary returned to work as a packer in a local factory, where she stayed until her retirement. In her personal community, Mary included her immediate family, her husband, daughters, sons-in-law, grand-sons and half-sister, all of whom, apart from her half-sister, live within a mile and were placed in the central ring. Mary is extremely fond of and close to her daughters and considers them friends, but, although they live locally, they are too preoccupied with their own families and with their work to be able to offer her much company. Her half-sister lives a hundred miles away and the two women are not particularly close. Mary's husband Jack is often busy with his hobbies, so that gardening and bowls take up much of his time.

Also included on Mary's map are some fun friends and a neighbour, but none of these is given the same prominence as family. Three of these friends, or ex-workmates as she called them, are from the packing factory. However, although they live only eight miles away Mary meets them just once or twice a year because she does not drive and finds the local buses inconvenient and expensive. Other friends are known through a neighbour, but they live more than eighty miles away and Mary only sees them when they come to visit. Recently, however, Mary has re-established a friendship with Dorothy, someone she has known for thirty-three years. The two women, whose children went to the same secondary school, used to chat at the school gates, but Dorothy had six children and Mary worked so there was little time to meet on other occasions. Now Dorothy is a widow and Mary has retired the two have started to spend time together. They regularly go on coach outings, and are planning to go on holiday together to Majorca. Mary considers Dorothy a very close friend and confides in her as much as she does with her daughters.

Typical of someone with a family-like personal community, Mary is very family-minded, and she considers family the most important people in her life. Her background, experience of working full-time outside the village, limited access to transport, and lack of geographical mobility, together with the proximity of her immediate family have not provided many opportunities or incentives over the years for her to form and sustain intimate local relationships outside the family circle. A crucial life-course transition, however, the experience of retirement, has brought some changes in her personal community. She now has more time on her hands but she has become cut off from her ex-workmates, and her daughters and husband are preoccupied with their own responsibilities and interests. In these circumstances she has looked beyond her family and established a very close friendship in the village.

Finally, we take the case of Gill, for whom life-course events have also been extremely influential in the development of her personal community. In Gill's case, her experience of further education and geographical mobility might have led us to expect a friend-based personal community, yet Gill's is firmly family-enveloped. Now in her fifties, Gill went to art college and then worked for a time in an advertising agency, moving a hundred and fifty miles away from home to live in London, while her parents and most of her siblings remained in Norfolk. Once in London, she met her husband who had been married before and had two children. The couple soon married and Gill gave up her job and looked after her step-children, later having two children of her own. In her personal community Gill lists mainly old friends of her husband and associates from her local church. She also includes two longstanding friends, one of whom she has known for eighteen years who now lives twelve thousand miles away so the women chat on the phone about once a year, and a friend from work, whom she has known for thirty years and who is essentially a fossil friend: she reflected that he had not even invited her to his wedding. None of these friendships is intimate or supportive, though Gill feels she could turn to the local priest and his wife if she needed to.

In practice, Gill is much more family-minded, placing more than thirty members of her family in the first two circles on her map: her husband, children and step-children; her parents; her five siblings and all their children; two great aunts and a great uncle. She relies totally on her husband and her family for help and support, even though most of her family do not live close by. As we saw in chapter 4, Gill attributes her lack of special friends to the fact that she has been caring for children for almost thirty years. When she was looking after her step-children none of her friends had children and she lost touch with her peers. Then when she had children of her own, she was older than the other mothers and did not make new friends. So, although Gill appears to have had an opportunity to make friends in a range of settings, such as at art college, by moving to London, through work, and as a mother, her strong sense of family, and the fact that her life-course transitions were out of kilter with those of her peers would seem to have worked against this and to have kept her firmly tied to kin.

Coda

As we have shown, although traditional sociological factors such as class, gender, life-course and cultural background can help us understand different patterns of sociability and reliance on family and friends, from these different case studies we can see just how complex is the interaction of influences that help shape the development of people's micro-social worlds. At different stages in their lives, and against a backdrop of class opportunities, gender socialization, cultural norms and experiences of geographical mobility, people make decisions about those whose companionship they enjoy, and those whom they trust and in whom they can confide. Given the range of cultural backgrounds in Britain today, and the diversity of resources and opportunities, it is likely that different kinds of personal community will continue to be found. As will become evident in the following chapter, understanding patterns of social support and appreciating the detail of people's micro-social worlds are vital if we are to evaluate the evidence and challenge those who would have us believe our social bonds have been irretrievably weakened, that we have somehow collectively fallen from grace.

CHAPTER EIGHT

Hidden Solidarities Revealed

I do not wish to treat friendships daintily, but with the roughest courage. When they are real, they are not glass threads or frostwork, but the solidest thing we know.

— Emerson

We return in our final chapter to the challenge set out in chapter 1. How does the detailed empirical evidence, presented in previous chapters, bear upon the strand of pessimistic thinking that has continued from de Tocqueville in the early nineteenth century through Durkheim, Lasch, Riesman and Putnam to Bauman and Castells in the early twenty-first century? In particular, have we anything to say to current commentators who have concluded that our informal personal ties are becoming increasingly transient and superficial, more liquid in Bauman's phrase, and that people are neglecting wider social responsibilities so that the quality of civil society is seriously compromised? Indeed, how far should we believe Bauman, perhaps the most despairing prophet of them all, who asserts that for him personal communities are

> as fragile and short-lived as scattered and wandering emotions, shifting erratically from one target to another and drifting in a forever inconclusive search for a secure haven; communities of shared worries, shared anxieties or shared hatreds – but in each case 'peg' communities: a momentary gathering around a nail on which many solitary individuals hang their solitary individual fears.[1]

The Discovery of Hidden Solidarities

As others before us have argued, over at least the last one hundred and fifty years, careful and detailed analysis of the human condition reveals a much more subtle and nuanced picture than is painted by the prophets of doom. The empirical diversity we report in this book, culminating in our typology of personal communities, confirms these earlier challenges by showing that criticisms of modern and late modern society have been overstated. Moreover, we argue that by overstating their case, some commentators unwittingly help to hide the complexities of people's lives in the broad sweep of their assertions, rather than illuminating them. The more we explore in detail the range and quality of people's actual rather than imputed social relationships, the more the intricacy of their micro-social worlds – and the hidden solidarities they contain – are revealed.

We chose the title of our book advisedly: the solidarities we explore are, indeed, largely hidden. This may be, in part, because certain commentators have continued to look for evidence of social solidarity in neighbourhoods or organizations, rather than search for 'supportive ties wherever located and wherever solidary'.[2] Consequently, where these place-based and organizational solidarities are in decline, commentators have drawn pessimistic conclusions about the state of community. By focusing, instead, on the nature and quality of people's informal personal relationships 'community *can* be seen'.[3] Furthermore, certain social solidarities are perhaps less visible now than they were in the past. Before people could easily communicate by telephone or the Internet, their social connections were mainly face-to-face and, literally, more visible. Only through detailed investigation can certain kinds of social connections – such as those made through phone calls, texts or emails – become evident to the observer.[4]

Since nowadays people are able to establish and maintain relationships in a wide variety of settings, across large geographical distances, social solidarities may also be hidden because, without some self-conscious reflection, people themselves may not always be readily aware of the overall set of social relationships in which they are embedded. They do not necessarily think about this collectivity in any methodical way, apart from, perhaps, at weddings, or significant birthdays, or other rites of passage such as christenings or bar mitzvahs. Of course, people are aware of individual solidarities, such as those found in particularly committed or trusting relationships; they recognize the solidarity of family groupings, or of clusters of friends, colleagues or neighbours, but they have not necessarily thought systematically about the overall set of people who are significant to them in some way. However, although people do not necessarily spontaneously see themselves as having a *personal community*, as we argued in chapter 2, we do not believe that we foisted on our participants an alien way of viewing their social world. On the contrary, once their personal community was mapped, people in our study became conscious of and recognized their map as a representation of their significant social world once they had helped us to construct it. We return to the implications of this new-found and emerging consciousness below.

Uncovering these hidden solidarities has been made possible because of the way we approached our research. Rather than asking directly about particular categories of relationship, or predetermining the contexts people should consider, or using proxy measures of social cohesion such as civic involvement, we simply asked people to tell us who is 'important to you now', and then explored the basis and quality of the relationships. Of course, our decision to concentrate on those relationships that our participants considered sufficiently important to be included means that we may have under-represented the more casual, fleeting ties that have attracted the attention of many commentators. However, this does not in any way undermine the fact that, among those relationships people claim are important, we find a range of different kinds of tie. Some relationships are based on strong trust, commitment, and have lasted in some cases over most of a lifetime. Others, to be sure, are more instrumental (if not calculative), or are recognized as being more light-hearted safety valves. But it is the very great diversity of ties, and the diversity of the circumstances or contexts that shape them, which provide the core finding of our study. How this understanding contributes to other debates is an issue we return to below.

DISTILLING OUR EVIDENCE

But what can our study tell us, in detail, about the state of community today? In particular, can our research shed any light on some of the major discontents we discussed in chapter 1? How can our knowledge of personal communities, and of the range of friendships and friend-like ties within them, address claims that, for example, place-based community has been lost, that people have 'few strong ties at

the neighbourhood level', that 'personal communities consist of networks of far-flung kinship, workplace and interest group relations',
that 'they are not place-based communities of geography'.[5] What can
we say about informal relationships today? Are people turning away
from their families? Are friendships nowadays more superficial and
transient?[6] Are 'long-term commitments thin on the ground, long-
term engagement a rare expectation, and the obligation of mutual
assistance "come what may" a prospect that is neither realistic nor
viewed as worthy of great effort'?[7] Finally, are most people vulnerable,
unhappy and socially isolated?

Community without Propinquity?

As we saw in chapter 1, for some pessimistic commentators, fears
about the dissolution of social bonds are associated with the alleged
decline of place-based communities. It is important, then, to stress
that our decision to focus on personal communities does not mean
that we think that personal communities have somehow replaced local
communities, or that the quality of life in particular locations or neighbourhoods is no longer important, simply that we have focused our
lens rather differently. As Wellman argues, studying personal communities

> does not preclude finding that communities are urban villages where
> everyone knows each other and provides the abundant, broadly based
> support that Tönnies. . . thought only to be a nostalgic relic of vanishing
> villages. . . [but] allows the discovery of other forms of community – per-
> haps sparsely knit and spatially dispersed. . . – perhaps loosely coupled
> or virtual.[8]

Yet, despite this different focus, we are still interested in the extent to
which personal communities are rooted in particular locales or, alternatively, made up of more dispersed ties. As we have already shown, in
chapter 7, people vary enormously in the extent to which those who
are important to them live close by. With a few exceptions, family-
enveloped personal communities seem to be the most locally embedded, with the majority of relationships based in the same neighbourhood or a short journey away. People with this kind of personal community tend to have lived in the same place for a long time, if not the
whole of their lives, and have several family members living close by.
By contrast, friend-like and friend-enveloped personal communities
appear to be the least local. People with these kinds of personal community have either been geographically mobile themselves, or family

and friends have moved away, yet we find that they still have important relationships with others in their local area.

Given some current fears about the fragmentation of social life, it is surely heartening to discover that, apart from the exceptions discussed below, people we interviewed still have local sources of fun, support and intimacy. Where people have not been very geographically mobile this is perhaps not so surprising, but where people's lives and relationships have been disrupted by their own or others' moves, it is even more reassuring to discover that they have formed a range of attachments within their local community, in particular where this has involved starting afresh in a new area without any close family around. Although these fresh local ties are often initially based on fun or favours, since people need some local sources of sociability and support, some of these new relationships develop over time into more confiding or intimate ties.

What might be considered even more heartening, however, is the discovery that people also sustain significant non-local relationships over time and space, especially when we have been led to believe that contemporary social relationships are fleeting and transient. So, far from concluding that personal communities containing dispersed ties are necessarily a sign of social fragmentation, we should perhaps acknowledge that dispersed ties could be construed as evidence of enduring attachments based on long-term commitment.

For example, as we saw in chapter 4, some people have an evolving pattern of making friends, whereby some friendships fade and new ones are formed but other friendships are maintained despite big geographical distances or long separations. By contrast, other people have a serial mode of friend-making, in which they replace all their friends at each new stage of the life-course or with each move to a new area. Interestingly, personal communities based on a serial mode of friend-making are likely to comprise a predominantly local set of relationships, yet these ties may well be more fleeting than those which have survived physical separation. So, in this case, very locally based personal communities might actually be less robust than those which contain a blend of local and more dispersed ties. Of course, personal communities consisting entirely of non-local relationships can be rather vulnerable, as we explore below, but the fact that significant ties are not confined to a small geographical area should not necessarily be a matter of great concern.

Arguably, in this context, some personal communities and patterns of friend-making may fit better with current realities of social and geographical mobility. Perhaps an evolving friendship mode is invaluable where people have to move on in their lives but wish to retain powerful social continuity as well. Some indication of people's desire to develop such a friendship mode is shown by the success of the 'Friends Reunited' website (http://www.friendsreunited.co.uk), which is designed to bring together those who were at school or college together but who now may be widely scattered. We return to the idea of personal communities being more or less appropriate below.

By revealing the way people vary in the extent to which they are embedded in their local community – through their significant relationships with others in their area – our study of personal communities can dispel some of the myths about people having become literally displaced, dislodged in the face of globalization and lacking any place-based roots. Additionally, we are able to challenge the notion that people with dispersed ties are necessarily more isolated and have fewer intimate or supportive relationships. However, it is important to remember that our research cannot address other fears about the state of place-based community. We cannot provide evidence, for example, about the quality of communal life in an area, or the extent to which local people share a commitment to the collective common good, since we have not conducted a place-based study. So, in this regard, we are not able to respond to commentators for whom these are their primary concerns.

The Quality of Personal Ties Today

Another major fear expressed by some who bemoan the loss of community is that the quality of social relationships has seriously declined, that we are now more instrumental, less caring, less trusting, and less committed. Family responsibilities are no longer honoured, or, according to the most pessimistic commentators, late modernity spells the end of family life altogether. Friendships are not what they used to be, but are superficial, casual and transient, an insubstantial form of social glue. In response to these dispiriting interpretations we have clearly shown that such sweeping conclusions are not supported by our study. Of course, we cannot estimate the numbers of people with different kinds of personal relationships, but the sheer diversity of relationships we encountered casts doubt on the idea that the quality of our social life today is in universal and terminal decline.

Take the importance of family, for example. In two of the seven kinds of personal community – family-like and family-enveloped – relatives outnumber friends as important people in our participants' lives. In friend-enveloped personal communities, family ties are considered the most important, taking central stage on people's maps, while even close friends are placed further out. Even friend-like personal communities, where friendships are considered among the most important relationships and placed in the centre of the map, significant family ties are also included.

Of course, including kin in a personal community does not of itself tell us about the quality of the tie, and we have evidence of a wide range of attachments. At one extreme, we have examples of immensely close and committed family relationships, between brothers and sisters, between parents and their children, between 'special' cousins, with grandchildren, 'favourite' aunts and uncles, nephews and nieces, where people refer to these relatives as 'a part of me', or 'one of the foundations of my life'. As we saw in chapter 5, sometimes these family relationships become suffused and take on a friend-like character, so that a sister, brother or cousin, for example, is also considered a friend. At the other extreme, however, we find cases of people including family members because of cultural expectations or a sense of duty, sometimes where the relationship is rather ambivalent, or even where the relative is actively disliked.[9]

We can also learn something about the quality of family ties today by hearing about relatives who have been excluded from people's maps. Sometimes these are members of a person's extended family, such as aunts, uncles, distant cousins, step-brothers and step-sisters, or they can be in-laws, but the relationship is simply not considered very significant. Sometimes, however, immediate family are not included, such as brothers or sisters, children or parents, and there has been some kind of breakdown in the relationship. We found this in our study where, for example, people have been brought up in foster homes and are alienated from their relatives, or where they are adopted and feel little sense of kinship with their adoptive family, where they are at odds with members of their family or have seriously fallen out.

Clearly, relationships in families are immensely diverse, from loving and committed, to distant, to estranged. However, the fact that people include all kinds of family ties in their personal communities tells something about the strength of the sense of familial connection and duty today. As we saw in chapter 7, particular cultural backgrounds place a strong emphasis on family ties, so, given the increasing cultural diversity in Britain, sombre forecasts that late modernity will spell the 'end of the family' seem overstated, to say the least.

Turning to relationships with friends, we find that both friend-like and friend-enveloped personal communities contain more friends than family and, in friend-like personal communities, some very important friends are placed in the centre of people's maps. Of course, the kinds of friends people consider important enough to be included vary considerably, and one of the key findings of our study is the diverse nature of friendship today. On the one hand, soulmates are the closest and most committed friends of all, exchanging support and confidences, sharing values and enjoying each other's company, knowing one other inside out. Then there are confidants, who share secrets and have fun together, comforters, who offer a shoulder to cry on, help-mates, who can rely on each other for practical help and who also socialize together. Other friends are neighbourly, doing small favours for each other; yet others are useful contacts, or associates who only meet in a particular context, for example, at the pub or a golf club. Finally, there are the sociable or fun friends, where the relationship revolves around going out, sharing a drink or a meal, chatting, but there is little intimacy and the friends do not rely on each other for help or support.[10]

Comforters, confidants and soulmates tend to be long-term, committed ties. Some of these relationships are so close that they may be seen as quasi-family. Other friendships, however, are quite casual and short-lived, the kind of relationships which have caught the attention of pessimistic commentators. For example, some associate, neighbourly or fun friendships may fade when people move, or follow different life-course trajectories. However, fun friendships can also be immensely affectionate and last almost a lifetime.

Not only are there different kinds of friendship, but people vary in their range or repertoire of friendships. So, for example, some people have basic or narrow repertoires in which all their friends are fun friends or associates; more intimate relationships are confined to family or partners or are missing altogether from their personal community. On the other hand, some people include only intimate friendships, considering more casual friendships not sufficiently important to include on their map. Yet others have broader types of repertoire, enjoying and including a range of different kinds of friendship, from close confidants to more casual, light-hearted ties.[11]

	High commitment	Low commitment
Given	Solid/foundational	Nominal
Given-as-chosen	Bonus	Neglected/abandoned
Chosen-as-given	Adopted	Heart sink
Chosen	Forged	Liquid

Figure 8.1. Commitment and choice in personal relationships.

Rather than subscribing to the view that informal personal relationships today are necessarily casual and fleeting, we should appreciate the fact that they come in many different forms and that, as usual, the devil is in the detail. Interestingly, the people in our study who were the most self-conscious and 'reflexive' – in Giddens's terms[12] – about their social world were not simply engaged in 'plastic', superficial, pick-up and put-down-again relationships. On the contrary, they had a range of close and more distant family ties and, in some cases, a few estranged relationships. They also had broad friendship repertoires that included soulmates, confidants, helpmates, favour friends and also some purely sociable fun friends. They were aware of the way in which friends may drift apart, and their personal communities actually relied on some friendships dropping off or at least fading in importance so that other friendships could blossom and come to the fore, becoming more committed but possibly also more demanding. Unlike some contemporary Jeremiahs, however, these reflexive participants did not consider their more light-hearted or short-lived friendships less valuable or worthwhile, but saw them as a vital counter balance to more serious relationships, referring to them as 'low maintenance' as distinct from 'high maintenance' friends, or as 'champagne bubbles', whose company acted as a refreshing tonic.

But how does the empirical diversity we have identified in our study link back to the classification of relationships introduced in chapter 2? There we discussed the notion that informal personal relationships could vary according to degrees of both commitment and choice, and put forward, as an analytical device, a set of eight different kinds of informal relationship, only two of which – neglected/abandoned and liquid – correspond with the uncommitted, low trust, transient ties that are supposed to be emblematic of Western society today. (The original diagram from chapter 2 is reproduced as Figure 8.1.)

Looking at the personal communities described in our study, we find some people's maps contain all eight kinds of relationships. Others include distinctive combinations of high and low commitment, given and chosen ties. Certainly, these kinds of personal community cannot be seen as evidence that personal relationships today are uniformly casual. Added to this, none of the personal communities we identified were made up entirely of nominal, neglected or liquid ties. However, and this is a serious matter of concern, we did find cases where these kinds of relationships were in the majority, and we consider the circumstances and contexts of such cases below.

Of course, some might argue that our approach did not enable us to pick up examples of more transient personal communities. As we acknowledged at the beginning of this chapter, the fact that we concentrated on relationships which people considered important may mean we have under-represented casual, fleeting ties. Also, the fact that our sample did not include people in highly transient circumstances may mean that we failed to capture the personal communities of the most isolated or global members of society.[13] Nor did we capture the micro-social worlds of celebrities – from whichever side of the Atlantic – or whatever groups the popular media report as having the most casual ties. What we can say, however, is that, apart from the cases and situations discussed below, among the men and women in our study we did not find much solid evidence of Bauman's world of 'liquid love'.

Personal Communities, Social Support and Health

As we saw in chapter 1, concern has also been expressed about increasing levels of depression and other mental health problems and there is a truly enormous scholarly literature on the connections between social support and health. Despite problems with the way social support has been defined and operationalized, there is now a body of evidence to suggest that 'little circles' and the support within them are crucially important for our psychological and biological well-being.

In our own study, we collected information about people's mental well-being using a well-known standardized method, the General Health Questionnaire (GHQ).[14] Across all our participants, scores on this measure varied widely, but when we looked at different kinds of personal community, some interesting patterns emerged. We found a cluster of people whose GHQ scores indicated poor mental health among those with partner-based and professional-based personal communities. In addition to this, poor mental health scores were found among some of the people with very small personal communities (which we were unable to fit into our typology), and, interestingly, these personal communities had elements of partner-based or professional-based types.

In friend-based and family-based personal communities, on the other hand, there are no clusters of people whose GHQ scores indicate poor mental health, but isolated cases can still be found. In these cases there appears to be a set of very particular circumstances associated with poor mental health, rather than a chronic lack of support within their personal community. For example, some people were in short-term stressful situations at the time of the interview, such as caring for young children while also experiencing serious relationship problems with a partner, being very unhappy at work, or having serious financial problems. In other cases, people were distressed about particular life-course events, such as being single and childless at an age where they felt they had 'missed the boat', the pain of which could not easily be assuaged, despite considerable love and support from friends and family. Interestingly, in one case, a woman in her forties had a long history of mental ill health, and in the past had lost a number of friends through her illness. At the time of interview, however, she was surrounded by friends she had made through her work in a mental health charity, all of whom had a greater understanding and were more supportive of her situation than she had experienced before. Although her GHQ score was high, it was not the highest score in our study.

It seems that some types of personal communities are more likely than others to provide the kind of social support which numerous studies have demonstrated is so important for people's sense of well-being and mental health. People with friend-like, friend-enveloped and family-like personal communities have a range of significant others – friends, family, neighbours – to whom they can turn, and it is this diversity of ties which, it had been argued, is associated with better physical and mental health. By contrast, those with partner-based and professional-based personal communities lack such diverse sources and, by having 'all their eggs in one basket', may become vulnerable if services are withdrawn or a partnership breaks down.

Although we have argued that fears about the state of society today appear to be overstated, clearly some people are isolated and unhappy, with unsupportive micro-social worlds. But how do people become embedded in fragile rather than robust personal communities? In chapter 7 we explored the influence of factors such as age, stage in the life-course, social class, gender and geographical mobility, and highlighted the complex interplay of different factors, but also drew attention to the diverse ways in which people themselves respond to the situations in which they find themselves.

There were, in fact, a range of circumstances and contexts in our study which were associated with fragile personal communities. For, example, some people have had little stability in their parenting or schooling. Being brought up in care and living with a series of different foster parents, or an 'army childhood' spent in many different countries, can lead to disrupted friendships or the formation of no significant childhood friendships at all. As adults, some people with this kind of background have still not formed any close friendships, and, where this is combined with the death or estrangement of key family members, they may become partner-based, professional-based or socially isolated. Interestingly, however, there can also be a different set of outcomes, as in the case of one young person brought up in care who was able to stay at the same secondary school throughout his teenage years, and who now has a robust friend-like personal community with a broad repertoire of friends.

Sometimes, people have fragile personal communities because they have simply not taken time to nurture friendships: for example, this happened to women who moved away from their family and friends to live with their husbands, or to relocate for their husband's work, putting all their energy into their role as wife and mother. It also happened to men who moved to a new area so that their children could grow up in a 'better' environment, but who then spent so much time travelling for their work that they neither kept up with old friends nor established new relationships in the local area. These people are vulnerable because they have no locally based significant ties, apart from their partner.

Some people have fractured personal communities, becoming alienated from family or losing friends, when they experience setbacks of various kinds, for example, difficult divorces, losing their jobs, becoming addicted to drugs or alcohol, or suffering a major illness which impairs their normal functioning. Sometimes people have vulnerable personal communities simply because they have traditionally relied on their family alone, but now none of their relatives lives nearby.

It is also important to recognize that, not only are some people living apart from their families, or even estranged from them, but it is certainly the case that there are people today who simply have no immediate family at all. For example, their parents and siblings are dead, they have no children of their own, nor any nephews or nieces, and their only relatives are distant and rarely seen.

So there are many different circumstances in which fragile personal communities may develop. But it is not the circumstances alone which lead to different kinds of personal community, since some people experience very similar situations or life events, but are nevertheless embedded in much more robust 'little circles'. In some of these cases, a loving family may provide a vital safety net, in others, however, where for whatever reason family members cannot provide support, it is the fact that close friendships have been established and nurtured which holds out a vital lifeline. Where family are no longer local, where family relationships have broken down, or people simply have no close relatives at all, then friendships can indeed provide an important form of social glue.

DRAWING WIDER IMPLICATIONS FROM OUR STUDY

Multifaceted Micro-Social Worlds

The diversity of informal personal relationships and the range of personal communities identified in our study have led us to question fears that social relationships today are necessarily instrumental, casual, fleeting or uncaring. Our exploration of people's micro-social worlds suggests that people's important relationships not only vary in the extent to which they are chosen or given, but also in their durability and degree of commitment. The argument that choice is a fate, a form of domination, may apply to consumer society and the marketizing of welfare, but seems less relevant to the sphere of informal personal relationships, which is so much more subtle and complex. Of course, in one sense, we exercise choice in deciding whom to include in our personal community, and there is no doubt that some people do choose the relatives they want to spend time with or support. However, these choices do not take place in a social vacuum, but within particular economic, cultural and political circumstances, and so may well be constrained by particular dependencies or feelings of duty or obligation. In effect, they may be more given than chosen.

Not only this, where relationships are freely chosen, it does not necessarily follow that they are casual. From the description of friendships found in our study, we can see that chosen relationships can be extremely close and long lasting, as well as short-term fleeting ties. In other words, people can choose commitment. To consider choice in personal relationships as some kind of universal and regrettable modern failing simply clouds rather than illuminates our understanding of social life today. Sweeping generalizations of this kind, which rightly warn us of the tyrannies of choice in some spheres, do not always recognize the tyrannies of no choice in others.[15]

Of course, some critics might add a sceptical note, suggesting that people could actually adopt 'commitment' as a lifestyle choice by, as it were, advertising the notion that one is a socially acceptable 'caring person', as a strategy to obtain status and influence among peers. Those subscribing to economic theories of the family following Gary Becker, or those invoking various social theories of rational action or exchange, might wish to criticize our distinctions between choice and commitment. Despite disclaimers to the contrary, such critics do have a rather pessimistic view of human nature where all our actions are driven by self-centred desires for psychological, social, economic or political advantage.[16] However, as sociologists, we argue that social facts cannot logically be reduced to individual motivations, an issue that has been developed by the most distinguished contemporary theorists such as James Coleman, David Lockwood and W. G. Runciman.[17]

In any case, our empirical analysis suggests that people have the personal communities they have because their informal social relationships are based on *different degrees of commitment and choice*. It is the emphasis on *difference* and *diversity* that provides the distinctive contribution of our approach. Personal communities are much more complex and multifaceted than traditional 'families of fate', dominated by ties of obligation and duty, or free-floating 'families of choice', collected like so many butterflies in a cage, though, of course, we are not suggesting that such 'families of fate' and 'families of choice' do not exist.[18] The overwhelming conclusion of our particular study, however, is that there is no single dominant kind of personal community; people live in micro-social worlds which differ enormously in their connectivity, their degree of commitment, and their pattern of reliance on given and chosen ties.

Identifying Robust Personal Communities

Network researchers inform us that large heterogeneous and loosely knit networks – those made up of people of different ages, in different employment situations, with different religious affiliations and educational levels, from different socioeconomic backgrounds, will give people greater access to a range of different kinds of social support. However, this appears to be based on findings from large-scale surveys which indicate that people nowadays have rather specialized sources of support:

> a good deal of research... has shown that most... ties are specialized, with... network members supplying only a few kinds of social support... The specialized provision of support... means that people must maintain differentiated portfolios to obtain a variety of resources. They can no longer assume that any or all of their network members will help them, no matter what the problem. In market terms, people must shop at specialized boutiques for needed resources instead of casually dropping in at a general store... Like boutique shoppers, people who only have a few network members supplying one kind of support have insecure sources of supply. If the tie ends – if the boutique closes – the supply of that particular support may disappear.[19]

These kinds of data are not necessarily very illuminating, however, since they represent statistical majorities, based on notions such as an 'average' tie or an 'average' personal network. One study, for example, reports that 87% of ties in a network provide just one kind of support, whereas 39% provide at least three types.[20] The problem with this kind of evidence is that it masks the really interesting and important finding which is that people's micro-social worlds vary enormously, and that some people do still get a lot of social support from a narrow range of multifaceted ties, whereas others rely on a diverse specialized set of ties. In this case, reducing this empirical complexity by giving statistical averages actually diminishes rather than enhances our understanding.

Added to this, there is an argument that different kinds of tie are important for different kinds of exchange and social support. So, it is not simply a case of specialization or diversity, but a question of having an appropriate set of ties. So, for example, we are told that 'strong' ties – with people we see frequently, usually taken to refer to immediate family and neighbours – are reportedly good for providing emotional support and material aid. On the other hand, 'weak', heterogeneous, bridging dispersed ties – with people we see less often, usually taken to be acquaintances, former colleagues and friends, or even friends of friends – are good for 'getting on', particularly for getting jobs.[21] Others have developed this idea further, demonstrating that, at different stages in the life-course, people need different concentrations of strong and weak ties. For example, young children need strong family support[22], frail elderly people, on the other hand, fare best with support from a number of sources such as local relatives, other family, friends and neighbours.[23] Hence, some commentators have argued that there could be different kinds of 'network poverty': 'isolation', where a network lacks both strong and weak ties; 'weak tie poverty', where adults lack sufficient bridging, social ties; 'strong tie poverty', where children and frail older people lack strong ties to kin and immediate neighbours; and 'network transition poverty', where at points of transition between adolescence and adulthood, and between active third age retirement and dependency, people fail to change their network configuration.[24]

Of course, our research is not about social networks but about personal communities, and we do not know about all the contacts in a person's overall network, only about those considered important now. Also, our study was confined to adults aged 18 to 75 so we have no data about the personal communities of children or frail older people. Nevertheless, our research on personal communities raises a number of issues in relation to some of these arguments. For example, we ask why frequency of contact should be taken as a measure of the strength of a relationship, since, as we saw in chapter 7, friends who are close confidants and soulmates need not live nearby or be in frequent contact. We also challenge the notion that strong ties are necessarily with family or neighbours, while weak ties are with friends, since, as we have already shown, the quality of family relationships and friendships varies hugely. It seems to us that the robustness of personal communities relates to their degree of *suffusion* and *redundancy*. Suffusion, as we saw in chapter 5, can give a degree of flexibility in personal communities because members play multiple, overlapping non-specialized roles. Redundancy, also gives flexibility because there are a number of different people who provide intimacy, help and sociability. Suffusion, without redundancy, however, can lead to vulnerability: if too much is vested in one or two key relationships, and something happens to weaken or break the tie, then people may be left without much needed sources of support.

If we were to offer a view about what may appear to be robust personal communities today, excluding the case of young dependent children or frail older people, then friend-like, friend-enveloped and family-like would be strong contenders. In the case of the friend-based personal communities, these are characterized by a high degree of suffusion and redundancy, containing a range of highly committed and supportive as well as more light-hearted friendships, some which have stood the test of time or separation, together with a range of family ties. They also usually contain local as well as dispersed sources of sociability and support. However, in certain contexts, for example, in highly stable populations, or for people who come from a cultural background which places great emphasis on family ties, family-like personal communities may well be more appropriate. In this kind of personal community people are very attached to and rely heavily on their relatives, but they have nevertheless formed some significant chosen ties. Family-enveloped personal communities, on the other hand, are potentially less robust since they are not as flexible. People with this kind of personal community have not had the experience of establishing any close or supportive ties outside the family, so, if they or their family were to move in the future, their source of social support might well be disrupted. As we have shown above, partner-based and professional-based personal communities are also vulnerable because they lack diverse sources of support.

More than One Kind of Social Capital

Not only does our research challenge the idea that the quality of social relationships today is in universal decline, but we would also argue that it calls into question the heavy emphasis, by some commentators at least, on social capital at the level of formal associational involvement rather than at the level of informal personal relationships. Might an awareness of different types of personal community lead to a re-evaluation of the importance of people's micro-social worlds? Of course, if all personal communities were inward-looking, based on unquestioned trust, fears about the implications of this for wider social integration might well be justified, but if, on the other hand, some personal communities were discovered to be outward-looking, micro-bridging cells, then commentators would surely not wish to neglect them in their analysis.

As others have already maintained, the implication that having large numbers of people actively involved in local associations – *machers* in

Putnam's terms – is necessarily conducive to a well-functioning society needs to be challenged.[25] There is a whole spectrum of possibilities for associational involvement, from being a key and hectic office holder to being a regular or one-off financial donor, and it is not clear why the active involvement of many is more effective than, say, the motivated involvement of a few. It could be argued that a small leaven in a large lump is a more effective way to get things done. As long as it is possible to reign in or vote out the more active office holders, modern democratic activity does not necessarily require an Athenian-type model for it to work effectively.[26] On the other hand, if the supposed advantage of *machers* is not just the effective accomplishment of tasks, but a kind of spin-off of social connection and trust, then, as we argue below, this is not always the outcome, and it may be that *schmoozers*, who commune with and support their friends and family, provide an under-recognized and under-valued social resource.

Turning to Putnam's iconic example in *Bowling Alone*, it is not clear what the direct benefit of people bowling in leagues rather than in informal personal groups might be. In some cases, for example, a strong sense of team loyalty may lead to the neglect of other responsibilities, or intense rivalry between team supporters may lead to serious outbreaks of violence.[27] Under these circumstances we might conclude that bowling – or playing tennis or any number of other activities – with friends and family, rather than in clubs or leagues, might be better for a nation's health and the smooth operation of its institutions.

Added to this, as many contributors to the social capital debate have recognized, some associations and alliances do not engage in the kind of institution-building activities that are the concern of political scientists and politicians. In some cases the institutions people support and the voluntary associations they join are in opposition to or subversive of the established political and economic institutions. For example, in Britain as we write there is strong opposition to the government's ban on fox hunting with dogs. A loose organization called the Countryside Alliance, bringing together disparate groups with different interests and values, has been formed and is, numerically, one of the largest oppositional forces in recent British history. Activists in anti-animal experimentation groups or anti-global capitalism groups are also examples of 'anti-establishment social capital'.

Finally, the idea that densely linked sets of social relationships are necessarily good for society has also been challenged by those who acknowledge a dark side to social capital. Drug-dealing gangs, various

kinds of Mafiosi and, of course, terrorist cells rely on close and trusting ties. Sometimes, the more impervious and closely bonded certain
collectives are, the greater the potential for illicit and subversive activity. The relationship between revolution and high trust among small
tightly knit groups is very well established.

If, instead of concentrating all our energies into compiling statistical evidence of the so-called breakup of the family or the decline
in associational memberships, we focused some of our attention on
the complexity of people's micro-social worlds, this would enable us
to evaluate more coolly the state of contemporary social life. It would
mean we could identify and celebrate situations where people are well-
embedded in flexible, supportive and robust personal communities,
while at the same time focusing our concern, and support, for cases
where people have more fragile, fractured personal communities. If
individuals themselves were more aware of being embedded in a personal community, recognizing it as a vital resource, they might be able
to cope better with the traumas and vicissitudes of life. As we have
discovered, some members of personal communities may offer support on a daily basis, providing much needed sociability or practical
assistance; others, however, may only come to the rescue at times of
major crisis. Acknowledging this, and understanding personal communities as a collectivity, might help people appreciate the support
that hitherto they had not recognized or had taken for granted, while
at the same time becoming aware of the efforts that have to be made
to keep it in good repair. Perhaps, rather than regretting the decline of
bowling leagues, we should look elsewhere for our missing social glue.

As we have already indicated earlier in this book, social capital is a
splendid metaphor but a confused concept. However, as an umbrella,
below which a robust debate can shelter, it serves an admirable purpose. While our research cannot tell us about the world of *machers*,
through our study of the world of *schmoozing* we hope we can make a
contribution to the social capital debate.[28]

FRIENDSHIP AND PERSONAL COMMUNITIES AT THE CORE

We have argued that a focus on the micro-social level, particularly
on personal communities, is a valuable way of understanding life in
the twenty-first century, since personal communities fit well with the
realities of social and geographical mobility and the contemporary
emphasis on personal development and fulfilment. Nevertheless, we

must face the question of how, if at all, a collection of personal communities, with different degrees and forms of friendship, relates to the age-old sociological problem of social integration and cohesion. Does it matter if the micro-social world of little circles is the most solid and enduring form of social capital in contemporary society? What are the implications for society if people prefer to be *schmoozers* rather than *machers*? What kind of a society is it if the basic social glue is made up of personal communities? How would such a social reality relate to various conceptions of 'the good society' put forward by political philosophers? These are clearly enormous questions and ones we can only tentatively address at this stage. Our hope is that others will be fired to join the debate, refining and adding to the points we make below.

In the first place, as we have already demonstrated, the fact that personal communities often contain chosen as well as given ties does not mean that they lack trust and commitment. Personal communities may be personal and individual, but they are not necessarily individualistic. Indeed, our research has demonstrated that far from being isolated, anomic or narcissistically self-focused, people may still feel connected and committed to others, through their personal communities, in a significant and meaningful way.

In addition to this, personal communities may contribute to social integration through a set of cross-cutting allegiances. So although some personal communities may be drawn from a narrow local base, containing a set of dense inward-looking ties, since barriers of class, age, religion and culture still remain and friends tend to have certain characteristics in common[29], others are much more broadly based, drawing their members from different organizations, occupations, age groups, interest groups, walks of life, neighbourhoods, and even continents.

People nowadays can be bound together in many different ways and the concept of a personal community enables us to identify and describe these different linkages. Some of these bonds are similar to ones we would expect to find in traditional communities of shared fate. For example, there is a still a place-based element to personal communities where important family and friends live nearby. There are also associational elements when members belong to the same church, society, club or workplace. There may also be a moral connection between members where people have a strong sense of obligation and responsibility towards each other. But focusing on personal communities also enables us to capture what have been proposed as late modern or postmodern traits. For example, as we saw in chapter 2, personal communities can provide a sense of belonging and identity, not simply through geographical proximity or shared occupational fate, but through biography and the active maintenance of longstanding relationships, and through the sharing of similar interests and values with others who are discovered to be 'on the same wavelength'. In this way, personal communities often contain elements of both 'fate' and 'choice', but, as we have already argued, fate may not necessarily be accompanied by commitment, and choice does not necessarily imply casual or fleeting relationships.

We also have to remember that personal communities are not isolated entities, jostling or bumping against one another. Each member of a personal community is also the focal person in his or her own set of significant relationships, so that we have an ever-increasing set of 'little circles', with some degrees of overlap. However, even if we were able to map and represent society in this way, as a set of overlapping circles,[30] to answer our question fully we would also need to know something about the resources of different personal community members, since individuals clearly differ in their access to goods and power. In other words, personal communities not only vary in their ability to provide robust social support, they also vary in their ability to shape social outcomes. Concentrations of especially robust or especially vulnerable personal communities among particular sectors of society or in particular locales are clearly a matter of concern for policy makers today. But linking the micro- and macro-levels has always been an enormous challenge for sociologists, and is something we can do no more than acknowledge here:

> It is the question of how to relate understanding of social life and the cohesion of social relationships based on actors and action to those based on notions of self-regulating systems, unintended functioning, or structure.[31]

Finally, our research shows that friendship can act as a vital safety-net providing much needed support and intimacy, but also as a safety-valve enabling people to relax and cope with the pressures of contemporary life. Not only this, friendship can be with partners or with other members of a natal family as well as with non-kin. It can take many forms but, at its strongest, it is based on trust, commitment and loyalty. As such, it deserves to be nourished and cherished.

Yet somehow friendship does not always receive the recognition it deserves. No one seriously disputes that friends and friendship are essential for our happiness and well-being yet there is very little public discussion beyond the trivial or anecdotal. Based on our research, we would argue that, far from being 'shards of community' or 'pieces of jetsam afloat on the seas of economic and political egoism',[32] friendships and friend-like relationships – in their robust and committed form – can provide an important form of social glue, holding personal communities together. The assumption that engagement in civic or voluntary associations is the prime measure of social capital, or that strong family ties alone form the core of community, overlooks the role of friendship. It is time for friendship to take its rightful place.

In particular, the importance of friends and friend-like relations among kin has been surprisingly underestimated in contemporary policy debates. It is possible that the importance of friends may have been neglected because of our sometimes ambivalent and equivocal attitudes to friendship as a form of social solidarity. On the one hand, friendship is valued as a way of binding us into society, albeit at a micro-level, but, on the other, it may be rejected as potentially subversive at a macro-level. E. M. Foster's dictum that if forced to choose between betraying his country or his friend, he hoped he would choose the former, is little comfort to those in power and authority over us. Such a stance implies too much independence and public leaders would find those strongly committed to their friends less easy to control or to manipulate. Too much social cohesion at a micro-level might reduce cohesion at a more macro-level and certainly the links between the two are less clear.

We have, however, provided a sound empirical base on which others may build, and which may help to modify the way we view micro-social worlds. We are inclined to agree with Allan that 'friendships may be recognised increasingly as one of the main sites of activity giving life meaning'[33] and with Delanty that 'Friendship may be seen as a flexible and de-territorial kind of community that can be mobilised easily depending on circumstances, and can exist on "thick" and "thin" levels, for friendship comes in many forms.'[34]

We hope that our work will feed into an ongoing debate about the extent to which there has been a major, and deleterious, change in the quality and basis of social relationships over the past two hundred years. By drawing attention to the diversity of personal relationships

today, and to recent historical research about the nature of social relationships in the past, we hope to discourage commentators from comparing 'our tawdry todays with past golden ages'.[35] We have opened a
window on a world of hidden solidarities, particularly the world of
friendship, which we hope others will be encouraged to explore.

How We Carried Out Our Study

BACKGROUND

Our study grew out of an interest in current debates about social solidarity and the state of community today.[1] Commentators, politicians and policy makers appear to be alarmed by what they perceive as a lack of civic responsibility and community values, coupled with a growth of consumerism and selfish individualism. Such concerns have been voiced since the middle of the nineteenth century but have been fed more recently by social scientists from Amitai Etzioni, Robert Bellah, to Robert Lane, Robert Putnam and Zygmunt Bauman.[2] We believed that there was a need to understand the nature of people's micro-social worlds and the importance of friendship and friend-like relationships within them. In the light of these concerns, we wanted to take a fresh look at friendship and explore friend-like relations with non-kin and kin alike.

AIMS AND OBJECTIVES OF THE STUDY

The overall aim of this study was to understand the role of people's micro-social worlds, and, in particular, the role of friends and friend-like relationships, in providing a form of social glue. Consequently one of our first objectives was to clarify what people meant when they used the term 'friend', since the term can cover a range of relationships from a close, supportive soulmate (perhaps increasingly also the individual's partner), to little more than an acquaintance. Secondly, because we were interested in a possible suffusion of roles between friends and family, we wanted to liberate participants from received categories and explore the actual set of social relationships in which individuals were embedded. In this regard, we found Wellman's definition of a personal communities, which referred to people's 'intimate and active ties with friends, neighbours and workmates as well as kin', especially helpful.[3]

This focus on personal communities meant that a further objective of the study was to devise a rigorous methodology for gathering the relevant data for constructing personal communities, and then for analysing and categorizing them. As we explain below, when asking people to tell us about the members of their personal community we used the phrase 'people who are important to you now', making it clear that all categories in Wellman's definition could be covered. Personal communities provide a set of social moorings, they embed people in society, and the degree of social affirmation and practical support they provide would, we hypothesized, be of fundamental importance in understanding patterns of social cohesion.

Research Strategy and Sampling

In-depth interviews were chosen as the most appropriate research method since these would enable us to explore issues flexibly, establishing what people meant by different terms, and examining the quality and content of different relationships. We decided to adopt an iterative, multi-staged approach to selecting our sample. In the first stage a heterogeneous purposive sample[4] was drawn to ensure a broad section of participants, chosen according to a number of socio-demographic characteristics and contexts such as age (from 18 to 75), stage in the life-course, occupation, geographical mobility, ethnic background and type of neighbourhood. Given the rich diversity of cultures and backgrounds in Britain today we had to make some key decisions about the range of ethnic groups we could incorporate. We concluded that it would be better to understand a few situations well, rather than spread our resources too thinly, and consequently interviewed people from white British and from black African and Caribbean backgrounds. Twenty-six people were recruited by a professional recruitment agency and interviewed by the research team as part of this first stage.

A second sample was then drawn using different purposive rationales. In the first place we wanted to adjust the overall balance of our sample by including undersampled cases, such as people with a non-heterosexual orientation, people who were unemployed, or in manual occupations, or living alone. Secondly, having carried out some preliminary analysis, we were keen to snowball from the initial sample and to interview people who had been nominated as friends by some of the first-stage participants. A further thirty interviews were carried out in this second stage. Finally, extreme-case sampling was used in order to explore situations where people might be at risk of exclusion and likely to have restricted friendship repertoires. Two young people who had been brought up in care and two people with mental health problems were included in the third stage of the project. We did not, however, interview homeless rough sleepers, or travellers, or asylum seekers, or international jet setters, so our study may fail to capture the personal communities of the most isolated or the most global citizens.

In all we interviewed seventy people: ten 'trial' interviews when we were developing our method, and sixty for the main study. We interviewed twenty-seven men and thirty-three women. Ten of our participants were aged between 18 and 30, nineteen were between 31 and 45, sixteen between 46 and 60, and the remaining fifteen were over 60. In terms of occupational classification, twenty-six people would be considered manual workers, thirteen as intermediate, and twenty-one as professional or managerial. The majority of the sample was white British, but we also interviewed six black British people from Caribbean backgrounds, two Irish people, one man from Africa, and two people from mixed race backgrounds. Eleven people were single and had no children; five were living with partners and were also childless; another five were lone parents; sixteen were married or cohabiting and had children living at home; a further sixteen were married but their children had flown the nest; the final seven were living alone in middle or older age. We took care to include some people who had been very geographically mobile as well as those who had lived in the same area for most of their lives. Our participants were based in East Anglia, inner London, mid Wales and the northwest of England (focused largely in Greater Manchester but stretching down as far as the Potteries).[5] (A more detailed profile of the overall sample can be found in annexe 2.)

GENERATING PERSONAL COMMUNITIES

An initial task we faced was to devise a way of generating participants' personal communities.[6] Since our developmental stage happened to be in the weeks running up to Christmas we arranged a few trial interviews in which we asked people to list those to whom they send Christmas cards. Of course, we had no intention of using this method in the main study, since the sending of Christmas cards is too culturally specific, but this simple exercise provided us with some interesting lessons.

Firstly, Christmas card lists include contacts which vary enormously in terms of their importance and role in people's lives. Secondly, although people found it illuminating to discuss these different relationships, the exercise was immensely time consuming. Exploring and comparing systematically the content of up to a hundred different relationships from 'very good friends', to 'friends at the office', to various fossilized links with social worlds long since left, together with all familial links bound along a continuum from love to duty, was daunting and unmanageable within the context of a single interview.

This experience showed that we had to find a way, without being too directive, of encouraging our participants to be more selective in their choice of people to include. We were keen, however, to try and avoid imposing any assumptions about the kinds of relationships which might be included in someone's personal community, and adopted a neutral approach, not taking it for granted that family would be included or presuming that people would necessarily have any friends. We also made the assumption that, for perhaps all except hermits or mystics, some relationships are likely to be considered more significant than others, and we therefore decided to focus on a smaller collective of relationships which were considered important in some way, rather than including everyone in a person's social circle no matter how casual or tenuous the tie.[7] Our solution was to ask about 'people who are important to you now', making it clear that such people 'could include a partner, family, friends, neighbours, people you work with and so on'. The word 'important' was chosen with care because it did not imply how 'importance' should be judged. At the beginning of each interview, however, we explored in detail how this instruction had been interpreted and the basis on which relationships had been included.

The word 'now' was added in order to set a time frame. We considered the possibility of asking about everyone who had ever been important and using a life-history approach, but rejected this. Because we wanted to explore relationships in depth, and to make comparisons between them, it made more sense to focus on current circumstances.

Nevertheless, once an initial list had been generated, we also asked some retrospective questions about earlier contexts or life-course stages – school or college, employment before marriage or cohabitation, the period of life with preschool children, other work experiences, after divorce, on retirement – to see if our participants could recall other relationships which had been important in the past but which had not yet been mentioned.

Our pilot interviews also demonstrated that constructing a list of 'people who are important to you now' could take up a great deal of the interview, leaving little time to explore the various relationships. Our participants had not necessarily thought about their personal community in a structured way before, except, perhaps, in the context of particular events such as weddings, significant birthdays or funerals, and so needed time to reflect. We therefore asked them to make their list in advance. We also realized we needed a system of recording and displaying the people who had been included so that we could keep track of the each relationship as it was discussed. A week before the interview participants were sent a letter asking them to list the names of people they wished to include. (A copy of the letter is included in annexe 3.) Twenty sticky labels were also included on which participants were invited to write the name of the important tie, together with details of their age and occupation (if appropriate), how far away (in miles) they lived, how the relationship was designated, for example, family member, friend, colleague, neighbour and so on, and the context of meeting (for non-kin ties).[8] However, we went to great lengths to stress that we were not suggesting that people had as many as, or as few as, twenty important relationships. Our aim was for participants to use the labels as flexibly as possible and so we encouraged them to use only the number of labels they needed, emphasizing that they were not obliged to use all the labels, but that if they wanted to write more than one name on a label they could do so. People were also free to add further names throughout the interview.

One concern we had about our approach was that, by issuing twenty labels, we might implicitly be suggesting that personal communities should be of a certain size, or that our participants should restrict themselves to a maximum of twenty people. Three of the sixty people we interviewed claimed they would have liked more labels, and, conversely, two people confessed that they had 'scraped the barrel', including some names simply because they felt they should use most of the labels. However, by asking people to talk us through their decisions we were able to identify cases where names were added as 'fillers', and by allowing further names to be added during the interview we were able to overcome any initial limitation on numbers. It seems that by stressing that people use only as many labels as they needed, and that they could put more than one name on each label, we seem to have given our participants enough flexibility to enable them to include the number of people they wished: from just five to forty-one.

THE INTERVIEWS

Having devised a method for constructing personal communities in advance of an interview, we had to determine how the interview itself should be handled. In other words we had to turn our research interests into a set of themes to be explored during the interview, and consequently designed and piloted a series of interview guides. (A copy of the main guide can be found in annexe 4.) The interview guide was used extremely flexibly, representing an aide memoire to be adapted as necessary, but essentially covered the following stages and themes:

Generating members of a personal community. Participants were asked how they had interpreted the phrase 'important to you now', what criteria they had used when deciding who to include or exclude, and whether they would have liked more labels.

Comparing importance. We asked participants to compare the people they had listed and to place them in order of importance on an 'affective map' consisting of five concentric rings intended to convey differing degrees of importance, with the centre of the map representing the most important (examples of maps can be found in chapters 2 and 6). Participants were encouraged to use as few or as many of the rings as they wished (they could place labels straddling more than one ring and request more rings), and to talk the interviewer through the basis of allocation.

Comparing relationships. We probed the difference between relationships in the different circles, why some relationships were described as friendships, what the term friend meant, whether there were different kinds of friendship, how relationships with friends compared to those with family, and to whom participants would turn in a range of situations.

Describing quality and content. Where people had listed a lot of names, we were unable to ask in detail about every single member of their community and, therefore, together with participants, we selected a number of ties to explore in more depth. Names were chosen according to the different qualities of the relationship and to represent different circles on the map. Participants were then asked how long they had known the person, how the relationship had developed, how frequently they had contact and the bases of the interaction.

Identifying social convoys. We were interested in the notion of a social convoy (how people's sets of significant others change through the life-course) and therefore asked participants about past members of their personal communities. We enquired about earlier stages or contexts in participants' lives (for example, school, college, sequence of jobs, child bearing, retirement), identifying people who had been important to them then, and asking what had happened to those relationships.

Plotting the structure and density of personal communities. Participants were asked about relationships between members of their personal community, whether members knew or were friendly with each other.

Checking participants' recognition of their personal community. As the study progressed, we decided in later interviews to ask participants to look at their map and to reflect on how accurately it represented their micro-social world.

Throughout the interviews, the meaning and role of friends and friend-like relationships was explored in a range of ways, for example, when

- names were allocated to different circles, and relationships in different circles were compared;
- general conceptions of friendship were discussed;
- relationships with friends and with family were compared;
- the role of members of the personal community in providing different kinds of social support was explored;
- details of the formation and development of selected friendships were given.

The interviews were carried out in participants' own homes during June and July 1999, between March and August 2000, and between February and July 2001. All were tape-recorded and transcribed verbatim. In three cases, however, there were recording difficulties and parts of the interview had to be reconstructed from memory.

ANALYSIS

We analysed our data using Framework, a thematic approach to qualitative analysis developed at the National Centre for Social Research in London.[9] Essentially, Framework is an interpretive, thematic method which concentrates on the substantive, common sense content of interviews rather than on the structure of accounts or the linguistic devices used within them.[10] Most approaches to qualitative data analysis involve a number of key stages, the first of which is data management, and Framework is basically a data management tool that helps the researcher sift, sort and summarize the voluminous and messy raw data according to key themes. This stage typically involves the researcher becoming familiar with the range and breadth of the data and identifying some descriptive categories and themes which comprise an initial conceptual framework. This set of categories and themes is then applied to the data through a process of indexing or labelling. Once the data have been indexed in this way, they are sorted and synthesized under the key categories. With Framework, synthesized and summarized data are displayed in matrix-based form through the production of thematic charts. Page references to the original transcripts are included so that the researcher can return to the raw data at any point. (Excerpts from a sample chart are included at annexe 5.) In our own study, in addition to thematic charts, we also made a set of individual charts for each participant in which we summarized all the information we had about each member of his or her personal community.

Once data management was complete, we were able to move to a more interpretive stage in which we attempted to produce both descriptive and explanatory accounts. At first this involved searching the thematic charts and identifying the elements and dimensions of categories, refining them and developing more abstract analytical constructs. Examples of such constructs include *friendship repertoires* (chapter 3), *friendship modes* (chapter 4) and *patterns of suffusion* (chapter 5).

Based on these constructs we drew up the classification of personal communities presented in chapter 6. As we explain in that chapter we could have identified our typology theoretically, by constructing all the possible combinations of analytical building blocks, but chose to do this empirically, based on the cases in our study. However, the distinctive feature of this approach is that, while our typology is firmly grounded in our findings, the analytical components allow us to recognize other kinds of community when we find them. Not everyone's personal community will necessarily match our types very neatly but the types described in chapter 6 are the 'best fit' in relation to the data, bearing in mind that these relate to a particular time and culture. The range of personal communities we have identified may develop in future, new types may need to be added, especially if the study were to be carried out in other contexts.

Qualitative studies are sometimes criticized for spattering cases or quotations through the text to support the author's argument. The reader has little means of judging how these cases or quotations relate to the body of data as a whole. Have particularly apposite quotations been chosen highly selectively to back up the author's position? Are they used to add a little 'local colour'? Or do they represent a perspective or position that has emerged from careful analysis of the data, chosen from a number of possible cases. Our approach to analysis, which involves looking at all the cases, not just those which fit recurrent types, means that when we cite a case or use a quotation in the main part of the book, these serve to illustrate a concept or idea which has been developed through a rigorous analytical process. They are not just 'cherry-picked' anecdotes.[11]

Having developed a set of analytical building blocks and devised a typology of personal communities, we were eager to discover whether there were any patterns in terms of the kind of people who had each type of personal community, and, if patterns could be found, to explore a range of possible explanations. The first stage in this process, described in chapter 7, involved searching for patterns of association in relation to a number of characteristics and factors. As part of this search we investigated the profiles of people with each kind of personal community and looked at their sex, age and stage in the life-course, their educational level, their occupational category, ethnic background, sexual orientation and experience of geographical mobility, not as deterministic personal traits, but as structural locations or parts of their social landscape. During this search we found a number of clusters and patterns of association. However, although the identification of these patterns involves some simple counting, the numbers have no statistical validity since this is a qualitative study with a purposive rather than a random probabilistic sample. Likewise, the patterns of association we identified do not represent statistical correlations between variables, nor are they results in themselves, but pointers to further analysis. They represent groups of factors that may have contributed to the development of different kinds of micro-social world.[12]

Interestingly, within each pattern of association there was no uniform set of characteristics or contexts for each type of personal community, but a set of different clusters. In order to unpack this complexity we first looked to other studies to establish if they could illuminate our findings, for example, through their analysis of differences linked to gender, social class, age and life-course stage, geographical mobility and ethnic background. Then we took a series of case studies for each type of personal community and explored the particular set of circumstances which could have helped shape different patterns of reliance on friends and family.

WIDER RELEVANCE

As we argue in the Introduction readers may well question the wider relevance of our qualitative study and, in particular, whether British data can have any bearing on patterns of sociability and support in other societies, particularly America, which is sometimes seen as the embodiment of individualized, isolated society. We maintain that our study does indeed have broader relevance, precisely because it is qualitative and because of the nature of generalization within qualitative research. In small-scale, purposively sampled studies, the reader makes a qualitative judgement about the wider applicability of the findings based on the detailed description of concepts and cases. Qualitative generalization, therefore, is based on assertional rather than probabilistic logic. It does not rest on statistical representativeness or sampling theory but on careful comparison and unassailable analysis. Essentially, the reader decides whether the concepts have wider analytical or explanatory power by looking in detail at both the 'sending' context (the setting of the initial study) and the 'receiving' context (the setting where the findings might be applied), by comparing those contexts, and judging whether the analysis and interpretation found in the initial study can help make sense of another setting. We are not making any claims about the frequency or ubiquity of any particular kind of friendship repertoire or personal community, simply that a range of types and patterns exist. We are mapping the territory, if you like, and the reader's main concerns should be, Can I recognize the map? How well does the map fit our situation or are some parts of the map less relevant? Are some parts of the map missing? By giving details of how the concepts and patterns were identified, and illustrating each with cases from our research, we enable the reader to check the applicability of the map to other settings. It is important to remember that even with a large quantitative study carried out in Britain there could be no automatic generalization to other countries, since a British sample would not be statistically representative of other populations. In this case, the reader would still have to make a qualitative judgement about the transferability of findings, and might well have less detailed information on which to make such a judgement.[13]

Annexe 1. Dramatis Personae.

Name	Age	Education/career/ occupation	Household, marital status, children	Occupation of spouse or partner	Location	Geographical mobility
Ben	37	Film technician University Chemistry teacher	Single No children		Manchester	Born and brought up in London. Went to university in the southeast before moving to Manchester.
Brenda	64	Shop assistant Part-time clerical work Part-time barmaid and cleaner	Twice divorced Widowed 3 adult children 3 grandchildren		Stockport	Born and brought up in Stockport, has lived in several parts of Britain, including Cornwall, with her two husbands.
Chantal	43	Physiotherapist University Teacher	Divorced 1 adult daughter 1 young son	Partner is a hospital consultant	Greater Manchester	Born in St Lucia, moved to the UK aged 12. Has lived in the same neighbourhood since then.
Charles	54	Sixth-form college University Teacher Self-employed translator	Divorced 3 daughters (one still living at home with her mother)		Town on the Welsh borders	Born in Cheshire, moved four times before the age of 18, to different parts of the UK; moved a further 9 times since then, but has spent the last 20 years in the same area.
Colleen	54	Office junior Full-time housewife and mother Telesales Childminder	Married 2 adult sons	Husband is retired civil servant	London	Born in the Republic of Ireland, moved to England when she was 12. Lived in India for fourteen years because of husband's job.
David	34	University Local government officer Trades union official Academic researcher	Single No children		London	Born and brought up by his adoptive family in Dorset.
Derek	66	University Journalist Now retired through ill health (aphasia)	Divorced 2 adult sons		London	Lived all his life in and around London.

Dramatis personae (*continued*).

Name	Age	Education/career/ occupation	Household, marital status, children	Occupation of spouse or partner	Location	Geographical mobility
Diana	51	Nurse Teacher Careers adviser	Single No children		Essex	Born in London, has lived in Essex for the past thirty years.
Don	18	Unemployed, looking for work	Single No children		Suffolk	Born in Suffolk. Lived with a series of foster parents but always within a few miles of each other.
Donald	67	Computer programmer Now retired	Married 2 adult sons	Wife is a retired financial adviser	Essex	Moved nine times in the southeast through his job.
Doreen	65	Seamstress Telephonist Now retired	Married 1 adult daughter 1 grandson	Husband is a retired taxi driver	Near Stockport	Lived in the same neighbourhood all her life.
Duncan	33	Art college University Teacher	Living with partner No children	Partner owns her own sandwich bar	Manchester	Born and brought up near Manchester, moved around the northwest and northeast before settling in Manchester.
Edith	70	Switchboard operator Knitting machinist University administrative assistant Now retired	Married 1 adult daughter 4 grandchildren	Husband is a retired corporate debt negotiator	Manchester	Lived in the same neighbourhood all her life.
Emily	26	Sixth-form college Union researcher Administrative work plus night school University About to go travelling	Single No children		Essex (temporarily with her parents after graduating from university)	Born in Lancashire, moved three times before the age of 18, to different parts of the UK.

Dramatis personae (*continued*).

Name	Age	Education/career/ occupation	Household, marital status, children	Occupation of spouse or partner	Location	Geographical mobility
Esther	38	Boarding school Beautician Proprietor of beauty parlour Manager of dental practice	Married 3 young children	Husband is a doctor	Manchester	Born in Nigeria, brought up in Nigeria and Ghana, attended boarding school in the UK.
Gary	37	Building and gardening work Unemployed, looking for work	Separated 1 child		London	Born in London and has lived there all his life apart from 1 year in Devon.
George	43	University in Ghana and Britain Doctor	Married 3 children	Wife manages a dental practice	Greater Manchester	Born in Nigeria, brought up in Nigeria and Ghana, attended university in Ghana and Britain.
Gill	49	Art college Typographer at advertising agency Full-time housewife and mother	Married 2 adult children 2 step children	Husband was copywriter in advertising agency, now retired	London	Born and brought up in Norfolk, moved to London to attend art college.
Gloria	44	Hospital cleaner At home looking after her daughter	Divorced Widowed 4 adult children 1 daughter living at home 3 grandchildren		London	Born in Jamaica, moved to Britain at the age of 4. Has lived in east London since then.
Harriet	36	University Administrative posts in: computer games company medical charity	Single No children		London	Born and brought up in London. Attended university in London, but spent 1 year of degree course in Germany.
Henrietta	57	Privately educated at home Boarding school Debutante Art school Part-time work in friends' shops Full-time wife and mother	Married 4 adult children	Husband is a merchant banker	Norfolk	Born and brought up in Hampshire, studied and lived in London before moving to Norfolk.

Dramatis personae (*continued*).

Name	Age	Education/career/ occupation	Household, marital status, children	Occupation of spouse or partner	Location	Geographical mobility
Huw	75	Farmer Now retired	Widowed 2 adult children		Montgomery-shire	Born and has lived all his life in the same village in Wales.
Ian	39	Boarding school College Medical technician	Married 2 children	Wife is at home looking after the children	Essex	Born in Libya (father in the army), and lived in several parts of Germany and Britain as a child. Has lived in Essex since he started work.
Jackie	38	Secretarial college Secretarial work Own catering business Part-time debt collector	Living with partner 3 young children	Partner is a painter and decorator	London	Has lived all her life in north and east London.
Jane	41	Secretarial college Secretarial work Part-time teaching assistant	Married 2 children	Husband is a solicitor	Suffolk	Born in London, moved three times in Kent and Essex as a child. Lived and worked in London, moved to Suffolk a year after youngest child was born.
Jenny	26	Sixth form college Further education college Proprietor of sandwich bar	Living with partner No children	Partner is a teacher	Manchester	Born in Cheshire, moved 12 times within the county before the age of 18, moved a further four times since then, always in the north of England, has been in Manchester for the past 4 years.
John	70	Laundry delivery boy Proprietor of shoe repair shop Salesman Corporate debt negotiator Now retired	Married 1 adult daughter 4 grandchildren	Wife is a retired university administrative assistant	Manchester	Lived in the same neighbourhood all his life.
Judy	26	Further education college Pensions administrator	Single, lives with parents No children		Essex	Born in Essex. Has lived all her life in the same neighbourhood, but commutes to London.
Mary	66	Packer in a factory Now retired	Married	Husband is a retired assembly line worker	Essex	Born in Essex. Has lived all her life in the same village.

Dramatis personae (*continued*).

Name	Age	Education/career/ occupation	Household, marital status, children	Occupation of spouse or partner	Location	Geographical mobility
Mervin	36	Loans and mortgage adviser	Married 2 children	Wife works in a friend's shop	Essex	Has lived all his life on the border between northeast London and Essex.
Michelle	36	Secretarial college PA Part-time shop assistant in friend's dress shop	Married 2 children	Husband is a loans and mortgage adviser	Essex	Has lived all her life on the border between northeast London and Essex.
Muriel	68	Insurance clerk Financial adviser	Married 2 adult sons	Husband is a retired computer programmer	Essex	Moved four times in the south-east through husband's job.
Patrick	42	Medical school Hospital consultant No children	Single, but has a partner	Partner is a teacher	Manchester	Born and brought up in Belfast, has lived in London and Liverpool before settling in Manchester.
Robert	52	Two part-time degrees Psychotherapist	Divorced Married for a second time 2 adult sons from first marriage 1 young son from second marriage	Wife is a social worker	Manchester	Born and brought up in Dominica. Came to the UK in his mid twenties.
Roger	52	Technical college Proprietor of small publishing company	Divorced 1 daughter still living at home		Essex	Born and brought up in Essex but has travelled extensively.
Ronald	59	Unskilled factory work Fitter in the army Part-time degree Teacher Administrator in health service Now retired	Married 3 adult children 5 grandchildren	Wife is a retired teacher	Shropshire	Born in the Midlands. Moved a great deal through his work, and was stationed abroad with the army.

Dramatis personae (continued).

Name	Age	Education/career/ occupation	Household, marital status, children	Occupation of spouse or partner	Location	Geographical mobility
Rupert	42	Boarding school University Solicitor	Married 2 children	Wife is a part-time teaching assistant	Suffolk	Born in the Cotswolds, brought up in Hertfordshire. Studied and worked in London. Moved to Suffolk a year after youngest child was born. Commutes to London.
Sarena	40	Further education college Social worker	Divorced Married for a second time 1 adult daughter from first marriage 1 young son from second marriage	Husband is a counsellor and psychotherapist	Manchester	Has lived all her life in Manchester.
Shelley	21	Unemployed, looking for work	Single No children		Suffolk	Born in Suffolk. Moved several times to different parts of the country to live with a series of foster parents.
Terry	66	Butcher's assistant National Service (RAF) Fitter in engineering company Taxi driver Now retired	Married 1 adult daughter 1 grandchild	Wife is a retired telephonist	Near Stockport	Has lived all his life in the same neighbourhood.
Wayne	26	Finisher in garage	Single, lives at home with his parents No children		Cheshire	Has lived all his life in the same neighbourhood.
Winston	40	Painter and decorator	Living with partner 7 children (4 from two previous partners, 3 with his current partner)	Partner is a part-time debt collector	London	Born in Tobago, moved to the UK when he was 17. Has lived in London ever since.

Annexe 2. Profile of the Sample

		Total = 60
Sex		
	Men	27
	Women	33
Age range		
	18–30	10
	31–45	19
	46–60	16
	over 60	15
Marital status/children		
	single, never married, no children	11
	married, living as married, no children	5
	married, living as married, children at home	16
	lone parents, children at home	5
	married, living as married, children left home	16
	single, divorced, separated, widowed, children left home	7
Occupational classification		
	manual	26
	intermediate	13
	professional managerial	21
Ethnic background		
	white British	49
	white Irish	2
	black British (Caribbean)	6
	black British (African)	1
	mixed race	2
Sexual orientation		
	heterosexual	55
	non-heterosexual	5
Geographical mobility		
	Stayed in same area all life (village, town, neighbourhood)	24
	Moved to new area(s) as a child, not as an adult	5
	Moved to new area(s) only as an adult	10
	Moved to new area(s) as a child and adult	21

ANNEXE 3. LETTER TO PARTICIPANTS

Dear . . . .

Informal social relationships and the new millennium

Thank you very much for agreeing to take part in this study. I look forward to meeting you on . . . . at . . . .

At the University of Essex we are interested in finding out what people's relationships are like with for example, family, friends, neighbours, people they work with or know in other contexts, and whether or not these relationships change at different stages in people's lives. We are also keen to discover how important these relationships are, and how easy or difficult it is for people to keep up with their family, friends and other contacts.

It would help the study a great deal if you could fill out the enclosed two sheets and have them with you when one of us comes to interview you.

The first sheet is made up of sticky labels on which we would ask you to list people who are important to you now – these could be family, friends, neighbours, a partner or spouse, or people you work with. When you have decided whom you want to include, please list them on the labels as follows. Please only use the number of labels you want to, you don't have to use them all. If you need more, just put more than one name on a label.

For each label you use, please fill in the following details

- Christian name(s) and initial of surname if there is more that one person with the same name
- age
- kind of relationship, e.g. brother, mother, partner, friend, neighbour, workmate
- how far away the person lives (in miles)

For family members this is all you need to write, but for any other relationships please also give

- the number of years you have known this person/these people
- how or where you met

If you cannot fit all the information on the label, don't worry, you can tell us during the interview. Please leave the labels stuck on to the blue sheet.

Here are some examples of completed labels.

Malcolm	Ann S	John	Julie
26	47	Mary	Chris
brother	colleague	76 63	32 31
4 miles	10 miles	neighbours	friends
	2 yrs	$\frac{1}{2}$ mile	150 miles
	work	5 yrs	22 yrs
		across fence	school

The second sheet is a short questionnaire about your personal history, which will help us to get an idea about different stages of your life.

We would like to assure you that your views will be enormously valuable to this study but that they will remain confidential and you will not be named or identified in anything we write.

Thank you very much indeed.

If you have any queries, please don't hesitate to contact us at the University of Essex on 01206 874809.

Yours sincerely

Liz Spencer

Ray Pahl

ANNEXE 4. INFORMAL SOCIAL RELATIONSHIPS: TOPIC GUIDE

1. Introduction

Introduce self, reaffirm confidentiality and restate aims of project:

- to find out more about informal personal relationships, the kind of ties people have with family, friends and neighbours or work-mates/colleagues
- to explore the quality of these relationships and how they change over time

Warm up – *check*

- – marital status
- – children
- – length of time in town, village, community
- – current or previous occupation

2. Ordering relationships

- – How drew up the list? How easy/difficult to limit to 20 labels?
- – Did you have to leave people out? What kind of people? How many?

If other names come up during interview, write on round labels

- – Are some of these people more important than others?

While the labels are being stuck on, briefly ask for each person:

- – Is he/she married/has got a partner?
- – What does he/she do for a living?

Probe criteria

- – Why have people been placed there?
- – What is the difference between relationships in the different circles? (What criteria are they using?)
- – How would you label/describe the different circles?

3. Comparing relationships

- – You have described some of the people on the map as a friend, what is a friend, what does it mean to have a friend?
- – Do you have a best friends or best friends? Why/why not? What is a best friend?
- – Are there any rules/expectations/dos and don'ts of friendship? What are they?
- – How do friends compare with family relationships?

- Do you get something out of friendship that you don't get out of family relationships?
- Do you get something out of family that you don't get from friends?
- What is the difference between friends in each circle – probe for basis. What do together/share?
- Which (if any) of these people would you turn to if, for example, you:

> Wanted to have some fun
> Were trying to find a job
> Were having financial difficulties
> Were having difficulties in a marriage or relationship
> Suffered a bereavement/lost someone close to you
> Became ill and needed help (self or partner)

- Why to those people in particular?
- Who do you tend to confide in? About what sorts of things?
- Who do you feel you have most in common with? What sorts of things?

4. Characteristics of Selected Relationships

Select relationships for more in depth exploration according to ring on map/type of relationship.

Start with friends
- How often do you keep in touch?
- What do you do when you contact each other?
- What do you talk about?
- Has the relationship developed and changed? Is it same as or different from when first met? How? Why?
- Were there any particular turning points? What are they?
- Has the friendship changed in importance or intensity?
- In what situations have you/would you turn to this person for support? Do they turn to you? [*Collect examples/stories/accounts*]
- Do you feel the relationship is reciprocal/there is the same amount of give and take?
- How important is the relationship?

For family:
- Describe relationship
- Do you have a friendship/friend-like relationship with any members of your family? How/why? Why not?

5. Dynamics of Social Convoys

Look at Personal History Questionnaire. For each domain/life-course stage...

- Are there any people from this stage who were important at the time who have not been already mentioned? Who?
- (*If not*) Why no important people from that stage?

Fill out a round label for each person mentioned

- What happened to the relationship? Why?
  [*Collect stories/examples, check whether want to add to the map*]
- Have you ever 'dumped' a friend/would you? What for/circumstances?
- Have you had fewer or more friends at different stages in your life? Why?
- Have friends been more or less important at different stages in your life? Why?
- (*If not mentioned parents*) Would your parents have been on the map? Where?

6. Structure of the Personal Community

- Do any of these people know each other?
- Are any friendly with each other? Which?
- Do any meet up as a group?
- Have there been any events recently where most people have met together? What?
- Any events planned for the future?

[*Using coloured felt tip pens, draw in the different connections, make a key afterwards*]

7. Recap

- Looking at the map, are you happy that this represents your social circle?
- How do you feel about where you have put people, now that we have discussed them a bit more?

Discuss aspects of the map, for example

- *Number and placing of family as against friends*
- *Number of circles used*
- *Whether map reflects quality/intimacy of relationships*

- Is there anything you would change?
- If you weren't limited in numbers, how many more would you add?
- What sort of people?
- Where would they go on map?
- What sort of people would go in the unused circles?

8. Health issues

Give out GHQ.

Instructions for completing the PC and map

Ask interviewees to take another look at the list and consider whether they would like to make any changes. If interviewees ask about children, say they can include them.

Reassure interviewees that there will be an opportunity later on to talk about people they have had to leave out. If they mention other people during the interview, *record them on the round labels*. Ask why have they forgotten them.

Get interviewees to order the labels in terms of closeness of the relationship, using the 'affective circles' record sheet. Tell interviewees that they do not have to use all the circles, of if they want more, you can draw them on. Start with the first, closest circle and ask interviewees to say who they would put in that circle. Stick the labels in that circle. Then move to the second circle and so on until the labels have all been allocated.

Discuss meaning, and title of each circle and difference between them.

At the end of interview ask if would have listed any other people? If so, how many? What sort of relationships? Where would they have been put on the circles? If they have not used some of the circles, what kind of people would have been put it them. What would they call these relationships?

Annexe 5. Excerpt from a Thematic Chart.
Chart 6. The meaning and role of friendship.

Participant	What is a friend?	Types of friends	Friends and family
No. 27 Female 55 yrs White Aristocratic wife of city financier 5 children, 4 are adults	You don't have to make an effort with great friends, they are not high maintenance (1) 'I think a great friend to me is somebody who, in spite of all your ghastly faults, still likes you' (1) Someone who still likes you even though they've seen your worst side. You don't have to put up any pretence, they know you as you truly are (9) A true friend you can phone them up if you are in trouble and waste their time for hours and they'll listen. Great friends are people who will put themselves out for you (14)	Some friends are absolute rocks – 'they'd absolutely come up trumps' and have done in the past. (11) Expect them to be rocks because that's why like them, but love other friends even though flighty or selfish, don't have same expectations of them (2, 3, 11) People who are fun to be with – 'On the whole, the flighty ones are the fun to be with' (12) Friends feel responsible for, have been ill, try to be a rock for them (12) Don't have same expectations of different friends (13) Best friend is someone who likes you in spite of it all, who knows you, you can't pretend with, knowing that you are also an important part of their life (13)	Family also comes up trumps in a crisis but quite irritated by some brothers and sisters. Would not choose to go on holiday with them! It's complete duty, family loyalty comes first. But cannot say what would do if there was a clash of responsibilities and had to choose between going to help family or friend (14) But feel you absolutely have to stand by your family and help them out (e.g. brother with financial difficulties), not quite the same with friends though you try – not quite the same sense of duty (15) Similarities are knowing them for a long time because have known friends 'forever' (16) 'Actually, I was just thinking, one's sisters aren't as much fun, I mean they are probably more critical. So I wouldn't go off with my family to have fun' (17) Was labelled as a flighty sort of menace when young. Brothers and sisters label you more than friends do (18)
No. 34 Female 64 yrs White Widowed part-time barmaid and cleaner 4 adult children	'A friend is someone you can turn to and ask anything. They are always there when you need them but a lot of friends are only acquaintances at the end of the day' (20) (e.g. the lads at work are acquaintances)	Difference between friends in 2nd and 3rd ring is I like the ones in the second better. Do different things. With friends in second circle, go to each other's houses, invite each other to parties, sell things to each other (catalogues, etc.) (11) [in third, don't go to each other's houses even if go out together outside work] Can tell different friends different things. Glenda only person could tell anything to. Lot of friends have a great sense of humour, but Doreen is a more reserved, serious friend, a friend who will help you out. 'You've got different friends for different things, haven't you' (20) Glenda is a best friend. Loads of acquaintances but would not call them best friends (21)	Family can really upset you and let you down. Children can be very hurtful. E.g. daughter uses me when she hasn't got somebody (boyfriend) but then she's up and left when she has got someone. But not sure what get out of friends. Don't get very close to them really (21–24)

Chart 6. *Continued.*

Participant	What is a friend?	Types of friends	Friends and family
No. 40 Male 36 yrs White, Jewish Mortgage adviser married 2 teenage sons	A friend is someone you can trust. If people are good enough friends, it does not matter if one is having a better time financially than the other – if going on holiday, then you find a place that is within everyone's price bracket. Or you treat each other. Another time you/they make it up. Don't keep a tally, it's an ongoing thing [but reciprocity is important] (17, 18) Don't like showy generosity, but don't tolerate hangers on – we are all genuine friends (19) A friend is someone you can discuss anything with, go anywhere with. You don't worry what they think (about you) and they don't worry what you think of them (41)	Don't have a best friend, don't believe in it. All my friends are close friends. 'Some people will say, "Oh, so and so, he's my best friend", you know, and then six months later – because you might not have got on so well with him or someone else becomes your best friend. Well, I class that as like being back at school. You know, "Oh, he's my best friend, he can sit next to me in class today". . . . They're all my best friends but rather than call them best friends, they're very, very, very close friends.' (20) Michelle (wife) is my best friend – can discuss anything. She's the person I'm with all the time so she's my closest friend (20)	Family have to come first, before friends, even though could trust all friends on the map with my life (11) With family there is always a bond, even with family you hardly ever see except at funerals – still have a hug, pleased to see them. You get a different type of closeness from friends. You get together, give each other a cuddle. You love each other. You have been through similar life experiences – having children, buying a house, going on holiday together (22)
No. 49 Male 48yrs White, Irish Hospital consultant, partner, no children	Someone you are pleased to hear from or to spend time with, there is a positive feeling about being or talking with them – warmth and enjoyment. People you can trust, whose opinion you value. (23) Mark a good example – admire his talents, enjoy being with him because would be both entertained and informed (22, 23)	Admire some friends for their talents or intellectual abilities but other friends are more active doers (23) With Chantal (partner) have a more complete and rounded type of friendship 'cos value a number of dimensions of her abilities, personality, humour, creativeness, attractiveness (23) Lust as basis of friendship with A but also more than that because enjoyed company and conversations. With Sarena and Robert it is generosity and warmth and discussion and learning – the ambience of their company (24) Malcolm is a zany and irresponsible friend (24)	Family relationships are carved in stone, don't question them, nurture them or withdraw from them. Expect them to be ongoing (27) Expect family to be there even though don't expect anything of them. It's one of the foundations of my life that my family are there, I know where they are – I would crumble if they moved and had not let me know. They provide the boundaries and structure of my life. Don't have same expectations of friends. I am so bad at keeping in touch would not be surprised if they moved and did not let me know (29)

ANNEXE 6. HEALTH QUESTIONS

Here are some questions regarding the way you have been feeling over the past few weeks. For each question please tick the box next to the answer that best describes the way you have been feeling. Have you recently...

Q1. Been able to concentrate on whatever you're doing?

Better than usual	❑
Same as usual	❑
Less than usual	❑
Much less than usual	❑

Q2. Lost much sleep over worry?

Not at all	❑
No more than usual	❑
Rather more than usual	❑
Much more than usual	❑

Q3. Felt that you were playing a useful part in things?

More than usual	❑
Same as usual	❑
Less than usual	❑
Much less than usual	❑

Q4. Felt capable of making decisions?

More so than usual	❑
Same as usual	❑
Less so than usual	❑
Much less capable	❑

Q5. Felt constantly under strain?

Not at all	❑
No more than usual	❑
Rather more than usual	❑
Much more than usual	❑

Q6. Felt you couldn't overcome your difficulties?

Not at all	❑
No more than usual	❑
Rather more than usual	❑
Much more than usual	❑

Q7. Been able to enjoy your normal day-to-day activities?

More so than usual	❏
Same as usual	❏
Less so than usual	❏
Much less than usual	❏

Q8. Been able to face up to problems?

More so than usual	❏
Same as usual	❏
Less able than usual	❏
Much less able than usual	❏

Q9. Been feeling unhappy or depressed?

Not at all	❏
No more than usual	❏
Rather more than usual	❏
Much more than usual	❏

Q10. Been losing confidence in yourself?

Not at all	❏
No more than usual	❏
Rather more than usual	❏
Much more than usual	❏

Q11. Been thinking of yourself as a worthless person?

Not at all	❏
No more than usual	❏
Rather more than usual	❏
Much more than usual	❏

Q12. Been feeling reasonably happy, all things considered?

More so than usual	❏
Same as usual	❏
Less so than usual	❏
Much less than usual	❏

INTRODUCTION

Ecclesiasticus 6. Quoted in *The Oxford Book of Friendship*, ed. D. J. Enright and D. Rawlinson (Oxford University Press, 1991), 30.

1. *World Health Report, 2001. Mental Health: New Understanding, New Hope* (Geneva: WHO, 2001).

2. For references to the term 'personal community', see B. J. Hirsch, 'Social networks and the coping process: creating personal communities', in *Social Networks and Social Support*, ed. B. Gottlieb (London: Sage, 1981), 149–70, B. Wellman, P. J. Carrington and A. Hall, 'Networks as personal communities', in *Social Structures: A Network Approach*, ed. B. Wellman and S. D. Berkowitz (Cambridge University Press, 1988), 130–84, and B. Wellman, 'The place of kinfolk in personal community settings', in *Families in Community Settings*, ed. B. Wellman (New York: Haworth Press, 1990), 195–228.

3. N. Cohn, *The Pursuit of the Millennium* (Oxford University Press, 1970).

4. W. F. Whyte, 'The slum: on the evolution of street corner society', in *Reflections on Community Studies*, ed. A. J. Vidich, J. Bensman and M. R. Stein (New York and London: John Wiley & Sons, 1964), 9. It is interesting that Part One of this book is entitled 'The community sociologist discovers the world'. It is arguable that the golden age of community studies was short-lived since, for a variety of reasons, few studies have been undertaken since the unintentional valediction in *Community Studies* by C. Bell and H. Newby (London: Allen and Unwin, 1971). See also M. C. Stein, *The Eclipse of Community* (Princeton University Press, 1960).

5. In the following chapters we make some highly selective references to specific pieces of historical anthropology, but, for those wishing to explore this area in greater depth, a good place to begin would be many of the papers published in *Continuity and Change: A Journal of Social Structure, Law and Demography in Past Societies* (Cambridge University Press, from 1986). This journal was founded in a collaborative venture between Tulane University Law School and the Cambridge Group for the History of Population and Social Structure. The editorial board is strongly international and interdisciplinary.

There are, of course, many other journals, such as the *Journal of Family History*, the *Journal of Interdisciplinary History* and similar journals in France, Italy and Germany. Perhaps the best known of these is *Annales ESC*, since the French were clearly among the pioneers of interdisciplinary history. Indeed, one should remember that Emile Durkheim was a regular author and reviewer for *L'Année sociologique*, which published much history and human geography from its foundation in 1886. The interdisciplinary school focused on *L'Année* has been described by Lewis Coser as 'probably the most brilliant ever gathered in the history of the discipline', *Masters of Sociological Thought* (London: Heinemann, 1971), 165. We feel sure that Durkheim would be an avid reader of *Continuity and Change* were he alive today, and his sociology would reflect that. It is contemporary sociology's loss that those with strong historical and cross-disciplinary interests are in a minority. However, it should be evident that we consider their work to be among the most exciting and rewarding.

6. With purposive sampling, the relationship between the sample and the wider group about which the study aims to speak is a conceptual rather than a probabilistic one, so that issues of sample size and statistical representativeness do not apply. See the appendix for further details of our sampling rationale.

7. We are grateful to the British Economic and Social Research Council for providing the funding for the study reported here (grant number R000237836).

CHAPTER ONE
THE FRAGMENTATION OF SOCIAL LIFE?

R. D. Putnam, *Bowling Alone* (New York: Simon and Schuster, 2000), 24.

R. A. Nisbet, *The Sociological Tradition* (London: Heinemann, 1967), 101.

G. A. Allan, 'Friendship, sociology and social structure', *Journal of Social and Personal Relationships* 15 (1998), 699.

1. For a wide-ranging and well-documented account of this putative growth of unhappiness, see R. E. Lane, *The Loss of Happiness in Market Societies* (New Haven, CT: Yale University Press, 2001).

2. Putnam, *Bowling Alone*.

3. However, 'the golden age of traditional morality is, typically, not very precisely described and, nor for that matter, are the future consequences for society of its "relinquished common morality" specified very clearly' (R. E. Pahl, 'The search for social cohesion: from Durkheim to the European Commission', *Archives européennes de sociologie* 32 (1991), 345–60, quoting B. R. Wilson, 'Morality in the evolution of the modern social system', *British Journal of Sociology* 36 (1985), 315–32; the phrase 'relinquished common morality' appears on p. 332).

4. This was a major concern for the Chicago School; see, for example, R. Lynd and H. Lynd, *Middletown* (New York: Harcourt Brace, 1929); R. Park, *Human Communities* (Glencoe, IL: The Free Press, 1952); L. Wirth, 'Urbanism as a way of life', *American Journal of Sociology* 44(1) (1938), 1–24.

5. See, for example, C. M. Arensberg and S. T. Kimball, *Family and Community in Ireland*, 2nd edn (Cambridge, MA: Harvard University Press, 1968 (first published 1940)); R. Redfield, *The Little Community* (University of Chicago Press, 1955); A. D. Rees, *Life in a Welsh Countryside: A Social Study of Llanfihangel Yng Ngwynfa* (Cardiff: University of Wales Press, 1950). For a review of some of the major studies, see R. M. French, *The Community: A Comparative Perspective* (Itasca, IL: Peacock Publishing, 1969). See also endnote 4 for the introduction.

6. S. Keller, *Community: Pursuing the Dream, Living the Reality* (Princeton University Press, 2003).

7. G. Delanty, *Community* (London: Routledge, 2003), 132.

8. H. Rheingold, *The Virtual Community: Homesteading on the Electronic Frontier* (Reading, MA: Addison-Wesley, 1993).

9. Keller, *Community: Pursuing the Dream*.

10. A. de Tocqueville, *Democracy in America* (London: Longman, Green and Co., 1889), volume 2, 90.

11. Ibid., 91–92.

12. A. Comte, *Systeme de politique positive*, cited in Nisbet, *Sociological Tradition*, 59.

13. A. Etzioni, *New Statesman* 25 (London, 12 May 1993).

14. F. Tönnies, *Gemeinschaft und Gesellschaft* (1887), translated and edited by C. Loomis as *Community and Society* (Harper Torchbook, 1963). For a discussion of these early sociological theories, see R. W. Connell, 'Why is classical theory classical?', *American Journal of Sociology* 102 (1997), 1511–57, and J. C. Alexander, 'Modern, anti, post and neo: how social theories have tried to understand the "new world" of "our time" ', *Zeitschrift für Soziologie* 23 (1994), 165–97. However, the conventional account is well presented by Nisbet in *Sociological Tradition*.

15. K. H. Wolff (ed.), *The Sociology of Georg Simmel* (Free Press, 1950), 326.

16. D. Riesman, *The Lonely Crowd*, with N. Glazer and R. Denney (New Haven, CT: Yale University Press, 1950). In the new preface to the abridged edition (1961), Riesman remarked, 'In stressing the passivity and joylessness of Americans, their obedience to unsatisfying values, we followed in the wake of other observers, notably Erich Fromm, Karen Horney, Harold Lasswell, C. Wright Mills and John Dollard', and went on to refer in the 'enormous meanness and mindlessness' of their fellow countrymen (p. xxxiii).

17. P. Slater, *The Pursuit of Loneliness: American Culture at Breaking Point* (Boston Beacon Press, 1970), 7.

18. Ibid., 10.

19. C. Lasch, *The Culture of Narcissism* (New York: Norton, 1979). See also P. Rieff, *The Triumph of the Therapeutic* (New York: Harper and Row, 1966).

20. R. Bellah, *Habits of the Heart: Middle Americans Observed* (University of California Press, Hutchinson Education London, 1985), 295.

21. Lane, *Loss of Happiness in Market Societies.*

22. *The Economist* (3 March 2005), 48.

23. Z. Bauman, *Liquid Love* (Cambridge: Polity Press, 2003), 69, his emphasis.

24. Ibid., 66.

25. Delanty, *Community,* 186.

26. Lasch, *Culture of Narcissism.*

27. A. Giddens, *Modernity and Self-Identity: Self and Society in the Late Modern Age* (Cambridge: Polity Press, 1991).

28. Bellah, *Habits of the Heart,* 295. Fears of a moral deficit were being raised at the beginning of the twentieth century, when, in 1906, Durkheim wrote: 'Today traditional morality is shaken and no other has been brought forward to replace it. The old duties have lost their power without our minds being able to see clearly and with assurance where our new duties lie. Different minds hold opposed ideas and we are passing through a period of crisis. It is not then surprising that we do not feel the pressure of moral rules as they were felt in the past. They cannot appear to us in their old majesty, since they are practically non existent.' E. Durkheim, *Sociology and Philosophy* (first published in 1906), translated by D. F. Pocock (New York: The Free Press, 1974), 68–69. A similar theme was taken up by Wilson in his Hobhouse Memorial Lecture some eighty years later, where he described the emergence of the 'anonymous individual – less powerfully socialized for moral response, and inhabiting new social contexts in which the old moral and personal prescriptions failed to apply, and liberated in considerable measure from self control of the old kind. In the civic arena, virtue has become a private predilection, and in a work order which depends on moral socialization, many partially de-moralized individuals inhabit public space.' Wilson, 'Morality in the evolution of the modern social system', 324.

29. See, for example, A. Etzioni, *The Spirit of Community: Rights, Responsibilities and the Communitarian Agenda* (New York: Crown, 1993), and, more generally, U. Beck and E. Beck-Gernsheim, *Individualization* (London: Sage, 2001). Nevertheless, some claim that individualism does not necessarily undermine wider social responsibility. Melucci, for example, views personal identities as more socially constructed, arguing that through chosen commitments to social movements, individuals express and discover their personal identity. A. Melucci, *Challenging Codes: Collective Action in the Information Age* (Cambridge University Press, 1996).

30. J. Davies, B. Berger and A. Carlson, *The Family: Is It just another Lifestyle Choice?* (London: Institute of Economic Affairs, 1995).

31. Z. Bauman, *Liquid Modernity* (Cambridge: Polity Press, 2000), chapter 2.

32. Z. Bauman, *The Individualized Society* (Cambridge: Polity Press, 2001), 46–47. Bauman is taking the term 'individuation' from U. Beck.

33. Bauman, *Liquid Modernity*, 36.

34. De Tocqueville, *Democracy in America*, volume 2, 93.

35. Ibid., 95–96.

36. Durkheim reversed the dichotomy between modern and traditional society by associating 'organic solidarity' with modern society. 'His own distinction was partly a way of stressing the social differentiation of "organized" societies, involving interdependent and multiplying specialized roles, beliefs and sentiments as opposed to the undifferentiated unity of uniform activities, beliefs and sentiments, and rigid social control found in "segmented" societies'. S. Lukes, *Emile Durkheim: His Life and Work* (London: Allen Lane, The Penguin Press, 1973), 148. Lukes's general discussion of Durkheim's *The Division of Labour in Society*, translated by G. Simpson (New York: Free Press, 1964 (first published 1893)), is exemplary. Durkheim did not adopt a universally gloomy perspective on the modern world. The morality of advanced societies 'required that we be kind to each other and be just, that we perform our duty well, and that we work to achieve a situation in which everyone will be called to the function that he can best perform, and receive a just price for his efforts' (translated by Lukes (1973), 157). Durkheim's vision of a universalized morality so that our 'collective ideal is that of humanity as a whole' (ibid.) was of course an ideal type. Getting there is quite a different matter.

37. H. J. Gans, *Middle American Individualism* (New York: Free Press, 1988), xi. Later on, Gans concedes 'I do not deny that the pursuit of individualism and self-development can turn into the pursuit of self-interest, and even to a concentration on selfishness to the exclusion of all communal concerns. However, I doubt that selfishness is as widespread in middle America as some observers believe, or that criticizing popular individualism will produce a decline in selfishness' (ibid., 108).

38. R. Williams, *The Country and the City* (London: Chatto and Windus, 1973), 26. Williams describes 'The conversion of a conventional pastoral into a localised dream' (ibid.), a theme that had previously been explored by R. E. Pahl in 'Class and community in English commuter villages', *Sociologia Ruralis* 5(1) (1965), 1–23, and 'The rural–urban continuum', *Sociologia Ruralis* 6(3–4) (1966), 299–329.

39. By contrast, it has been argued that, in America, notions of community are rooted in a very different 'frontier' experience associated with westward expansion: 'the unusual environment and the continuous rebirth of society in the western wilderness, endowed the American people and their institutions with characteristics not shared by the rest of the world'. R. A. Billington, *Westward Expansion* (New York: Macmillan, 1949), 3.

40. E. A. Wrigley, 'A simple model of London's importance in changing English society and economy 1650–1750', in *Towns and Societies*, ed. P. Abrams and E. A. Wrigley (Cambridge University Press, 1978), 215–243, 221.

41. E. Jones, 'Tregaron: the sociology of a market town in central Cardiganshire', in *Welsh Rural Communities*, ed. D. Jenkins, E. Jones, J. Jones Hughes and T. M. Owen (Cardiff: University of Wales Press, 1960), 65–117, see pp. 79–80.

42. F. Godwin and S. Toulson, *The Drovers' Roads of Wales* (London: Whittet Books, 1977), 16.

43. P. Clark, 'Migration in England during the late seventeenth and early eighteenth centuries', *Past and Present* 83 (1979), 64–71; 'Right back into the medieval period it is clear that the English (and probably also the Welsh and Scots) were migratory people', M. Anderson, 'The social implications of demographic change', in *The Cambridge Social History of Britain 1750–1950*, ed. F. M. L. Thompson (Cambridge University Press, 1990), 1–70, see p. 10. See also, in particular, J. J. Hart, *The Domestic Servant Class in Eighteenth Century England* (London: Routledge and Kegan Paul, 1956), chapter 1.

44. See endnote 39 above.

45. F. J. Fisher, 'The development of London as a centre of conspicuous consumption in the sixteenth and seventeenth centuries', *Transactions of the Royal Historical Society*, 4th Series, no. 8 (1948), 110–23.

46. B. Wellman, 'The network community', in *Networks in the Global Village: Life in Contemporary Communities*, ed. B. Wellman (Boulder, CO: Westview, 1999), 1–48.

47. S. Ozment, *Ancestors: The Loving Family in Old Europe* (Cambridge, MA: Harvard University Press), 53. Such an understanding is very recent and makes E. Shorter's book, *The Making of the Modern Family* (London: Fontana, 1975), seem outmoded. Shorter had argued that intimate and close conjugal relations did not develop until the eighteenth century when, quite seriously, he claimed that true love between the sexes finally emerged. Equally outmoded is sociology's uncritical acceptance that a new emotional order began in the eighteenth century. Giddens, for example, in his widely read book, *The Transformation of Intimacy*, quotes a fellow sociologist to assert that 'prior to the late eighteenth century, if love was spoken about at all in relation to marriage, it was as companionate love, linked to the mutual responsibility of husbands and wives for running the household or farm'. See A. Giddens, *The Transformation of Intimacy* (Cambridge: Polity Press, 1992), 43. Another fascinating piece of research that shatters conventional stereotypes is B. A. Hanawalt, *The Ties That Bound: Peasant Families in Medieval England* (New York: Oxford University Press, 1986): 'Friends played a more important part in wills than did extended family, with 419 receiving bequests. Some of the male testators who had children still at home relied on friends to act as executors along with their wives and rewarded them in their wills. Money payments went to a quarter of

the friends receiving bequests, animals to 22 percent, personal effects to 19 percent, and grain to 8 percent. Surprisingly, testators felt so strongly about some of their friends that 7 percent of friends receiving bequests were given land or a house. Others offered their friends the first option or a discount in buying the home tenement. In general, the value of bequests was greater than the ceremonial gifts to godchildren, grandchildren, and other kin. In other words, the wills tend to confirm the conclusion that neighbours and friends, rather than extended kin, played a significant role in daily life' (ibid., 267). Hanawalt's research was based on Bedfordshire wills between 1480 and 1519. Clearly, strong sentiments and choice in relationships have long existed, which is not really that surprising to those not trapped in various forms of academic conventional wisdom.

48. D. O'Hara, 'Ruled by my friends: aspects of marriage in the Diocese of Canterbury, c. 1540–1570', *Continuity and Change* 6(1) (1991), 9–41, 14.

49. Ibid., 14.

50. Ibid., 15. Clearly, we would like to know who, precisely, are these 'freendes'. In the case of another dispute there was a gathering of some sixteen or seventeen people who met to have dinner together. These included 'kin', 'friends' and many other 'neighbours'. Interestingly, this personal community is about the same size as the average size for the twentieth-century studies we refer to in the appendix, that is, 18.5 (see endnote 8). Some members of the community were more important in the decision-making process about the marriage and some friends withdrew at the crucial time. Those who were actively involved in the marriage process could be a variety of different people, including 'members of the nuclear family and such persons as friends, kinsmen, kinswomen, cousins, uncles, aunts, in-laws, neighbours, "fellows" (associates), bed fellows, gossips, the godmother of a kinsman, masters and mistresses. Connections appear to derive, therefore, from family and the surrogate family of masters, mistresses and fellow servants, from biological kin, affines and a range of what may loosely be termed fictive kin' (ibid., 22).

51. A. Macfarlane, *Origins of English Individualism* (Oxford: Basil Blackwell, 1978), 5.

52. L. Stone, *The Family, Sex and Marriage in England, 1500–1800* (London: Weidenfeld and Nicholson, 1977), 95.

53. Ibid.

54. R. Williams, *The Country and the City* (1973), 37.

55. Ibid., 11 and chapter 2 more generally. See also, for the United States, Stein, *Eclipse of Community*.

56. Much of this is also accessible through government websites. See, for example, http://www.statistics.gov.uk.

57. S. McRae, *Changing Britain: Families and Households* (Oxford University Press, 1999). The availability of longitudinal and panel studies has greatly increased the reliability and depth of social arithmetic. The National Child

Development Study began its survey of a nationally representative sample when the children were aged seven and has published the results of surveys of the same respondents over the years. See the fifth follow-up study, E. Ferri (ed.), *Life at 33* (London: National Children's Bureau, 1993). The British Household Panel Study, which began in 1991, makes annual sweeps of some 10,000 British people, so that there is now a substantial source for the analysis of social change. Research publications are available at http://iserwww.essex.ac.uk/pubs/. Two early reports are: N. Buck, J. Gershuny, D. Rose and J. Scott, *Changing Households: The British Household Panel Survey 1990–1992* (Colchester: ESRC Research Centre on Micro-Social Change, University of Essex, 1994), and R. Berthoud and J. Gershuny (eds), *Seven Years in the Lives of British Families* (Bristol: Policy Press, 2000).

58. For example, the number of divorces granted in the United Kingdom increased by 3.7% between 2002 and 2003 and is the third successive increase but it is still 7.4% less than the peak of 180,000 in 1993 (http://www.statistics. gov.uk); sources include the Office for National Statistics, the General Register Office for Scotland, and the Northern Ireland Statistics and Research Agency.

59. The percentage of women aged 18–49 who are married has declined continuously from 74% in 1979 to 49% in 2002 and the proportion of unmarried women cohabiting has increased from 11% in 1979 to 29% in 2002; among single women, the proportion cohabiting has almost quadrupled. Ibid.

60. N. Buck and J. Scott, 'Household and Family Change', in *Changing Households*, N. Buck et al. (1994).

61. J. Haskey, 'One parent families – and the dependent children living in them – in Great Britain', *Population Trends* 109 (2002), 46–57.

62. See R. Hall, P. E. Ogden and C. Hill, 'Living alone: evidence from England and Wales and France for the last two decades', in *Changing Britain: Families and Households in the 1990s*, ed. S. McRae (Oxford University Press, 1999), 265–97.

63. *The Economist* 373(8399) (October 2004).

64. For aspects of the debate, see P. Abbott and C. Wallace, *The Family and the New Right* (London: Pluto Press, 1992); M. Durham, *Sex and Politics: The Family and Morality in the Thatcher Years* (Basingstoke: Macmillan, 1991); A. Etzioni, *The Parenting Deficit* (London: Demos, 1993). The following publications from the London-based Health and Welfare Unit of the Institute of Economic Affairs are perhaps the most powerful statements of this position. The authors are all established British and American academics: N. Dennis and G. Erdos, *Families Without Fatherhood* (with a foreword by A. H. Halsey), 2nd edn (1993); J. Davies, B. Berger and A. Carlson, *The Family: Is It just another Lifestyle Choice?* (1993); and N. Dennis, *Rising Crime and the Dismembered Family: How Conformist Intellectuals Have Campaigned against Common Sense* (1993).

65. Interestingly, the government website, http://www.statistics.gov.uk, contains hardly any statistics about friends, but does include an entry about contacts and trust between friends as a form of social capital.

66. For a summary of some of these studies, see R. Blieszner and R. G. Adams, *Adult Friendship* (Newbury Park, CA: Sage, 1992).

67. P. Willmott, *Social Networks, Informal Care and Public Policy* (London: Policy Studies Institute, 1986).

68. F. McGlone, A. Park and C. Roberts, 'Kinship and friendship: attitudes and behaviour in Britain 1986–95', in *Changing Britain: Families and Households*, ed. S. McRae (1999), 139–55.

69. A. Park and C. Roberts, 'The ties that bind', in *British Social Attitudes: The 19th Report*, ed. A. Park et al. (London: Sage, 2002), 185–207.

70. For an excellent example, see the article in *The Sunday Times*, 'Britons have average of 14 close friends', news section, 9, 1 December 2002, by John Elliott and Jane Mulkerrins, which is based partly on the Park and Roberts article referred to above, and partly on saloon-bar journalism. It also misleadingly reports some of the findings of this book. We could add many examples gathered during the writing of this book, if justification is needed for the clichés and stereotypes we have mentioned. One further example will have to suffice. Suzanne Moore, writing in the *New Statesman* 26 (April 1999): 'People may be wealthier, but we are in many ways lonelier. If we are so preoccupied with our job that we don't have the time or energy for other people, then can we really be said to be living the good life?'. And then, later, she states: 'Men, we know, particularly suffer from a lack of intimate friendships'.

71. See, for example, C. Calhoun, 'Community without propinquity revisited: communications technology and the transformation of the urban public sphere', *Sociological Inquiry* 68 (1998), 373–97.

72. J. Gershuny, 'Web use and the Net nerds: a neofunctionalist analysis of the impact of information technology in the home', *Social Forces* 82(1) (2003), 141–68, 165–66.

73. K. N. Hampton and B. Wellman, 'The not so global village of Netville', in *The Internet in Everyday Life*, B. Wellman and C. Haythornthwaite (Oxford: Blackwell Publishing, 2002), 345–71, 367. Regardless of the findings of this particular study, the statement 'most North Americans' is surely too sweeping, especially in the light of the very great ethnic, cultural, class and regional diversity of North American life. The authors quote Fischer in support of this generalization but we are not sure that he would accept this interpretation of his monograph: C. S. Fischer, *To Dwell among Friends: Personal Networks in Town and City* (Chicago University Press, 1982).

74. C. Licoppe, 'Connected presence: the emergence of a new repertoire for managing social relationships in a changing communication technoscope', *Environment and Planning: Societies and Space* D 22 (2004), 135–56.

75. Ibid., 149.

76. Ibid., 145.

77. Ibid., 146.

78. Putnam, *Bowling Alone*.

79. Hall, who has reviewed the literature on social capital for Britain, concludes, 'Although aggregate levels of social capital and political engagement in Britain remain high, they are distributed very unevenly across the population. For the most part, political activism and the associational life that sustains it have remained middle-class phenomena in Britain and the preserve of those in middle age. We should not let the relatively good aggregate figures for social capital confuse us into summoning up the image of a polity uniformly criss-crossed by organizational networks and participatory citizens. The more accurate image is of a nation divided between a well-connected and highly active group of citizens with generally prosperous lives and another set of citizens whose associational life and involvement in politics is very limited.' P. A. Hall, 'Social capital in Britain', *British Journal of Political Science* 29 (1999), 471–61, 455.

80. J. Curtice and B. Seyd, 'Is there a crisis of political participation?', *British Social Attitudes, 20th Report, Continuity and Change over Two Decades* (London: Sage, 2003), 93–107.

81. For example, Putnam has argued that social capital develops through extensive and time-consuming interaction, and is essentially a *local* phenomenon. In his view, this social contact and the development of a wider set of social relationships among people sharing the same norms and values coalesce, as it were, into forms of mutual collaboration. R. D. Putnam and L. M. Feldstein with D. Cohen, *Better Together* (New York: Simon and Schuster, 2003).

82. In essence, the notion of social capital builds on a sociological truism that society is bound together by social ties and therefore the quality of these social ties relates to the quality of society as a whole. The idea of adding the word 'capital' carries overtones of a resource that can be invested to produce benefits or, conceivably, can be transferred from one owner to another. Evidently, this could be a useful metaphor to describe qualities which may accrue to individuals or groups. Thus, Pierre Bourdieu, one of the earliest scholars to use this term, was concerned with the way members of elite groups could individually use their social connections or networks to improve their social position. Those so connected could then acquire, so to speak, through the values they shared and the trust they generated, a collective social capital that would establish their ascendancy. See P. Bourdieu, *Reproduction in Education, Society and Culture* (London: Sage, 1977), and P. Bourdieu, 'The forms of capital', in *Handbook of Theory and Research for the Sociology of Education*, ed. J. G. Richardson (New York: Greenwood Press, 1986), 241–58. Over time, the metaphor of social capital has been conceptualized and used in different ways, and studies which purport to show the beneficial outcomes of 'high' social capital often operationalize the concept differently, adopting

a range of proxy measures. For a useful summary, see J. Field, *Social Capital* (London: Routledge, 2003). In Putnam's case, the precise mechanisms through which more trusting face-to-face relationships develop into stronger patterns of communal life are not entirely clear, and he has been accused of 'conceptual stretch', expecting social capital to be too versatile in its meaning. He has also been accused of being tautological – communities that are more civic-minded are more civic – and it is not clear whether increased trust between people is a cause, an ingredient or a consequence of higher levels of social capital. Despite these caveats, by drawing attention to the relevance of the content and quality of personal relationships for broader questions of social cohesion and solidarity, Putnam has created an international awareness of the importance of micro-social worlds.

In an attempt to bring some order into the debate, Portes argued that 'as shorthand for the positive consequences of sociability, social capital has a definite place in sociological theory. However, excessive extensions of the concept may jeopardize its heuristic value.' A. Portes, 'Social capital: its origins and applications in modern sociology', *Annual Review of Sociology* 24 (1998), 1–24, 1. However, neither he, nor anyone else, has much hope of limiting its 'excessive extensions'.

83. For example, the term 'social capital' is increasingly used by policy makers as another way of describing 'community', but it is important to recognize that a 'traditional' community is just one of many forms of social capital. Work-based networks, diffuse friendships and shared or mutually acknowledged social values can all be seen as forms of social capital.

84. See R. E. Pahl, 'Social capital in its place', The Bi-annual Donald Robertson Memorial Lecture (University of Glasgow, 2004), 7. Pahl argues that, in practice, there is likely to be what Gunnar Myrdal long ago referred to as cumulative and circular causation, which may be illustrated diagrammatically as follows:

Social capital: circular and cumulative causation

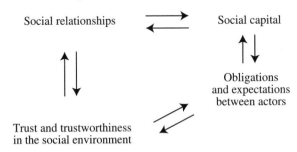

85. Ibid., 7.

86. We return to this theme in chapter 8, but for a highly sophisticated discussion of this point see A. McCulloch, 'An examination of social capital in neighbourhoods in the British Household Panel Study', *Social Science and Medicine* 56 (2003), 1425–38. This is not an easy paper for non-specialists but

one of the key findings has already been noticed by an American sociologist, namely, that 'social capital within a *single group* need not be positively related to social capital *at the community level*', P. Paxton, 'Is social capital declining in the United States?', *American Journal of Sociology* 105(1) (1999), 88–127, 96 (emphasis in the original).

87. Putnam, *Bowling Alone.*

88. *World Health Report, 2001.*

89. See, for example, P. Martin, *The Sickening Mind: Brian, Behaviour, Immunity and Disease* (London: Harper and Collins, 1997).

90. R. E. Lane, 'The road not taken: friendship, consumerism and happiness', *Critical Review* (fall 1994), 521–54, 525.

91. C. Campbell with R. Wood and M. Kelly, *Social Capital and Health* (London: Health Education Authority, 1999). Two socio-economically matched wards were selected in Luton, England, but one had indicators of higher levels of health than the other. The hypothesis was that some factors connected with higher levels of social capital would be associated with the higher levels of health in one of the wards. In the qualitative component of this study, researchers took Putnam's definition of social capital as community cohesion based on high levels of local identity, trust, reciprocal help and support, and civic engagement, and tried to measure these factors empirically. One of the main conclusions of the study was that conceptualizations of social capital which emphasize civic participation fitted more easily into 'people's romanticised reconstructions of an idealised past rather than to people's accounts of the complex, fragmented and rapidly changing face of contemporary community life – characterised by relatively high levels of mobility, instability and plurality', ibid., 156

92. Ibid., 155.

93. The British Household Panel Study (BHPS), started in 1991, is an ongoing annual panel survey of a nationally representative sample of over 5,000 households resulting in approximately 10,000 individual interviews of adults. Original sample members (OSM, $N = 10,264$) of the initial sample in 1991 continue to be followed, even if they leave the original household. New individuals enter the panel if they move into a household containing an OSM, are born to an OSM, or an OSM moves into a household with one or more new people. In this way the sample remains broadly representative of the British population. In waves 3, 5, 7, 9 and 11, questions were asked about the social support available to respondents. The questions asked if there was someone who will listen, help in a crisis, be there to relax with, who really appreciates you and whom you can count on to offer comfort. These five items were combined to make an additive scale. See D. J. Pevalin and D. Rose, *Social Capital for Health* (London: Health Development Agency, 2003).

94. D. J. Pevalin and D. P. Goldberg, 'Social precursors to onset and recovery from episodes of common mental illness', *Psychological Medicine* 33 (2003), 299–306.

95. Ibid., 303.

96. L. F. Berkman, 'Social support, social networks, social cohesion and health', *Social Work in Health Care* 31(2) (2000), 3–14, 10. See also the earlier study, L. F. Berkman and S. L. Syme, 'Social networks, host resistance and mortality: a nine year follow-up study of Alameda County residents', *American Journal of Epidemiology* 109 (1979), 186–204. Another early classic statement is S. Cobb, 'Social support as a moderator in life stress', *Psychosomatic Medicine* 38(5) (1976), 300–14.

97. J. S. House, K. R. Landis and D. Umberson, 'Social relationships and health', *Science* 241 (1988), 540–45; S. A. Stansfeld, 'Social support and social cohesion', in *Social Determinants of Health*, ed. M. Marmot and R. G. Wilkinson (Oxford University Press, 1999), 155–78.

98. S. Cohen, W. J. Doyle, D. P. Skoner, B. S. Rabin and J. M. Gwaltney, 'Social ties and susceptibility to the common cold', *Journal of the American Medical Association* 277 (1997), 1940–44.

99. While not wishing in any way to undermine the implications of all these studies, there are undoubtedly difficulties in making our understanding of 'social support' cumulative, given the variety of different measures used in analyses. See R. E. Pahl, 'Some sceptical comments on the relationship between social support and well-being', *Leisure Studies* 22 (2003), 357–68.

100. The recognition of this unsurprising finding has provoked a huge research interest. It has been calculated that over 3,000 papers on 'stress and health' were published in psychological and sociological journals between 1985 and 1995. P. Thoits, 'Stress, coping, and social support processes: Where are we? What next?' *Journal of Health and Social Behaviour*, extra issue (1995), 53–79. See also the introduction by the editors, S. Cohen, L. G. Underwood and B. H. Gottlieb, *Social Support Measurement and Intervention* (Oxford University Press, 2000).

101. B. N. Uchino, J. T. Cacioppo and J. K. Kiecolt-Glaser, 'The relationship between social support and physiological processes: a review with emphasis on underlying mechanisms and implications for health', *Psychological Bulletin* 119 (1996), 488–531. On unpacking social support, see Pahl, 'Some sceptical comments'. Where researchers have compared the role of different kinds of tie, some interesting counterintuitive results have been found. For instance, in a review of research among older people on the link between emotional well-being and contact with friends or family, it was concluded that contact with friends rather than family was positively related to morale. The key role of friends in providing companionship and engaging in spontaneous, rather than routine, domestic activities emerged as a key theme in a number of studies; see, for example, K. S. Rook, 'Social relationships as a source of companionship', in *Social Support: An Interactional View*, ed. B. R. Sarason, I. G. Sarason and G. R. Pierce (New York and Chichester: John Wiley & Sons, 1990).

102. A recent UK government discussion paper concluded, 'Social capital should be seen as giving policy makers useful insights into the importance of

community, the social fabric and social relations at the individual, community and social level'. See *Social Capital: A Discussion Paper*, UK Government Performance and Innovation Unit (April 2002), para. 184, 73. In fact, there are several pages on the government's website (http://www.statistics.gov.uk) devoted to the subject of social capital.

103. *Strategic Audit*, Summary Pack, UK Strategy Unity (November, 2003), 103, citing source as Future Foundation; N Vision. The shift in influences is striking, with television and newspapers showing declines of around ten percentage points and friends and family increasing by around five percentage points. While the church or political parties were claimed to be influential for less than 10% of respondents, friends influenced about 25% and family nearly 40% of respondents.

104. E. Le Roy Ladurie, *Montaillou: Cathars and Catholics in a French Village 1294–1324* (London: Scolar Press, 1978). R. Gough, *The History of Myddle* (first published in 1834), ed. D. Hey (Harmondsworth: Penguin Books, 1981).

105. M. Maffesoli, *The Time of the Tribes: The Decline of Individualism in Mass Society* (Minneapolis, MN: Minnesota University Press, 1996), 23.

106. Delanty, *Community*, 144.

CHAPTER TWO
CAPTURING PERSONAL COMMUNITIES

Calhoun, 'Community without propinquity revisited', 391.

1. See also R. E. Pahl and E. Spencer, 'Capturing personal communities', in *Social Networks and Social Exclusion*, ed. C. Phillipson, G. A. Allan and D. Morgan (Aldershot: Ashgate, 2004), 72–96.

2. In his report, Willmott lamented, 'How can the relevance of friends to informal support be sensibly examined if there is no agreement about who they are?' (P. Willmott, *Friendship Networks and Social Support* (London: Policy Studies Institute, 1987), 2). We consider this in more detail in the next chapter.

3. *The Sunday Times*, 1 December 2002 (see endnote 70 for chapter 1 for a discussion of this article). Another report in *The Times* ('What happened to wotsisname? He was one of 396 friends', 28 November 2003), compiled by the commercial organization MSN Messenger, claimed 'whether they are pals, mates, chums or buddies, you will go through 396 friends in a lifetime, but will have only 33 at any one time'. The national average number of friends was 33 but it rose to 38 in the northeast region with an average of 28 in the southwest. See also Park and Roberts, 'The ties that bind'.

4. For further and more detailed discussions of Aristotle's views on friendship, see, for example, J. M. Cooper, 'Aristotle on the forms of friendship', *The Review of Metaphysics* 30 (1976), 619–48; J. M. Cooper, 'Aristotle on friendship', in *Essays on Aristotle's Ethics*, ed. A. Rorty (Berkeley, CA: University of California

Press, 1980), 301–40 ('A human being cannot have a flourishing life except by having intimate friends [with whom] he can share the activities that are most central to his life', ibid., 330). A very interesting exploration of these issues has recently been developed by M. Vernon in *The Philosophy of Friends* (Palgrave Macmillan, 2005).

5. K. E. Davis and M. J. Todd, 'Assessing friendship: prototypes, paradigm cases and relationship description', in *Understanding Personal Relationships: An Interdisciplinary Approach*, ed. S. W. Duck and D. Perlman (London: Sage, 1985), 17–38.

6. J. Carsten (ed.), *Cultures of Relatedness: New Approaches to the Study of Kinship* (Cambridge University Press, 2000).

7. See the admirably clear discussion by Carsten in her introduction to *Cultures of Relatedness*. She points out the pivotal role of D. M. Schneider's more recent work and that of Needham before him, who actually claimed: ' "Kinship" is certainly a thoroughly misleading term. . . It does not denote a discriminable class of phenomena or a distinct type of theory', in *Rethinking Kinship and Marriage*, ed. R. Needham (London: Tavistock, 1971), cviii; 'Schneider's *Critique* was very successful in demonstrating the Eurocentric assumptions at the heart of the anthropological study of kinship. This was undoubtedly one of the many nails in the coffin of kinship', Carsten, 'Introduction', *Cultures of Relatedness*, 8.

8. M. Strathern, *After Nature: English Kinship in the Late Twentieth Century* (Cambridge University Press, 1992).

9. J. Edwards and M. Strathern, 'Including our own', in *Cultures of Relatedness*, ed. J. Carsten (2000), 149–66, 160–61.

10. B. P. McGuire, *Friendship and Community: The Monastic Experience 350–1250*, Cistercian Studies Series no. 95 (Kalamazoo, MI: Cistercian Publications Inc., 1988).

11. A. Macfarlane, *The Family Life of Ralph Josselyn* (Cambridge University Press, 1970).

12. N. Tadmor, *Family and Friends in Eighteenth Century England* (Cambridge University Press, 2001).

13. K. D. M. Snell, *Annals of the Labouring Poor: Social Change and Agrarian England, 1660–1900* (Cambridge University Press, 1987), 321, quoting J. Arbuthnot, *An Inquiry into the Connection Between the Present Price of Provisions and the Size of Farms* (1773), 26. Thomas Turner, the subject of Tadmor's book, wrote in his diary, 'My whole family at church – myself, wife, maid and the two boys', quoted in Snell, ibid.

14. These have been usefully reviewed in J. Klein, *Samples from English Cultures*, 2 vols (London: Routledge, 1965). See also R. Frankenberg, *Communities in Britain* (Harmondsworth: Penguin Books, 1966); Bell and Newby, *Community Studies*. Two classic studies of particular interest in the present context

are Rees, *Life in a Welsh Countryside*, and Arensberg and Kimball, *Family and Community in Ireland*, 196.

15. C. S. Fischer et al., *Networks and Places: Social Relations in the Urban Setting* (New York: The Free Press, 1977); Willmott, *Social Networks, Informal Care and Public Policy*; Phillipson et al., *Social Networks and Social Inclusion*.

16. G. A. Allan, *Kinship and Friendship in Modern Britain* (Oxford University Press, 1996); J. Ermisch and M. Francesconi, 'Cohabitation in Great Britain: not for long, but here to stay', *Journal of the Royal Statistical Society* A 163 (2000), 153–71; J. Haskey, 'Stepfamilies and step-children in Great Britain', *Population Trends* 74 (1994), 17–28; J. Haskey, 'Trends in marriage and cohabitation: the decline in marriage and the changing pattern of living in partnerships', *Population Trends* 80 (1995), 5–15; Y. Weiss, 'The formation and dissolution of families: Why marry? Who marries whom? And what happens upon divorce?', in *Handbook of Population and Family Economics*, ed. M. R. Roszenweig and O. Stark (Amsterdam: Elsevier Science, 1997).

17. T. Noble, 'Post modernity and family theory', *International Journal of Comparative Sociology* 39(3) (1998), 257–77; C. L. Johnson, 'Perspectives on American kinship in the later 1990s', *Journal of Marriage and the Family* 62 (2000), 623–39. For an interesting empirical study, see L. Jamieson, R. Stewart, Y. Li, M. Anderson, F. Bechhofer and D. McCrone, 'Single 20-something and seeking?', in *Social Relations and the Life Course*, ed. G. A. Allan and G. Jones (Basingstoke: Palgrave Macmillan), 135–54.

18. Willmott's typology is usefully discussed by M. Bulmer, *The Social Basis of Community Care* (London: Unwin Hyman, 1987), chapter 3. See also P. Willmott, *Kinship and Urban Communities: Past and Present*, The Ninth H. J. Dyos Memorial Lecture (Victorian Studies Centre, University of Leicester, 1987).

19. Aristotle, *The Eudemian Ethics*, quoted in S. Stern-Gillet, *Aristotle's Philosophy of Friendship* (Albany, NY: State University of New York Press, 1995), 50–51.

20. Cicero, 'De amicitia', in *Other Selves: Philosophers on Friendship*, ed. M. Pakaluk (Indianapolis, IN: Hackett, 1991), 88. The excerpt is taken from the translation by F. Copley, *Cicero: On Old Age and Friendship* (University of Michigan Press, 1967). Cicero also argues that 'the true friend is, so to speak, a second self' (Pakaluk, *Other Selves*, 108). He also remarks, 'Friendship, as you know, is the one thing in human life which all men with one voice agree is worthwhile' (Ibid., 109–10).

21. Ibid., 66–67.

22. Ibid., 67.

23. K. Horney, *The Neurotic Personality of Our Time* (New York: Norton, 1937).

24. A. Swidler, 'Love and adulthood in American culture', in *Themes of Work and Love in Adulthood*, ed. N. J. Smelser and E. H. Erikson (Cambridge, MA: Harvard University Press, 1980), 126.

25. For example, S. W. Duck, *Personal Relationships and Personal Constructs: A Study of Friendship Formation* (London: John Wiley & Sons, 1973); S. W. Duck and G. Craig, 'Personality similarity and the development of friendship', *British Journal of Social and Clinical Psychology* 17 (1978), 237–42.

26. There is a very large literature on this topic. A classic early study is M. Roff, 'Childhood social interactions and young adult psychosis', *Journal of Clinical Psychology* 19 (1963), 152–57. More recent material is gathered in J. M. Gottman and J. G. Parker (eds), *Conversations of Friends: Speculations on Affective Development* (Cambridge University Press, 1986). See especially pp. 5–21 and W. M. Bukowski, A. F. Newcomb and W. W. Hartup (eds), *The Company They Keep: Friendship in Childhood and Adolescence* (Cambridge University Press, 1996). In recent years there has developed a rather more self-critical note among some developmental psychologists. An excellent review is T. J. Berndt and L. M. Murphy, 'Influences of friends and friendships: myths, truths and research recommendations', *Advances in Child Development and Behaviour* 30 (2002), 275–310.

27. See Bukowski et al., *The Company They Keep*, 11–13, and D. Ginsberg, J. Gottman and J. Parker, who comment, 'Despite the increasing interest in friendship, there has been very little descriptive research on its natural formation and maintenance in ongoing relationships. Little is known about what friends talk about or do together... There is, therefore, a need for basic descriptive research in this area. Most work has been conducted in the laboratory', in Gottman and Parker, *Conversations of Friends*, 41.

28. D. Cocking and J. Kennett, 'Friendship and the self', *Ethics* 108 (April 1998), 502–27. For a more extended view of this argument, see R. E. Pahl, *On Friendship* (Cambridge: Polity Press, 2000), 81–86.

29. M. Strathern, *The Gender of the Gift: Problems with Women and Problems with Society in Melanesia* (Berkeley, CA: University of California Press, 1988).

30. For those who are attracted by these kinds of arguments and issues, there is perhaps no better starting point than the collection of essays edited by S. Bell and S. Coleman, *The Anthropology of Friendship* (Oxford and New York: Berg, 1999).

31. A. Silver, 'Friendship in commercial society', *American Journal of Sociology* 95 (1990), 1474–504; A. Silver, 'Two different sorts of commerce – friendship and strangership in civil society', in *Public and Private Perspectives on a Grand Dichotomy*, ed. J. Weintraub and K. Kumar (University of Chicago Press, 1998), 43–74.

32. Allan, 'Friendship, sociology and social structure', 698. See also R. G. Adams and G. A. Allan (eds), *Placing Friendship in Context* (Cambridge University Press, 1998).

33. Even as late as 1851, 25% of nineteen-year-old girls and 17% of nineteen-year-old boys were living in as servants or apprentices in Britain; see Snell, *Annals of the Labouring Poor*. The mean age of leaving the family of origin for

the family of service or apprenticeship between 1700 and 1860 was 14.3 for males and 15.5 for females. Ibid., 324.

34. Wellman, 'The place of kinfolk in personal community settings', 197. See also B. Wellman, 'Studying personal communities', in *Social Structure and Network Analysis*, ed. P. Marsden and N. Lin (Beverly Hills, CA: Sage, 1982), 61–80, and Wellman et al., 'Networks as personal communities', 130–84.

35. See Bell and Newby, *Community Studies*; Delanty, *Community*.

36. Giddens has proposed that, 'In the post-industrial order of modernity, and against the backdrop of new forms of mediated experience, self-identity becomes a reflexively organised endeavour. The reflexive project of the self, which consists in the sustaining of coherent, yet continuously revised, bio-graphical narratives, takes place in the context of multiple choice as filtered through abstract systems. In modern social life, the notion of lifestyle takes on a particular significance. The more tradition loses hold, and the more daily life is reconstituted in terms of the dialectical interplay of the local and the global, the more individuals are forced to negotiate lifestyle choices amongst a diversity of options'. Giddens, *Modernity and Self-Identity*, 5.

37. Calhoun, 'Community without propinquity revisited', 391.

38. M. Castells, *The Rise of Network Society* (Oxford: Blackwell, 1996), 3. In a later volume, however, Castells takes issue with Giddens, arguing that 'reflexive life-planning becomes impossible except for the elite inhabiting the timeless space of flows of global networks and their ancillary locales'. M. Castells, *The Power of Identity* (Oxford: Basil Blackwell, 1997), 11. Castell's thesis is fun-damentally pessimistic as he documents the dissolution of shared identities which, as he says, is 'tantamount to the dissolution of society as a meaning-ful social system'. Ibid., 355. His best hope is for people to form identities of resistance.

39. J. Gusfield, *Community: A Critical Response* (Oxford: Basil Blackwell, 1975), 41.

40. We stress our particular use of the term 'personal community' so as to avoid any confusion, since we appreciate that the term has come to have a number of different meanings. Despite Wellman's earlier formulation – see Wellman, 'The place of kinfolk in personal community settings', 197 – he has gone on to use the term as almost interchangeable with a 'personal (ego-centred) network', which includes a much wider set of ties than those which are intimate or significant. (B. Wellman and S. Potter, 'The elements of per-sonal communities', in *Networks in the Global Village*, 49–82.) Indeed, Well-man states that personal communities typically consist of '3 to 6 socially close intimate ties, 5 to 15 less strong but still significant ties, and approximately 1000 acquaintances and latent (but often still mobilizable) relationships'. See B. Wellman and M. Gulia, 'The network basis of social support: a network is more than the sum of its ties', in *Networks in the Global Village*, 85.

41. These problems had already been faced by Hirsch in his paper, 'Social networks and the coping process'. His argument for the use of personal communities rather than social networks is that 'By expressing and embedding our social identities in a social network, we make our social network a personal community. These personal communities reflect our involvement in the major spheres of life, as well as the degree to and manner in which these spheres are integrated or segregated. These personal communities also reflect our values and choices. In creating and maintaining a particular personal community, we are at least implicitly choosing, from among feasible alternatives, how we seek to achieve meaningful participation in our culture and society' (ibid., 161). We return to such issues in chapter 8.

42. One well-advertised networker has written a popular and chatty guide to networking: C. Stone, *Networking: The Art of Making Friends* (London: Vermilion, 2002).

43. The exploration of social networks is a large and complex field of study with its own journal, *Social Networks*. The International Network for Social Network Analysis was founded by Wellman in 1976 and Freeman founded *Social Networks* in the same year. Very useful reviews of the field are B. Wellman, 'Structural analysis: from method to metaphor to theory and substance', in *Social Structures: A Network Approach*, ed. B. Wellman and S. D. Berkowitz (Cambridge University Press, 1988), 19–61, and J. Scott, *Social Network Analysis* (London: Sage, 2000).

44. A focal individual surrounded by a number of associates is referred to as a 'primary star'. It matters not whether those in a primary star know each other. As long as they are all connected with the focal individual they are referred to as a network. We consider that this can be misleading because so-called personal networks may contain 'mini-networks' based on family, work, church, etc., contexts in which all members do know each other. Thus a so-called primary star could include within it a number of networks and this is what we consider to be confusing. See also endnote 7 for the appendix.

45. Calhoun, 'Community without propinquity revisited', 391.

46. Delanty, *Community*, 187.

47. See, for example, Granovetter's classic and influential study, 'The strength of weak ties', *American Journal of Sociology* 78 (1973), 1360–80, where frequency of contact was used as an indicator of the strength of a relationship. Wellman and Potter used a number of different proxy measures in their recent reanalysis of a dataset originally collected in the 1970s. They admit that this dataset had significant weaknesses: 'Brief answers to the short, closed-ended survey questions reveal little about the subtleties and details of interaction' ('Elements of personal communities', 56). In order to construct variables for their oblique promax factor analyses, the construct of 'contact' was based on the median annual rate of phone contact with an intimate (times per year), mean residential distance (miles) and median annual rate of face-to-face

contact with an intimate (times per year); see Table 1.5 (ibid., 58) for the variables used in the analysis.

48. This is the kind of issue that Wellman and others such as Van der Poel simply cannot address: Wellman and Gulia, 'Network basis of social support'; M. Van der Poel, *Personal Networks: A Rational Choice Explanation of Their Size and Composition* (Lisse: Swets and Zeitlinger BV, 1993). Similarly, in one attempt to tease out the relative importance of friends and family, tabulations show siblings and friends, for example, as separate non-overlapping categories. See F. McGlone, A. Park and C. Roberts, 'Relative values: kinship and friendship', in *British Social Attitudes Survey: The Thirteenth Report*, ed. R. Jowell et al. (Aldershot: Dartmouth, 1996), 53–72.

49. Our decision to adopt a qualitative approach with a small-scale purposive sample inevitably implies there are some questions our research can answer and some that lie outside its scope. We are able to describe in detail the complexity and diversity of personal communities and the role of friends and family within them. We can also describe different kinds of personal community and be confident that these exist in the wider population; see J. Lewis and J. Ritchie, 'Generalising from qualitative research', in *Qualitative Research Practice*, ed. J. Ritchie and J. Lewis (London: Sage, 2003), 263–86, and E. Spencer, J. Ritchie, J. Lewis and L. Dillon, *Quality in Qualitative Evaluation: A Framework for Assessing Research Evidence* (London: The Strategy Unit, Government Chief Social Researcher's Office, 2003). We have rich data on how people make friends, how friendships vary, how friendships develop or fade, how different stages of the life-course act as opportunities but also as threats for the friend-making enterprise, and how friendships compare with different kinds of family relationships. We can illustrate these findings by describing individual stories and by using our participants' own language. We cannot, however, report statistical regularities or trends, since we rejected survey research methods as insufficiently flexible to cope with the issues we wished to explore. See, in this context, J. Ritchie, 'The applications of qualitative methods to social research', in *Qualitative Research Practice*, 24–46.

50. Details of the sample are given in the appendix. In each case study, the name and other details of participants have been changed to preserve their anonymity.

51. For example, people have been asked about their contacts in a range of settings such as family life, neighbourhood, work and leisure; see M. Cochran, M. Larner, D. Riley, S. Gunnarsson and C. Henderson, *Extending Families: Social Networks of Parents and their Children* (Cambridge University Press, 1993); K. C. P. M. Knipscheer, J. Van de Jong Gieveld, T. G. Tilburg and P. A. Dykstra (eds), *Living Arrangements and Social Networks of Older Adults* (Amsterdam: VU University Press, 1995); J. Sokolovsky, 'Network methodologies in the study of aging', in *New Methods for Old Age Research*, ed. C. Fry and J. Keith (Chicago, Centre for Urban Policy, South Hadley: Bergin and Garvey Publishers, 1986). Alternatively, people have listed those with whom they have had contact

within a specified time period; see, for example, Willmott, *Friendship Networks and Social Support*. Finally, people have named those with whom they feel they have a 'special' relationship; see, in particular, the work of T. C. Antonucci, 'Personal characteristics, social support, and social behaviour', in *Handbook of Aging and the Social Sciences* (ed. R. Binstock and E. Shanas) (New York: Greenwood Press, 1985), 94–126; T. C. Antonucci and H. Akiyama, 'Convoys of social relations', in *Handbook of Aging and the Family*, ed. R. Blieszner and V. H. Bedford (New York: Greenwood Press, 1995), 355–71; and K. C. P. M. Knipscheer and T. C. Antonucci (eds), *Social Network Research: Substantive Issues and Methodological Questions* (Amsterdam: Swets and Zeitlinger BV, 1990). See also the useful review in chapter 2 of C. Phillipson, M. Bernard, J. Phillips and J. Ogg, *The Family and Community Life of Older People: Social Networks and Social Support in Three Urban Areas* (London: Routledge, 2001). Fischer and his colleagues, in their benchmark 1970s study, used a combination of frequency and closeness. In this survey of men's social relationships in Detroit participants were asked to name 'the three men who are your closest friends and whom you see most often'. Other questions also asked the participants to describe the characteristics of their friends and aspects of the friendship. This was not an entirely satisfactory strategy as the authors confess, acknowledging that the definitions of 'friend' that people adopted were often idiosyncratic. 'Even in the Detroit data 5% of those "closest" men [i.e. friends] were later labeled "acquaintances" and 20% of the "most often" seen men were seen, off the job, less than once a month'. Fischer et al., *Networks and Places*, 45. See also Fischer, *To Dwell among Friends*.

52. This mapping method is not, of course, original and is used in psychotherapy and counselling. Interestingly, it was used by Macfarlane in his detailed analysis of the diary of a seventeenth-century clergyman and, indeed, is illustrated on the cover of *Family Life of Ralph Josselyn*, and is employed to good effect by R. L. Kahn and T. C. Antonucci, 'Convoys over the life course: attachment, roles and social support', in *Life Span Development and Behavior*, ed. P. B. Baltes and O. Brim (New York: Academic Press, 1980), volume 3, 253–86. This approach was also used in Phillipson et al., *Family and Community Life of Older People*. However, as far as we are aware, we are the first to use the 'sticky label' technique!

53. These included: wanting to have fun, looking for a job, being in financial difficulty, falling ill, being bereaved, and experiencing difficulties in a personal relationship.

54. A detailed description of our analytical procedure is given in the appendix. An excerpt of a thematic analysis chart can be found in annexe 4. See also J. Ritchie, E. Spencer and W. O'Connor, 'Carrying out qualitative analysis', in *Qualitative Research Practice*, 219–62.

55. T. Lott, *White City Blue* (London: Viking, 1999), 41. The rest of the chapter is a brilliant description of Frankie's personal community. He is later encouraged

by his partner, Veronica, to make decisions about who should be invited to their wedding. She suggests that he stick colour-coded pins into a photograph of his friends to group them into categories. We shall see how Frankie responded to this in endnote 8 for chapter 3.

CHAPTER THREE
THE NATURE OF FRIENDSHIP

A. Nin, *The Diary of Anaïs Nin* (Harvest Books, 1970), volume 2, 4.

Quoted in B. Fehr, *Friendship Processes* (Thousand Oaks, CA: Sage, 1996), 1.

Vatican Collection. Quoted in *The Changing Face of Friendship*, ed. L. S. Rouner (University of Notre Dame Press, 1994), 15.

1. As Silver remarked, 'Are the intense loyalties, coexisting with the frank expectation of reward, found in the richly elaborated cultures of honour the same "conceptual stuff" as the loyalties of modern friends and the instrumentalism of market society?' ('Two different sorts of commerce', 68–69).

2. R. Firth, Preface, in Bell and Coleman, *Anthropology of Friendship*, xiv.

3. A London socialite with a highly visible public presence and who prides herself on her capacity to bring people together at her 'salon' claims to have well over a thousand friends. Stone, *Networking*. See the article by S. Gordon in *The Observer*, 'Friends like these', 30 November 2003.

4. President George W. Bush referred to Britain as 'America's closest friend' during a state visit to Britain in November 2003 and in April 2004 made much of the point in a press conference outside the White House that he preferred to think of the British Prime Minister as 'my friend Tony'. As Mr Bush had just done a unilateral deal with Mr Sharon, Prime Minister of Israel, at odds with British foreign policy, the television pictures of Mr Blair's face on hearing such a protestation of 'friendship' was a study to behold. Friendship has a price!

5. Wellman, an American sociologist who writes about social networks, has a personal email list of '80 best friends' whom he defines as 'people socially close enough to give me a friendly critique' (of a draft academic article). B. Wellman, 'Physical place and cyberplace: the rise of personalized networking', *International Journal of Urban and Regional Research* 25(2) (2001), 241. In all, Wellman maintains an email address file of more than 1800 members of his 'personal community', which he now defines as 'an individual's social network of informal personal ties, ranging from a half-dozen intimates to hundreds of weaker ties': B. Wellman and M. Gulia, 'Net-surfers don't ride alone: virtual communities as communities', in *Networks in the Global Village*, 331–66, 35l.

6. The literature on this issue is too large to cite in detail but we may direct the interested reader to the following references as being particularly useful. C. S. Fischer, 'What do we mean by "friend"? An inductive study', *Social Networks* 3 (1982), 287–306; Davis and Todd, 'Assessing friendship'; L. Weiss and M.

Lowenthal, 'Life-course perspectives on friendship', in *Four Stages of Life*, ed. M. Lowenthal, M. Thurnher and D. Chiriboga (San Francisco, CA: Jossey-Bass, 1975), 48–61; M. Argyle and M. Henderson, 'The rules of friendship', *Journal of Social and Personal Relationships* 1 (1984), 211–37.

Two monographs that grapple with the problem of definitions are J. B. Gurdin, *Amitié/Friendship: An Investigation into Cross-Cultural Styles in Canada and the United States* (Bethesda, MD: Austin and Winfield, 1995), and C. Bidart, *L'Amitié: un lien social* (Paris: Editions La Découverte, 1997). G. A. Allan's student text, *Friendship: Developing a Sociological Perspective* (New York: Harvester Wheatsheaf, 1989), is still very useful, as is Fehr's *Friendship Processes*. Among the more popular books, by far the best is R. Brain, *Friends and Lovers* (London: Hart-Davis, MacGibbon, 1976). Written by an anthropologist, it is much less stodgy than student texts but is very illuminating and the author wears his knowledge lightly.

7. The idea that friends help to establish a better sense of self-identity has been well explored by developmental psychologists. However, in a review of the topic, Berndt has to concede that 'the direction of causality could be from psychological adjustment to friendship quality rather than the other way round'. T. J. Berndt, 'Exploring the effects of friendship quality on social development', in Bukowski et al., *The Company They Keep*, 346–65, 358. According to two leading sociological authorities on the study of contemporary friendship, 'there can be little doubt that identity is a more variable and fluid social property than it was. Within this context friendship is likely to become of more rather than less salience... And as, over time, different projections or images of self develop, informal solidarities like those of friendship will be a means of establishing and sustaining these new identities'. Allan and Adams, 'Reflections on context', in *Placing Friendship in Context*, 183–94, 193.

8. For an amusing account of the less than ideal nature of some friendships, see Lott's *White City Blue*, 38–49. When asked how many varieties of friend there are, Frankie replies, 'Oh loads. For a start there are friends you don't like. I've got plenty of those, then there are the friends you do like, but can't stand their partners. There are those you just have out of habit but can't shake off. Then there's the ones you're friends with not because you like them, but because they're very good-looking or popular and it's kind of cool to be their friend. Trophy friends. Most of the time they're what I call VCSPs, although you can be a trophy friend without being a VCSP. It's just that the two tend to go together.

'What does VCSP stand for?

'Very Charming Selfish People. I've got two of them, and a third borderline. They hold you on a string. Then when they feel you're getting far enough out for the string to break, they pour charm on, draw you back in again... Then there are sports friends. There are friends of convenience – they're usually work friends. There are pity friends who you stay with because you feel sorry for them. There are acquaintances who are on probation as friends...' (ibid.,

45–46). And so on. The object of the exercise is to cut down the list of 'friends' to determine who is to be invited to Frankie's wedding. The task is not simple, but Frankie's lengthy attempt to do a kind of friends' spreadsheet is witty and insightful.

9. One of the earliest and most frequently cited studies was of men's social relationships in Detroit in the early 1970s by Fischer and his colleagues. The men were asked to name 'the three friends who are your closest friends and whom you see most often'. On the basis of 2935 'friendship links', the authors constructed five variables according to which they analysed friendships:

intimacy: the reported 'closeness' of the friendship;

frequency: how often the pair 'got together outside of work';

duration: the number of years a man knew his friend;

role multiplexity: the number of role relations involved in a link;

attributed source: the social context from which the friendship emerged.

See Fischer et al., *Networks and Places*. Although men's friends were the main topic of this study, the researchers admitted, however, that their treatment of friendship was somewhat crude, for example, the assumption that 'frequent interaction promotes intimacy, or men seek out intimate friends more frequently, or both' (ibid., 47).

10. This is an extremely important aspect of our understanding of friendship. Others, of course, have identified different kinds of friends, but sometimes it seems that friends are classified into types according to a single dimension, rather than according to different combinations of characteristics.

11. The significance of context is well explored in the essays in the collection edited by Adams and Allan, *Placing Friendship in Context.*

12. Whether particular categories of people – defined by gender, cultural differences or whatever – have greater difficulty in forming close and expressive attachments is a large and complex issue. Clearly, the very notion of a 'mature adult' is highly culture-specific. Post-Freudians such as Fromm and Horney writing in America in the 1930s and 1940s detected a kind of general cultural neurosis. More recently, see the collection edited by Smelser and Erikson, *Themes of Love and Work in America.* A useful review of childhood influences on adult behaviours is C. L. Bagwell, A. F. Newcomb and W. M. Bukowski, 'Preadolescent friendship and peer rejection as predictors of adult adjustment', *Child Development* 69 (1998), 140–53. For a general and accessible overview of the issues, see Pahl, *On Friendship*, 84–142. Further aspects of this issue are discussed in chapter 7.

13. Further to the references cited in the previous note, the relevance of attachment theory should be recognized. Holmes has done much to emphasize the contemporary significance of the theory; see J. Holmes, *John Bowlby and Attachment Theory* (London: Routledge, 1993). For a very accessible introduction to the question of linking early socialization to wider societal and political concerns, see S. Kraemer and J. Roberts (eds), *The Politics of Attachment*

(London: Free Association Books, 1996). There is an extensive sociological literature on putative gender difference in the capacity to establish deep and lasting friendship relations. Some of these studies, however, report counterintuitive findings that rebut the cultural stereotypes. For example, one study by K. Walker, 'Men, women and friendship: what they say, what they do', *Gender and Society* 8(2) (1994), 246–65, concluded: 'To the extent that discussing problems is a mark of intimacy for many individuals, working-class men appeared to have more intimate friendships than professional men and women' (p. 261). For a more detailed discussion of this issue, see chapter 7.

14. For a brilliantly insightful and illuminating discussion of affection, loving and liking, *The Four Loves* by C. S. Lewis (London: Geoffrey Bles, 1960) is hard to beat. His exploration of Affection, Friendship, Eros and Charity has a wisdom not always evident in the literature on the sociology of emotions or the social psychology of attraction.

15. See Davis and Todd, 'Assessing friendship', for a discussion of active and dormant ties.

16. It is a commonplace in sociological analysis that aging affects the pattern, style and content of friendship. See G. A. Allan and R. G. Adams, 'Aging and the structure of friendship', in *Older Adult Friendship*, ed. R. G. Adams and R. Blieszner (Newbury Park, CA: Sage, 1989), 45–64; Weiss and Lowenthal, 'Life-course perspectives on friendship'; C. A. Stueve and K. Gerson, 'Personal relations across the life-cycle', in *Networks and Places*, 79–98; C. S. Fischer and S. J. Oliker, 'A research note on friendship, gender and the life cycle', *Social Forces* 62 (1983), 124–33; R. B. Brown, 'A life-span approach to friendship: age-related dimensions of an ageless relationship', *Research in the Interweave of Social Roles: Friendship* (JAI Press, 1981), 2, 23–50; S. H. Matthews, *Friendship through the Life-Course: Oral Biographies in Old Age* (Newbury Park, CA: Sage, 1986); R. B. Hays, 'A longitudinal study of friendship development', *Journal of Personality and Social Psychology* 48 (1985), 909–24; M. Dainton, E. Zelley and E. Langan, 'Maintaining friendships through the life span', in *Maintaining Relationships through Communication: Relational, Contextual, and Cultural Variations*, D. J. Canaray and M. Dainton (Hillsdale, NJ: Lawrence Erlbaum, 2003), 79–102. Again, these issues are discussed in more detail in chapter 7.

17. This is in sharp contrast to many studies which take frequency of contact as an indicator of the closeness of the tie. See endnote 47 for chapter 2.

18. The nuanced distinctions between 'friendships and friendly relations' has been usefully discussed by S. B. Kurth in her eponymous chapter in *Social Relationships*, ed. G. J. McCall (Chicago, IL: Aldine, 1970), 137–70. See also J. Bensman and R. Lilienfeld, 'Intimacy as the basis of social networks and culture' in their *Between Public and Private: The Lost Boundaries of the Self* (New York: The Free Press, 1979), 147–70. On the somewhat neglected topic of neighbouring see M. Bulmer, *Neighbours: The Work of Philip Abrams* (Cambridge University Press, 1986), and *The Social Basis of Community Care*.

19. The fact that people can have quite distinctively different relationships in mind when responding to, say, questions in a survey, which also probably includes questions on many other matters, may account for the wide variations in the number of 'friends' reported in different studies. We are not saying that large-scale surveys about 'friends' are all misleading but simply that considerable caution in their interpretation is required. The same ambiguity applies to 'best friends'; see the following endnote.

20. This has important implications for those devising questions for large-scale surveys. It may well be that the notion of 'best friend' is more significant among young people who are largely taken care of by their parents. Thus most practical matters of getting through life do not pose any problems, leaving their friendships to be based on pure sociability. Asking questions about 'closest friends' will have different significance at different stages of the life-course.

21. It is surprising that there has been relatively little sociological research on groups of varied types of friends, though the idea of a constellation of friends is somewhat similar to our concept of a friendship repertoire, see E. Litwak, 'Forms of friendships among older people in an industrial society', in *Older Adult Friendship*, 65–88. An emphasis on dyadic friendship is to be expected in social psychology and philosophy but sociologists have also made only modest contributions in this area. We are not referring to studies of, say, peers or co-workers, since clearly they have not been neglected. Rather, we are referring to distinctive mixes of different types of friends. Clearly, this is the stuff of most novels but somehow the subtlety and complexity has eluded social scientists. Perhaps the social anthropologists have come closest to it, for example, J. Pitt-Rivers in *The People of the Sierra* (Chicago University Press, 1961) (1st edn 1954) writes of 'lop-sided friendship' going on to assert, 'It is a commonplace that you can get nothing done in Andalusia save through friendship... The more friends a man can claim the greater his sphere of influence; the more influential his friends are the more influence he has... So while friendship is in the first place a free association between equals, it becomes in a relationship of economic inequality the foundation of the system of patronage' (p. 140). This political use of friendship is just one way in which a particular constellation can be mobilized and the actual repertoire could be larger and more complex. For a discussion on the wider sociological significance of friendship, see the debate between J. Ede and R. E. Pahl in *Archives européennes de sociologie* 43(3) (2002), 386–423.

22. Stern-Gillet, *Aristotle's Philosophy of Friendship*, 57. 'Truly friends are an aid – to the young in keeping them from making mistakes; to the old in supplying their wants and doing for them what in the failure of their physical powers they cannot do for themselves; to those in the prime of life by making it possible to get fine achievements brought to accomplishment... It is not only that friendship is necessary to the good life, it is in itself a good and beautiful thing', *The Ethics of Aristotle*, translated by J. A. K. Thomson (Harmondsworth: Penguin Books, 1955), 228. Later, Aristotle claims that 'In true

friendship between good men we do not hear complaints. In it the benefit is considered to be measured by the intention expressed in the deliberate action of the benefactor. For the intention is the mainspring of character and moral excellence', ibid., 255. Of course, there are debates about the meaning of the term 'moral' in Aristotle's time, see Vernon, *Philosophy of Friends.*

23. Psychologists have tried to establish informal rules of friendship which operate cross culturally. See, for example, Argyle and Henderson, 'The rules of friendship'.

24. Allan: 'maintaining reciprocity is not always a straightforward matter', in *Kinship and Friendship*, 90. See also the discussion in the report by Willmott, *Social Networks, Informal Care and Public Policy.* For a social psychological perspective, see M. J. Mendelson and A. C. Kay, 'Positive feelings in friendship: does imbalance in the relationship matter?', *Journal of Social and Personal Relationships* 20(1) (2003), 101–16.

25. On this topic see, for example, K. Werking, *We're Just Good Friends: Women and Men in Non-Romantic Relationships* (New York and London: The Guilford Press, 1977); G. Meilaender, 'When Harry and Sally read the Nicomachean Ethics: friendship between men and women', in *Changing Face of Friendship*, 183–96; D. W. Heibert, 'Toward cross-sex friendship', *Journal of Psychology and Theology* 24(4) (1996), 271–83; C. S. Schneider and D. A. Kenny, 'Cross-sex friends who were once romantic partners: are they platonic friends now?', *Journal of Social and Personal Relationships* 17 (2000), 451–66; A. L. Busbroom, D. M. Collins, M. D. Givertz and L. A. Levin, 'Can we still be friends? Resources and barriers to friendship quality after romantic relationship dissolution', *Personal Relationships* 9 (2002), 215–23; L. Gee, *Friends: Why Men and Women Are from the Same Planet* (London: Bloomsbury, 2004).

26. For a detailed discussion of friendship among non-heterosexual men and women, see J. Weeks, B. Heaphy and C. Donovan, *Same Sex Intimacies: Families of Choice and Other Experiments* (London and New York: Routledge, 2001).

CHAPTER FOUR
PATTERNS OF FRIEND-MAKING

A. Pope, letter to the Earl of Oxford (7 November 1725).

Willmott, *Friendship Network and Social Support* (1987).

1. Among the standard sociological texts are the following: G. A. Allan, *A Sociology of Friendship and Kinship* (London: Allen and Unwin, 1979); Allan, *Friendship* and *Kinship and Friendship*; Blieszner and Adams, *Adult Friendship*; Fischer, *To Dwell among Friends*; Matthews, *Friendships through the Life-Course*; W. K. Rawlings, *Friendship Matters: Communication, Dialectics and the Life Course* (Hawthorne, NY: Aldine de Gruyter, 1992). A very useful review of the psychological literature is provided by Fehr, *Friendship Processes,*

although again it is primarily a student text. Pahl, *On Friendship*, provides a general overview of a large field.

2. For a discussion of the concept of a social convoy, see T. C. Antonucci, *Convoys of Social Relations* (1995).

3. Of course, there is the perennial issue of whether birds of a feather flock together or whether their coming together produces commonalities. For an early social psychological approach, see Duck, *Personal Relationships and Personal Constructs*, and see also Fehr, 'Friendship formation', in *Friendship Processes*, chapter 3. The classic sociological statement of homophily is P. Lazarsfeld and R. Merton, 'Friendship as a social process', in *Freedom and Control in Modern Societies*, ed. M. Berger, T. Able and C. N. Page (Princeton, NJ: Van Nostrand, 1954). More recently there is the professional review by M. McPherson, L. Smith-Lovin and J. M. Cook, 'Birds of a feather: homophily in social networks', *Annual Review of Sociology* 27 (2001), 415–44. The discussion in J. M. Pahl and R. E. Pahl, *Managers and Their Wives* (London: Allen Lane, The Penguin Press, 1971), is highly relevant in this context: 'If [a manager's wife] feels that she needs friends, but yet does not find that all potential friends are equally acceptable, she is faced with the problem of differentiating those who will be her friends, from those who will be merely acquaintances or less... In the context of making friends, however, the situation may be one in which a woman, not knowing exactly what sort of person she ought to be, sets out to make a relationship, the warmth and depth of which she does not yet know, with another woman, about whom she possesses little information and who is probably equally unsure about the sort of person she is' (p. 152). See also endnotes 80–82 for chapter 7.

4. Since this is a study of adult friendships, we did not interview anyone at school. However, there is a voluminous literature on this area and a good place to start is Bukowski et al., *The Company They Keep*.

5. This idea of 'framing' of sets of friends in specific contexts has been noted by others. Framed groups of friends may be investigated as cliques, gangs, action sets, factions and so on. See J. Boissevain, *Friends of Friends: Networks, Manipulators and Coalitions* (Oxford: Basil Blackwell, 1974), especially chapter 7.

6. This may be encouraged in various ways, for example, reunions of alumni with the only mildly camouflaged hidden agenda of soliciting donations and bequests helps to track the movement of college peers. Likewise the hugely successful website 'Friends Reunited' provides a good vehicle for tracking old friends (http://www.friendsreunited.co.uk).

7. The huge expansion of tertiary education over the past fifty years provides an extended fertile breeding ground for the establishment of friendships. Since life at college is structured by the syllabus and the provision of collective facilities, pure 'expressive' friendships are likely to dominate over more 'instrumental' ones. See Blieszner and Adams, *Adult Friendship*, for a useful summary of

literature on friendships among college students or, more readably, T. Wolfe's *I Am Charlotte Simmons* (Jonathan Cape, 2004).

8. This point is well recognized in the sociological literature, e.g., Allan, *Kinship and Friendship*, 96. Some of the most perceptive studies have focused on the impact of marriage on women's friendships. See S. J. Oliker, *Best Friends and Marriage: Exchange among Women* (Berkeley, CA: University of California Press, 1989); K. Harrison, 'Rich friendships, affluent friends: middle class practices of friendship', in *Placing Friendship in Context*, 92–116; T. Cohen, 'Men's families, men's friendships: a structural analysis of constraints on men's social ties', in *Men's Friendships*, ed. P. Nardi (Newbury Park, CA: Sage, 1992).

9. One of the themes noted in E. Bott's study, *Family and Social Network* (London: Tavistock, 1957).

10. Evidently, divorce, separation and widowhood may have a dramatic impact on existing friendship patterns and this issue has been well explored by sociologists and social psychologists. Many studies show the increasing importance of friends for the newly divorced or widowed. See, for example, G. Arling, 'The elderly widow and her family, neighbours and friends', *Journal of Marriage and the Family* 38 (1976), 757–68, and B. L. Wilcox, 'Social support in adjusting to marital separation: a network analysis', in *Social Networks and Social Support*, 97–115.

11. In addition to the references in endnote 7, see the useful summary in chapter 3 of P. O'Connor, *Friendships between Women: A Critical Review* (New York and London: Harvester Wheatsheaf, 1992). For a spirited account of how children foster competition and aggression between their mothers, see R. Coward, *Our Treacherous Hearts* (London: Faber and Faber, 1993).

12. Or new enemies; see Coward, *Our Treacherous Hearts*.

13. This may be encouraged by the breakdown of the 'psychological contract' between employer and employee. For the changing nature of the employment contract see the Special Issue of *Human Resource Management* 33(3) (1994) and C. Heckscher, *White Collar Blues: Management Loyalty in an Age of Corporate Restructuring* (New York: Basic Books, 1995).

14. Many studies in industrial sociology focus on the strong ties that may develop in different occupational contacts but do not always explore the notion of friendship in any detail. Notable exceptions include S. R. Marks, 'The gendered contexts of inclusive intimacy, Hawthorne women at work and home', in *Placing Friendship in Context*, chapter 3, 43–70, and Bidart, *L'Amitié*, who most interestingly compares the context of factory work with that of the supermarket and the office on forms of friendship.

15. This theme is also well discussed in Bidart, *L'Amitié*, and was also the central focus of Fischer, *To Dwell among Friends*. In a recent review of the relationships between different localities and personal well-being, it was shown that community socio-economic contexts contribute to health, independently of community members' own social status. S. A. Robert, 'Socio-economic position and health: the independent contribution of community socio-economic

context', *Annual Review of Sociology* (Palo Alto, CA, 1999), 489–516. The current political and policy-orientated interest in social capital has led to many empirical studies exploring the links between community structure and individual well-being reported in such journals as *Health and Place* or *Social Science and Medicine.*

16. These issues are very well reviewed in the empirical studies by Willmott, *Social Networks, Informal Care and Public Policy*, and *Friendship Networks and Social Support.* See also S. Keller, *The Urban Neighborhood: A Sociological Perspective* (New York: Random House, 1968); Bulmer, *Neighbours*; Phillipson et al., *Family and Community Life of Older People.*

17. The classic statement for family relationships is E. Litwak, 'Geographical mobility and extended family cohesion', *American Sociological Review* (1960), 305–94, but see also Pahl and Pahl, *Managers and Their Wives*, for a discussion on the relationship between mobility and friendship. For a more recent account of geographical mobility and the middle class see A. Fielding, 'Migration and middle class formation in England and Wales 1981–1991', in *Social Change and the Middle Class*, ed. T. Butler and M. Savage (London: UCL Press, 1995).

18. We owe this phrase to C. S. Fischer.

19. See endnote 2 above.

20. The relationship between illness and social support including friendship is a large and complex question. See endnotes 93–106 for chapter 1. A general overview is the editors' introduction, 'Social relationships and health', Cohen et al. (eds), in *Social Support Measurement and Health*, 3–25. Two pertinent case studies are H. Hammer, 'Social support, social networks and schizophrenia', *Schizophrenia Bulletin* 7 (1981), 45–57, and P. S. Bearman and J. Moody, 'Suicide and friendships among American adolescents', *American Journal of Public Health* 94(1) (2004), 89–95.

21. In developing our notion of friendship modes we were influenced by Matthews's concept of friendship styles where she distinguished between an 'independent' style in which people are 'friendly' throughout life but do not form close friendships, a 'discerning' style characterized by a few close friends, and an 'acquisitive' style where people have a large number of friends made throughout their life. We unpacked these friendship styles into friendship repertoires and friendships modes. Matthews, *Friendships through the Life-Course.*

22. The idea of a 'friendship budget' is discussed by H. Gouldner and M. S. Strong, *Speaking of Friendship: Middle-Class Women and Their Friends* (New York: Greenwood, 1987).

CHAPTER FIVE
FRIENDS AND FAMILY: THE CASE FOR SUFFUSION

Charles is a participant in our study.

Firth, Preface, in Bell and Coleman, *Anthropology of Friendship.*

Giddens, *Transformation of Intimacy*, 155.

1. For a clear sociological account of the differences, see Allan, *Sociology of Friendship and Kinship* and *Kinship and Friendship*.

2. Classic studies include D. Forde and A. R. Radcliffe-Brown (eds), *African Systems of Kinship and Marriage* (Oxford University Press, 1950), or E. E. Evans-Pritchard, *Kinship and Marriage among the Nuer* (Oxford University Press, 1951).

3. A very useful summary which is also very well documented, especially for the American literature, is Wellman, 'The place of kinfolk in personal community networks'. Recent British studies exploring issues of obligation and responsibility in the contemporary family are J. Finch, *Family Obligations and Social Change* (Cambridge: Polity Press, 1989), and J. Finch and J. Mason, *Negotiating Family Responsibilities* (London and New York: Tavistock/Routledge, 1993).

4. See the discussion in chapter 2, p. 35.

5. Finch, *Family Obligations*, and for a broader historical perspective, see H. Medick and D. W. Sabean (eds), *Interest and Emotion: Essays on the Study of Family and Kinship* (Cambridge University Press, 1984).

6. The notion that exploring internal family dynamics opens up a can of worms is as old as recorded history and was given prominence in the twentieth century by Freud and his adversaries and followers. See B. Simon and R. B. Blass, 'The development and vicissitudes of Freud's ideas on the Oedipus complex', in the *Cambridge Companion to Freud* (ed. J. Nell) (Cambridge University Press, 1991), 161–174. In Britain the writings of D. W. Winnicott have been very influential, see D. W. Winnicott, *The Family and Individual Development* (London: Tavistock, 1965). The baleful effects of parents on children is the theme of countless books on self-analysis. Larkin's poem, 'This be the Verse', begins, 'They fuck you up, your mum and dad. / They may not mean to, but they do. / They fill you with the faults they had / And add some extra, just for you.' P. Larkin, *Collected Poems* (London: Faber and Faber, 1988), 180.

7. The idea that friends feel freer to talk to each other than to relatives without fear of being ridiculed or judged is discussed by H. Lewittes, 'Group cohesiveness, communication level, and conformity', *Journal of Abnormal and Social Psychology* 62 (1961), 408–12.

8. In this context we are most grateful to G. Hyssain of the University of Leeds, who wrote to us after a seminar in which we acknowledged that we had only interviewed people from white European, black Caribbean and black African backgrounds. Her comments are particularly appropriate.

'For the south Asian families, there is a preference for a multi-generational household and an extended family. But this has meant that although it may be physically impossible for all family members to live in one house, family members are now buying houses near the parental home. This has an effect on the social dynamics. Social interaction is favoured amongst family members more readily than that within non-family. Therefore when talking to south Asians about their concept of friendship, more than likely they will talk about friends who are actually cousins. In the transnational kinship study individuals put down names on the concentric diagram who are their friends but when probed they are revealed to be cousins – this is interesting. The reason why this has occurred is that they have been encouraged to develop those links through parents, siblings, etc., and in developing the relationship the individuals are more likely to become friends. Gender is important here also.

'Furthermore, the concept of *bridari* – which is the wider family unit within the south Asian family framework – has meant that other individuals who are not actual family members are brought into the realm of family also, purely through interaction. Friends compensate for family because real family members live abroad so that interaction with them is far more limited than with the friends who live next door, perhaps. But ultimately the friends are compensated as family members. They become members of a bridari, a family network which isn't really a family network but basically made up of friends who are trying to reconstruct a bridari in Britain.'

9. See L. Davidoff (ed.), *Worlds Between: Historical Perspectives on Gender and Class* (Cambridge: Polity Press, 1995); L. White, 'Sibling relationships over the life course', *Journal of Marriage and the Family* 63 (2001), 551–68; T. R. Lee, J. A. Mancini and J. W. Maxwell, 'Sibling relationships in adulthood: contact patterns and motivations', *Journal of Marriage and the Family* 52 (1990), 431–40.

10. It is a strange folk belief in the middle class that teenage children are all 'difficult' and hard to communicate with. This comes out very clearly in many contemporary novels where the authors delight in putting on the agony. Two good excerpts from A. Lurie's *The War between the Tates* (London: Heinemann, 1974) and B. Bainbridge's *Injury Time* (London: Duckworth, 1977) are reproduced in C. Tomalin's charming little anthology *Parents and Children* (Oxford University Press, 1981) (significantly, this book was given to Ray Pahl by his son, Nick, when he was 15!). The sociological literature is, of course, awash with endless stories of 'youth cultures' in different class, gender and ethnic contexts. That it would be very 'uncool' to refer to his parents as friends is well expressed by the remarks of Duncan which follow. In the days of apprenticeships young men and women aged 15 or 16 worked alongside older adults in field or factory and the communication divide did not exist. However, this did not stop rural youth in Wales in the 1940s from embarrassing its elders and indulging in practical jokes, see Rees, *Life in a Welsh Countryside*, 83.

11. See Davidoff, *Worlds Between*.

12. Anthropologists have been more alert to problems of nomenclature and the status of quasi-kin than have sociologists. For an excellent collection of

essays which explore in various contexts suffusions of family and friendship, see, in general, E. Leyton (ed.), *The Compact: Selected Dimensions of Friendship* (Institute for Social and Economic Research, Memorial University of Newfoundland, 1974), and, in particular, the chapters by E. Schwimmer, 'Friendship and kinship: an attempt to relate two anthropological concepts", 49–70, and, especially, E. Leyton, 'Irish friends and "friends": the nexus of friendship, kinship, and class in Aughnaboy', 93–104. The following quotation gives some indication of the complexities involved:

'Whilst friendship as a voluntary and preferential alliance is an important segment of village social life, the word "friend" is rarely used to describe this relationship. "Friend" means kinsman in Ireland, even in this entirely English-speaking, Protestant and Northern Irish village. Although use of the term is occasionally ambiguous such as in the remark by one informant, "Och, he's no friend of mine; he's more a friend, if you know what I mean" (that is, he is not a relative, but rather a friend in the English sense). "Friends" is more commonly used to designate kinsmen, and "mates" or "chums" for non-kin friendships'. Ibid., 95.

Investigating suffusion between friends and family in England is difficult enough, but as Leyton demonstrates it would be a problem of a different order in Ireland. In Aughnaboy, 'for the majority of the adults in the village, friendship can only be found among one's "friends", that is one's close cognative kin' (ibid.). It is only at certain points in the life cycle can the villagers enjoy the 'luxury' of friendship with non-kin, namely, 'during childhood and adolescence, and often in old age' (ibid., 97). It seems clear that whatever the ideas about suffusion which we are developing in this chapter, they cannot be readily transferred to Ireland, where it may be 'difficult or even impossible for most men to find intimacy and brotherly love with non-kin after marriage' (ibid., 98).

Returning to the question of quasi-kin, anthropologists working in the Spanish-speaking world have focused on the distinctive role of godparents or *compadres* and the relationship that is created between the parents and the godparents (*compradazgo*): 'It is a bond of formal friendship more sacred than any personal tie outside the immediate family. Its seriousness is stressed by the fact that, in the popular conception though no longer in the Canon Law, it creates an incest taboo – you cannot marry your *compadre* or padrino.' Pitt-Rivers, *People of the Sierra*, 107.

13. In the words of Macfarlane, 'Many people who marry in most societies end up as affectionate friends. But one of the major lessons to be learnt from the anthropological discussions of marriage is that the Western concept of 'companionate' marriage is unusual... Usually the worlds of men and women are separate, and this is the case after marriage as it was before. A wife will remain closer to her female kin and neighbours than to her husband; a man will spend his time and share his interests with other men. The couple will often eat apart, walk apart, and even, for most of the time, sleep apart. They may even dislike each other intensely and yet both honestly proclaim that it is a satisfactory

marriage because the economic, political and reproductive ends have been satisfied.' A. Macfarlane, *Marriage and Love in England 1300–1840* (Oxford: Basil Blackwell, 1986), 154. Nevertheless, the companionly ideal of marriage – or marriage for friendship – fits the Christian tradition where 'mutual society, help, and comfort, that one ought to have of the other is enshrined in the book of Common Prayer's marriage service. Clearly, companionate marriage was widespread and not simply in the middle class in early modern England. The close conjugal attachment of couples in England was contrasted with the more segregated pattern in France in the eighteenth century (ibid., 156). 'Moving back to the middle of the seventeenth century, model letter writers assuming that the central advantage of marriage was the mutual society and companionship, the identity of interests in an otherwise competitive and individualistic world – in other words true friendship' (ibid., 157).

Sociologists without the benefit of historical scholarship have claimed that companionate marriage is a relatively recent phenomenon. 'Although the phrase "companionate marriage" had been employed as early as the 1920s, it is in the post-war period that it appears more widely'. J. Finch and P. Summerfield, 'Social reconstruction and the emergence of companionate marriage, 1945–59', in *Marriage, Domestic Life and Social Change*, ed. D. Clark (London and New York: Routledge, 1991), 7–32 and 7. For a brilliant review of English working-class marriage and family life from 1890 to 1914 by an American historian, see S. Meacham, *A Life Apart* (London: Thomas and Hudson, 1977). Anyone seeking a benchmark about 'ordinary' family life a century ago would be hard pressed to improve on Meacham's account, based as it is on meticulous analysis of documentary sources and oral history. Significantly, neither 'friendship' nor 'companionship' appears in the index of Meacham's book.

Another particularly fine study of working-class family life in America is the mid twentieth century is M. Komarovsky, *Blue Collar Marriage* (New York: Random House, 1962). Komarovsky showed that for the 1950s almost a third of her sample of husbands and wives could not be said to friends with each other (p. 140). More recently, see L. B. Rubin, *Worlds of Pain: Life in the Working-Class Family* (New York: Basic Books, 1976).

14. Arguably, this was not always the case as there has been a substantial shift in working-class conjugal relations over the last sixty years, since studies such as those by Komarovsky in American or those British community studies reviewed by Klein in *Samples from English Cultures*. The so-called 'Demeter system' was based on conjugal role segregation, a strong bond between mothers and daughters, and a close-knit family circle (ibid., 185). The family was also strongly matrifocal. Again, arguably the Demeter-system has re-emerged with the growth of marriage dissolution and partner changes so that maternal grandmothers play a more influential role as male partners come and go. We have very little serious study of upper-class family life on which to base similar generalizations, since most sociological analysis stops short at the middle class. In some respects upper-class liaisons have much in common with

traditional working-class patterns. The couple may lead separate professional lives and have separate lovers and mistresses. A well-publicized example in Britain is the case of Lord Archer and Lady Archer, both of whom appear to have separate lives and relationships and much of the time live in separate houses but still gain many social and probably financial benefits in remaining married. This is evidently a large and fascinating topic on which we could write at considerable length. The volume edited by D. Clark, *Marriage, Domestic Life and Social Change*, addresses some of these issues. For a more up-to-date account, based on a longitudinal study of 10,000 men and women, we urge readers to consult the work of our colleagues in the Institute of Social and Economic Research at the University of Essex. See Berthoud and Gershuny, *Seven Years*, chapters 1–3. See also R. E. Pahl, *Divisions of Labour* (Oxford: Basil Blackwell, 1984).

15. Of course, arranged marriages are very much the norm in other parts of the world, and among some cultural groups in Britain.

16. For extended discussions of these issues, see Giddens, *Transformation of Intimacy*, and, perhaps more judiciously, L. Jamieson, *Intimacy: Personal Relationships in Modern Societies* (Cambridge: Polity Press, 1998). Anyone seeking a general introduction to many of the issues on which we focus in our study would find Jamieson's account very useful. In some respects her chapter 4 – 'Are good friends all you need?' – is a sceptical note on an aspect of our present thesis. However, we confidently hold our ground.

17. An excellent historical study is Tadmor, *Family and Friends*. See also our more extended discussion, R. E. Pahl and E. Spencer, 'Personal communities: not simply families of "fate" or "choice" ', *Current Sociology* 52(2) (2004), 199–221.

CHAPTER SIX
PERSONAL COMMUNITIES TODAY

G. C. Homans, *Social Behaviour: Its Elementary Forms* (London: Routledge and Kegan Paul, 1961).

1. *Research note on other typologies of personal communities/personal networks.* Analysing and classifying personal communities is not a new idea and readers may wish to compare our typology with ones devised by other researchers. From the many different typologies of personal networks, family networks, support networks, personal communities and so on that have been developed over the past sixty years, we give a few examples here. One of the earliest and most cited studies was carried out by Elizabeth Bott and her colleagues at the Tavistock Institute in London in the early 1950s. Based on a study of twenty couples with school-age children, Bott explored the relationship between the degree of segregation in a couple's conjugal roles and the degree of connectedness of their networks. She classified conjugal roles into *segregated*, where couples had separate roles and looked to external sources of

help, support and sociability; *intermediate*, where couples had some shared and some overlapping roles; *joint*, where couples shared tasks and looked to each other for practical and emotional support.

The personal networks of each spouse were also categorized as follows: *close-knit*, where the network contained a high proportion of kin who shared similar views and exerted informal normative pressures; *medium knit*; *transitional*; *loose-knit*; where the network contained a lower proportion of kin, few members knew or interacted with each other, and there were fewer shared norms.

Bott then classified each of her families by type of occupation, type of network and then arranged these in order of conjugal segregation. Where husbands and wives had segregated conjugal roles, their own networks were close-knit. By contrast, where couples had joint conjugal roles they had loose-knit networks. Between these two extremes, couples with intermediate conjugal roles had medium knit or transitional networks.

However, although the study gathered detailed information about relationships with kin, information about friends and neighbours was far less comprehensive. See Bott, *Family and Social Network*.

Social networks have also been a topic of considerable interest in the field of gerontology, where the focus has been on social support. Wenger, for example, has developed a typology based on research on older people in North Wales. Taking a number of differentiating criteria, including the availability of local close kin, the frequency of contact with significant others in the personal social network, and measures of integration in the local community, she has identified five network types: *family-dependent* small groupings, where people rely on close family members; *locally integrated* large groupings, which include friends and neighbours as well as families; *locally self-contained* small groupings, where people are mostly reliant on neighbours; *wider community-focused* large groupings, where people rely on friends and distant kin; *private-restricted* very small groupings, where there is little reliance on local kin and minimal ties to neighbours. See C. Wenger and V. Burholt, 'Relationships between older people and support network members' (Centre for Social Policy Research and Development, 1997).

Also in the field of gerontology, Litwin has identified the support networks of older people in Israel. Based on factors such as the composition of the network (proportion/types of kin or non-kin), size of network, percentage of intimates, duration of tie, frequency of contact and proximity, Litwin distinguished the following main types of support network: *diverse*, variety of sources of different types of support; *friends*, variety of sources, especially friends, but only minimal contact with neighbours; *neighbours*, few have spouse, rely mainly on neighbours and adult children but not friends; *family network*, frequent contact with proximate children; *restricted*, without spouse, little contact with friends or neighbours. See H. Litwin, 'Social network types and morale in old age', *The Gerontologist* 41 (2001), 516–24.

Numerous other typologies have been developed in this field, for example, in America, England, France, the Netherlands and Canada. For a brief and succinct summary of this work and some indication of its significance, see C. Phillipson, 'Social networks and social support in later life', in Phillipson et al., *Social Networks and Social Exclusion*, 35–49, and the monograph by Phillipson et al., *Family and Community Life of Older People*.

As we have noted in chapters 1 and 2, one of the most active popularizers of the notion of a personal community is Barry Wellman, who, together with Stephanie Potter, has devised a typology containing sixteen kinds of personal community. These sixteen types are based on different configurations of the following elements: *range*, which includes both network size and heterogeneity (influencing people's access to different resources); *intimacy*, which refers to the special nature of a tie, the interest in spending time together, and the sense of mutuality in the relationship; *contact* between members of a personal community in terms of accessibility and amount of actual contact; the *proportion of immediate family* vis-à-vis friends in the network.

These four elements were based on oblique promax factor analyses of interview data. Wellman and Potter, 'Elements of personal communities'.

In addition to this classification of personal communities, Wellman has also proposed a typology of particular geographical areas or neighbourhoods on the basis of the kinds of personal relationships and networks found within them. Wellman's community typology incorporates a number of elements, for example, the size of people's networks; the basis of intimacy, the basis of assistance, the mode and frequency of contact between members, the proportion of kin, neighbours and friends; the extent to which people know each other and interact together, and the extent to which people have similar characteristics. Based on different configurations of elements, Wellman proposed a threefold typology: *community lost*, communities have lost their dense family base and are made up of weak ties; *community saved*, communities have maintained their dense interconnected 'traditional' form; *community liberated*, communities are made up of more dispersed, heterogeneous and loosely knit networks. See B. Wellman, 'The community question', *American Journal of Sociology* 84 (1979), 1201–31, and Wellman and Potter, 'Elements of personal communities'.

Interestingly, where authors have compared different typologies and analysed their construction, they have found a number of similar elements or dimensions. For example, Wenger has concluded that the seven different typologies she reviewed were each based on a continuum from high density, close knit, to low density, loose-knit networks. Moreover, denser networks were linked to a higher proportion of family members, and to small stable neighbourhoods. Loose-knit networks were more common among the middle class. See G. C. Wenger, 'Social network research in gerontology: how did we get here and where do we go next?', in *Sociology of Aging: International Perspectives*, ed. V. Minichello, N. Chappell, H. Kendig and A. Walker (International Sociological

Association Research Committee on Aging, Melbourne: Thoth, 1996), 60–79.

Wellman and Potter have compared Wellman's community typology with the Bott's family network typology, Wenger's social support typology, and Granovetter's comparison between strong and weak ties. Elements which are common to each of these schema include overall network size, proportion of kin, density, role multiplexity, and heterogeneity. Other factors which appear in some but not other typologies include proportion of friends or neighbours, frequency of contact, intimacy, proximity, and level of support. See Wellman and Potter, 'Elements of personal communities'.

The dimensions which underpin our own classification of personal communities (see p. 129) have elements in common with a number of other typologies that are based on: the overall composition of a network or personal community (relative numbers of family, friends, neighbours and so on), aspects of intimacy (importance and content of relationships), and role multiplexity (the notion of suffusion in our study). Where our typology differs from others, however, is in the detailed consideration of different kinds of friendship and friendship repertoires, and different patterns of friend-making. But this is hardly surprising given our particular interest in the role of friendship and friend-like ties.

Although we refer in chapters 2 and 6 to factors such as the size of personal communities, their density, the proximity of members and their frequency of contact, we decided against using these as dimensions of the typology itself. This was because we found that these factors were not linked to different kinds of personal community in any systematic or clearly patterned way. In the case of size, for example, a similar broad range was evident in friend-like, friend-enveloped and family-like personal communities. Across family-enveloped personal communities this range was particularly wide. Only in partner-based and professional-based personal communities, and those we were unable to classify, did we find consistently small personal communities. In terms of density, the most common pattern across friend-like, friend-enveloped and family-like personal communities was for separate clusters of friends and relatives to know each other. Dense interconnections were found mainly but not exclusively in family-enveloped personal communities. Frequency of contact did not appear to be linked to the type of personal community but to the location of particular ties and the nature of the particular relationship. Given this diversity we were keen to avoid devising a very cumbersome typology, allowing for all the different permutations of these additional factors.

In fact, this is one of our reservations about the work of Wellman and Potter. Their sixteenfold classification is very unwieldy, especially when it relates to 33 cases. A decade after his 1960s study of a random sample of 845 adult residents of a Toronto ward, Wellman followed up with in-depth interviews with 33 people chosen from the original sample. While it is understandable that Wellman and his colleagues analysed their 1960s data quantitatively, it is perhaps surprising that they also used hierarchical cluster analysis and multidimensional scaling on the 33 in-depth interview data. Using the four constructed variables outlined above, Wellman and Potter classified the 33 cases according to their high or low scores on each, and then presented the distribution of the 33 cases across the sixteen types, expressed as percentages.

2. For a discussion of 'families of choice' and friendships among non-heterosexual men and women, see Weeks et al., *Same Sex Intimacies.*

CHAPTER SEVEN
MICRO-SOCIAL WORLDS IN THE MAKING

Allan, *Friendship*, 19.

1. M. Q. Patton, *Qualitative Evaluation and Research Methods* (Thousand Oaks, CA: Sage, 2002), 423.

2. To illustrate the nature of qualitative explanation, Patton recounts an old Sufi story:

'Walking one evening along a deserted road, Mullah Nasrudin saw a troop of horsemen coming towards him. His imagination started to work; he imagined himself captured and sold as a slave, or robbed by the oncoming horsemen, or conscripted into the army. Fearing for his safety, Nasrudin bolted, climbed a wall into a graveyard, and lay down in an open tomb.

'Puzzled at this strange behaviour the men – honest travellers – pursued Nasrudin to see if they could help him. They found him stretched out in the grave, tense and quivering.

' "What are you doing in that grave? We saw you run away and see that you are in a state of great anxiety and fear. Can we help you?"

'Seeing the men up close Nasrudin realised that they were honest travellers who were genuinely interested in his welfare. He did not want to offend the travellers or embarrass himself by telling them how he had misperceived them. Nasrudin simply sat up in the grave and said, "You ask what I am doing in this grave. If you must know, I can tell you only that I am here because of you, and you are here because of me." ' Ibid., 425. (Adapted from I. Shah, *The Exploits of the Incomparable Mullah Nasrudin* (New York: E. P. Dutton, 1972), 16.)

Patton suggests attempting to explain the story in two quite different ways: by identifying the independent and dependent variables, or by distinguishing the different meanings and understandings that contributed to the outcome.

3. See endnote 12 for the appendix.

4. We began by classifying members of personal communities in terms of their distance in miles from the focal person, but quickly decided that a less mechanistic classification would serve our purposes better. Instead of exact distances, we devised another classification based on the likely length of journeys (walking distance; return visit possible in under half a day or within an evening; return visit possible in a whole day; in the United Kingdom but a return visit requires an overnight stay; and overseas). This was then simplified

into 'local', referring to people who lived within half a day's or evening's return journey, and 'non-local', which referred to those living further away. Interestingly, Savage and colleagues also talk in terms of lengths of journeys; see M. Savage, M. Bagnall and B. Longhurst, 'Local habitus and working class culture', in *Rethinking Class: Identities, Cultures and Lifestyles*, ed. F. Devine, M. Savage, R. Crompton and J. Scott (Palgrave Macmillan, 2004).

5. U. Beck, *Risk Society* (London: Sage, 1992); S. Lash and J. Urry, *Economies of Signs and Places* (London: Sage, 1994).

6. C. Bell, *Middle Class Families* (London: Routledge and Kegan Paul, 1968); M. Castells, *The Information Age*, vol. 1, *The Rise of the Network Society* (Oxford: Blackwell, 1996).

7. Allan, *Friendship*, 19.

8. For a fuller discussion of the way qualitative analysis should attempt to account for all the data, and search for negative cases, rather than being content with explaining most of the variance, see D. Silverman, *Doing Qualitative Research* (London: Sage, 2000).

9. Hall, 'Social capital in Britain'.

10. See Weeks et al., *Same Sex Intimacies*.

11. See among others: A. Booth, 'Sex and social participation', *American Sociological Review* 37 (1972), 183–92; P. Marsden, 'Core discussion networks of Americans', *American Sociological Review* 52 (1987), 122–31; J. S. Hurlbert and A. C. Acock, 'The effects of marital status on the form and composition of social networks', *Social Science Quarterly* 71(1) (1990), 163–74; G. Moore, 'Structural determinants of men's and women's personal networks', *American Sociological Review* 55 (1990), 726–35; as against Fischer, *To Dwell among Friends*; S. Van Leeuwen, H. Flap and M. Tijhus, 'Cohesion in Dutch society: the relationship between integration, heterogeneity and social support', *Sociale Wetenschappen* 36 (1993), 23–44; and Van der Poel, *Personal Networks*.

12. See, for example, Weiss and Lowenthal, 'Life-course perspectives on friendship', as against A. Booth, and E. Hess, 'Cross-sex friendship', *Journal of Marriage and the Family* 36 (1974), 38–47.

13. See, for example, D. L. Gillespie, R. S. Krannich and A. Leffler, 'The missing cell: amiability, hostility, and gender differentiation in rural community networks', *The Social Science Journal* 22 (1985), 17–30; Fischer and Oliker, 'A research note on friendship, gender, and life cycle'.

14. Some have argued that affluent women who work part-time have plenty of opportunity to make and enjoy friendships. See, for example, Harrison, 'Rich friendship, affluent friends'.

15. For a review of the literature, see Blieszner and Adams, *Adult Friendship*.

16. See, for example, R. J. Barth and B. N. Kinder, 'A theoretical analysis of sex differences in same-sex friendships', *Sex Roles* 19 (1988), 349–63; P. H. Wright, 'Men's friendships, women's friendships, and the alleged inferiority of the latter', *Sex Roles* 8 (1982), 1–20.

17. F. L. Johnson and E. J. Aries, 'The talk of women friends', *Women's Studies International Forum* 6 (1983), 353–61, 354. It is argued that women talk with friends more than with husbands and talking with female friends helps resolve problems with husbands. See, for example, Oliker, *Best Friends and Marriage*; D. Jerrome, 'Good company: the sociological implications of friendship', *Sociological Review* 32 (1984), 696–715.

18. J. Pulakos, 'Young adult relationships: siblings and friends', *Journal of Psychology* 123 (1989), 237–44.

19. L. B. Rubin, 'On men and friendship', *Psychoanalytic Review* 73 (1986), 165–81, 166.

20. Wright, 'Men's friendships, women's friendships'.

21. M. Caldwell and L. Peplau, 'Sex differences in same-sex friendship', *Sex Roles* 8 (1982), 721–32; L. Bendtshneider and S. W. Duck, 'What's yours is mine and what's mine is yours: couple friends', in *Interpersonal Communications: Evolving Interpersonal Relationships* (ed. P. Kalbfleisch), 169–86 (Hillsdale, NJ: Lawrence Erlbaum, 1993); D. G. Williams, 'Gender, masculinity-femininity, and emotional intimacy in same-sex friendship', *Sex Roles* 12 (1985), 587–600; F. L. Johnson and E. J. Aries, 'Conversational patterns among same-sex pairs of late adolescent close friends', *Women's Studies International Forum* 6 (1983), 353–61; A. Haas and M. A. Sherman, 'Reported topics of conversation among same-sex adults', *Communication Quarterly* 30 (1983), 332–42; Oliker, *Best Friends and Marriage*; Booth, 'Sex and social participation'.

22. See Fischer, *To Dwell among Friends*; Rubin, 'On men and friendship'.

23. For a review of the literature, see Fehr, *Friendship Processes*.

24. R. B. Hay and D. R. B. Oxley, 'Social network development and functioning during a life transition', *Journal of Personality and Social Psychology* 50 (1986), 305–13; R. Aukett, J. Ritchie and K. Mill, 'Gender differences in friendship patterns', *Sex Roles* 19 (1988), 57–66.

25. See, for example, T. J. Berndt, 'The features and effects of friendship in early adolescence', *Child Development* 53 (1982), 1447–60; W. M. Bukowski, A. F. Newcomb and B. Hoza, 'Friendship conceptions among early adolescents: a longitudinal study of stability and change', *Journal of Early Adolescence* 7 (1987), 143–52; W. Furman, 'Children's friendships', in *Review of Human Development*, ed. T. M. Field, A. Huston, H. C. Quay, L. Troll and G. E. Finley, 327–39 (New York: John Wiley & Sons, 1982); E. E. Maccoby, 'Gender relationships: a developmental account', *American Psychologist* 45 (1990), 513–20; M. Raffaelli and E. Duckett, ' "We were just talking…": Conversations in early adolescence', *Journal of Youth and Adolescence* 18 (1989), 567–82; L. A. Tedesco and E. L. Gaier, 'Friendship bonds in adolescence', *Adolescence* 23 (1988), 127–36.

26. Rubin, 'On men and friendship'.

27. V. Seidler, 'Rejection, vulnerability and friendship', in *Men's Friendships*. Some have argued that differences between men and women are not universal patterns but that there are important cultural differences; for example, in India

men are not socialized into rugged individualism, they display more physical affection, such as holding hands; see J. J. Berman, V. Murphy-Berman and A. Pachauri, 'Sex differences in friendship patterns in India and the United States', *Basic and Applied Social Psychology* 9 (1988), 61–71.

28. For a discussion of many aspects of men's friendships and the extent to which differences have been overstated, see Nardi, *Men's Friendships*.

29. Walker, 'Men, women and friendship'.

30. See, for example, P. Camarena, P. Saigiani and A. Peterson, 'Gender-specific pathways to intimacy in early adolescence', *Journal of Youth and Adolescence* 19 (1990), 19–32; F. M. Cancian, 'The feminization of love', *Signs: Journal of Women in Culture and Society* 11 (1986), 692–709; B. Wellman, 'Men in networks: private communities, domestic friendships', in *Men's Friendships*. Other writers, however, have shown that self-disclosure is still ranked by men and women as the meaning of intimacy. See, for example, M. Monsour, 'Meanings of intimacy in cross-sex and same-sex friendships', *Journal of Social and Personal Relationships* 9 (1992), 277–95.

31. Walker, 'Men, women and friendship'.

32. Johnson and Aries, 'Conversational patterns'. L. Davidson and L. Duberman, 'Friendship: communication and interactional patterns in same-sex dyads', *Sex Roles* 8 (1982), 809–22.

33. Fehr, *Friendship Processes*; Wellman, 'Men in networks'.

34. Wright, 'Men's friendships, women's friendships'; Hays, 'A longitudinal study of friendship development'. Other studies, however, have still found gender differences in the degree of intimacy with close, long-lasting friendships; see, for example, Barth and Kinder, 'Theoretical analysis of sex-differences'; Caldwell and Peplau, 'Sex differences in same-sex friendships'.

35. S. Swain, 'Covert intimacy: closeness in men's friendships', in *Gender in Intimate Relationships*, ed. B. J. Risman and P. Schwartz (Belmont, CA: Wadsworth, 1989), 71–86.

36. H. T. Reis, M. Senchak and B. Solomon, 'Sex differences in the intimacy of social interaction: further examination of potential explanations', *Journal of Personality and Social Psychology* 48 (1985), 1204–17. However, this idea has been challenged by Reisman, who found that men would like to talk about personal problems more often than they do and self-disclosure and satisfaction with friendship positively correlated for both men and women; see J. M. Reisman, 'Intimacy in same-sex friendships', *Sex Roles* 23 (1990), 65–82.

37. Wright, 'Men's friendships, women's friendships', 4.

38. Weeks et al., *Same Sex Intimacies*.

39. See, for example, E. P. Thompson, *The Making of the English Working-Class* (London: Gollancz, 1963); R. Hoggart, *The Uses of Literacy* (London: Chatto, 1957); R. Williams, *The Long Revolution* (London and New York: Columbia University Press, 1961); J. H. Goldthorpe, D. Lockwood, F. Bechhofer and J. Platt,

The Affluent Worker (Cambridge University Press, 1968–69); P. Willis, *Learning to Labour* (London and New York: Columbia University Press, 1977); J. L. Applegate, B. R. Burleson and J. G. Delia, 'Reflection-enhancing parenting as antecedent to children's socio-cognitive and communicative development', in *Parenting Belief Systems: The Psychological Consequences for Children*, ed. I. E. Siegel, A. V. McGillicuddy-Delisi and J. J. Goodnow (Hillsdale, NJ: Lawrence Erlbaum, 1992), volume 2, 3–39. See also Bourdieu's concept of cultural capital, or the idea that people vary in their ability to secure educational and social advantage, Bourdieu, 'The forms of capital'.

40. For example, M. Young and P. Willmott, *Family and Kinship in East London* (London: Routledge and Kegan Paul, 1957); J. Mogey, *Family and Neighbourhood* (London: Oxford University Press, 1956); K. Coates and R. Silburn, *Poverty: The Forgotten Englishman* (Harmondsworth: Penguin, 1970). More recently, however, it has been argued that the picture of 'traditional' working-class life painted in some of the British studies is very much coloured by the particular estates chosen and the patterns of migration which were taking place at the time, and that working-class sociability today may not be as sharply distinguished from middle-class patterns as the studies suggest. See G. A. Allan and G. Crow, *Families, Households and Society* (Basingstoke: Macmillan, 1999).

41. H. G. Oxley, *Mateship and Local Organisation* (Brisbane: University of Queensland Press, 1974); J. Rosecrance, 'Racetrack buddy relations: compartmentalized and satisfying', *Journal of Personal and Social Relationships* 3 (1986), 441–56.

42. Numerous studies have found a relationship between class and network composition, for example, Hurlbert and Acock, 'The effects of marital status on the form and composition of social networks'; Marsden, 'Core discussion networks of Americans'; Moore, 'Structural determinants of men's and women's personal networks'; Fischer, *To Dwell among Friends*; C. S. Fischer and S. Phillips, 'Who is alone? Social characteristics of people with small networks', in *Loneliness: A Source Book of Current Theory Research, and Therapy*, ed. L. Peplau and D. Perlman (New York: Wiley Interscience, 1982), 21–39; Van der Poel, *Personal Networks*.

43. M. Lowenthal and B. Robinson, 'Social networks and isolation', in *Handbook of aging and the social sciences*, ed. R. Binstock and E. Shanas (New York: Van Nostrand Reinhold, 1976), 432–56; P. Keith, 'Isolation of the unmarried in later life', *Family Relations* 35 (1986), 389–95.

44. Bott, *Family and Social Network*, 113.

45. B. Wellman, 'Domestic work, paid work and net work', in *Understanding Personal Relationships*; Allan, *Friendship* and *Kinship and Friendship*; Oxley, *Mateship and Local Organisation*.

46. See Allan, *Friendship*, 138.

47. J. Cornwell, *Hard-Earned Lives* (London: Tavistock, 1984); Allan and Crow, *Families, Household and Society*.

48. F. Devine, *Affluent Workers Revisited: Privatism and the Working Class* (Edinburgh University Press, 1992).

49. Buddy is a parallel concept in the United States, which appears to have similar connotations to 'mate'; see Rosecrance, 'Racetrack buddy relations'.

50. Allan, *Kinship and Friendship*, 75.

51. For a fuller discussion of habitus, see P. Bourdieu, *Pascalian Meditations* (Cambridge: Polity Press, 1999); see also Giddens's notion of practical versus discursive consciousness, A. Giddens, *The Constitution of Society* (Cambridge: Polity Press, 1984).

52. Gershuny's work on cultural capital develops an innovative approach to social class; see J. Gershuny, *A New Measure of Social Position: Social Mobility and Human Capital in Britain* (ISER Working Paper 2002-2). His position is further developed in the following working papers: 2001-20, 2002-16, 2002-17, 2002-18. These are all available and can be downloaded from www.iser.essex.ac.uk.

53. See Van der Poel, *Personal Networks*.

54. Marsden, 'Core discussion networks of Americans'; Fischer, *To Dwell among Friends*. Interestingly, there is evidence that these adult sons and daughters may also be considered friends, see R. E. Pahl and D. J. Pevalin, 'Between family and friends: a longitudinal study of friendship choice', *British Journal of Sociology* 56 (2005), 433–50. There is a rich literature on the personal or support networks of older people. See, for example, Wenger, 'Social network research in gerontology'; Phillipson et al., *Family and Community Life of Older People*. Because older people have been the subject of so many studies, we deliberately excluded older frail people from our study.

55. For a discussion of the literature on friendship and aging, see endnote 16 for chapter 3.

56. See J. Reisman, 'Adult friendship', in *Personal Relationships 2*, ed. S. W. Duck and R. Gilmour (London: Academic Press, 1981).

57. T. L. Huston and G. Levinger, 'Interpersonal attraction and relationships', *Annual Review of Psychology* 29 (1978), 115–56.

58. J. Davitz and J. Davitz, *Making It from 40 to 50* (New York: Random House, 1976) argue that there is less time in middle age for friendship but that this is the time to savour old established friendships, whereas B. Hunt and M. Hunt, *Prime Time* (New York: Stein and Day, 1975), maintain that this is a time for making new friends.

59. B. L. Neugarten and N. Datan 'The middle years', in *American Handbook of Psychiatry 1*, ed. S. Arieti (New York: Basic Books, 1974).

60. C. Marsh and S. Arber, 'Research on families and households in modern Britain: an introductory essay', in *Families and Households: Divisions and Change*, ed. C. Marsh and S. Arber (Basingstoke: Macmillan, 1992), 1–25.

61. G. L. Creasey, 'The association between divorce and late adolescent grandchildren's relations with grandparents', *Journal of Youth and Adolescence* 22

(1993), 513–29; G. Dench, J. Ogg and K. Thompson, 'The role of grandparents', *British Social Attitudes, 16th Report, Who Shares New Labour Values?* (Aldershot: Ashgate, 2000), 135–56; G. E. Kennedy and C. E. Kennedy, 'Grandparents: a special resource for children in step-families', *Journal of Divorce and Remarriage* 19(3–4) (1993), 45–68; P. Thompson, 'The role of grandparents when parents part or die: some reflections on the mythical decline of the extended family', *Aging and Society* 19 (1999), 471–503.

62. See, for example, W. W. Hartup and N. Stevens, 'Friendship and adaptation in the life-course', *Psychological Bulletin* 121 (1997), 335–70.

63. Weiss and Lowenthal, 'Life-course perspectives on friendship'.

64. Since ours is not a longitudinal study, we cannot say how personal communities will change at future stages in the life-course. It is possible that people may change from having a friend-like to a friend-enveloped personal community when partner and children become the core of their lives or as their children grow up take on the mantle of friend. It seems unlikely, however, that people would change from a friend-like to family-enveloped personal community since the two represent such different approaches to and valuations of friendship.

65. We know, for example, that there are different patterns of kinship within Britain today, ranging from cases where most family members, including extended family, live in the same neighbourhood, to cases where the immediate nuclear family live together but other family members are dispersed and have little contact, to cases where people have no local family at all; see Willmott, *Social Networks, Informal Care and Public Policy*. See also Wellman and Potter, 'Elements of personal communities'. The personal networks of older people also reflect major differences in the extent to which they have local sources of support from kin, neighbours or friends; see Van der Poel, *Personal Networks*.

66. For a summary of the literature, see Allan, *Friendship*.

67. See, for example, the work of Savage and colleagues at Manchester University, who have discovered what they call the northern middle class, who are committed to the northwest, and who are different from both the local middle class and the true cosmopolitans who have little sense of spatial belonging. M. Savage, G. Bagnall and B. Longhurst, 'Ordinary, ambivalent and defensive: class identities in the northwest of England', *Sociology* 35 (2001), 875–92. In our own study, we found some interesting cases of middle-class participants who have very local personal communities and a very strong sense of neighbourhood. Amanda, for example, a part-time drama teacher with two young children, lives in what she describes as 'a middle-class ghetto' in northeast London. She is strongly involved with the local primary school, and expressed the sense of betrayal she and other local friends felt when they heard that 'yet another middle-class family' had moved out of the area.

68. R. G. A. Williams, 'Kinship and migration strategies among settled Londoners', *British Journal of Sociology* 34 (1983), 386–415.

69. Ibid.

70. Some studies have shown that women are closest to longstanding friends who no longer live close by and who are rarely seen face-to-face, and have more casual relationships with local friends whom they see quite frequently. See R. G. Adams, 'The demise of territorial determinism: online friendships', in *Placing Friendship in Context*; M. Rohlfing, ' "Doesn't anyone stay in one place anymore?" An exploration of the understudied phenomenon of long-distance relationships', in *Understudied Relationships: Off the Beaten Track*, ed. J. T. Wood and S. W. Duck (Newbury Park, CA: Sage, 1995). Our own study showed that people with friend-based personal communities tended to have some long-distance confidants. Some also had the resources to retain friendships with fun friends who lived a considerable distance away. For younger people, email was their main way of keeping in contact with friends who had moved abroad, though they also hoped to be able to visit these friends at some stage in the future.

71. For a discussion of the literature on territory and friendship, see R. G. Adams and R. Blieszner, 'Resources for friendship intervention', *Journal of Sociology and Social Welfare* 20 (1993), 159–75.

72. Allan, *Friendship*.

73. D. Mason, *Race and Ethnicity in Modern Britain* (Oxford University Press, 1995).

74. S. Westwood and P. Bachu, *Enterprising Women: Ethnicity, Economy, and Gender Relations* (London: Routledge, 1988).

75. S. Warrier, 'Gujerati Prajapatis in London: family and sociability networks', in *Desh Pradesh: The South Asian Presence in Britain* (ed. R. Ballard) (London: Hurst, 1994).

76. See B. de Vries, C. Jacoby and C. G. Davis, 'Ethnic differences in later life friendship', in *Canadian Journal on Aging* 15(2) (1996), 226–44.

77. W. Samter, B. B. Whaley, S. T. Mortenson and B. B. Burleson, 'Ethnicity and emotional support in same-sex relationships', in *Personal Relationships* 4 (1997), 413–30.

78. E. T. Hall, *Understanding Cultural Differences* (Yarmouth, ME: Intercultural Press, 1989).

79. Swidler, 'Love and adulthood in American culture'.

80. The terms status homophily and value homophily were originally used by Lazarsfeld and Merton, 'Friendship as a social process'.

81. For example, Marsden, 'Core discussion networks of Americans', found a high degree of homophily in relation to race, sex, age and education among a national sample of American adults, but a lower level in terms of religion. Fischer et al., *Networks and Places*, found men's closest friends tended to be aged within eight years of each other. A high degree of homophily in relation to education, occupation and social class was found by, for example, E. O. Lauman, *Bonds of Pluralism: The Form and Substance of Urban Social Networks*

(New York: John Wiley & Sons, 1973), and H. Louch, 'Personal network integration: transivity and homophily in strong tie relations', *Social Networks* 22 (2000), 45–64. Other studies have found that friendship similarity is a relative rather than an absolute criterion in friendship selection, so that friends may be similar in some respects, but dissimilar in others, and that the bases of similarity or difference vary between different ethnic groups, for example. See J. Hamm, 'Do birds of a feather flock together? The variable bases for African American, Asian American, and European American adolescents' selection of similar friends', *Developmental Psychology* 36 (2000), 209–19. Broad boundaries such as black–white in the United States and Arab–Jewish in Israel are strong factors in friendship selection, but class appears to be stronger basis of homophily than ethnic origin for friendships within white ethnic groups in America, or within Jewish groups in Israel; see H. Ayalon, E. Ben-Rafael and S. Sharot, 'Ethnicity, class and friendship: the case of Israel', *International Sociology* 4(3) (1989), 293–310.

82. See, for example, McPherson et al., 'Birds of a feather'. For an example of this multifactor approach in relation to cross ethnic friendships, which examines the role of educational level, length of time in the country, experience of intergroup contact, intermarriage, income and local neighbourhood, as well as ethnic origin, see E. Fong and W. W. Isajiw, 'Determinants of friendship choices in multiethnic society', *Sociological Forum* 15(2) (2000), 249–69.

CHAPTER EIGHT
HIDDEN SOLIDARITIES REVEALED

R. W. Emerson, 'Friendship', in Pakaluk, *Other Selves.*

1. Bauman, *Liquid Modernity*, 37.

2. Wellman, 'The network community', 13.

3. Ibid., 21, our emphasis.

4. In this context it is as well to remember the magisterial work of Castells, who, in a series of books, has shown how the technology of network societies has extended our range of possible contacts, thus extending our social space, enabling new and disparate linkages to form new sources of social meaning. See Castells, *Rise of Network Society*. See also the discussion of Licoppe's work in chapter 1, p. 25.

5. Hampton and Wellman, 'The not so global village of Netville'.

6. D. Anderson, *Losing Friends* (The Social Affairs Unit, 2002).

7. Bauman, *Liquid Love*, 66.

8. Wellman, 'The network community', 17.

9. See chapters 2 and 6 for further details about the bases of inclusion for family ties.

10. See chapter 3 for a more detailed discussion of different kinds of friendship.

11. For a more detailed description of friendship repertoires, see chapter 3

12. Giddens's discussion of reflexivity is subtle and complex; see chapter 2, endnote 36. For a lively continuation of the debate about these issues, see U. Beck, A. Giddens and S. Lasch, *Reflexive Modernization* (Cambridge: Polity Press, 1994).

13. See the introduction and the appendix for a discussion of the implications of our sampling decisions.

14. This asks people a range of questions about how they have been feeling over the previous month compared to how they usually feel. A high score indicates poor mental health. See annexe 6 in the appendix. See also Pevalin and Goldberg, 'Social precursors to onset', 299–306. A. J. Martin, 'Assessing the multidimensionality of the 12-item General Health Questionnaire', *Psychological Reports* 84 (1999), 927–35.

15. It is part of the project of the liberal enlightenment that individuals should be free to choose how they live their lives, so long as they do not harm others. This is, of course, not universally accepted and the tensions between, say, limiting the choice of marriage partners to maintain cultural continuity, as opposed to following the inclination of love, is a good example. William Shakespeare's *Romeo and Juliet* recognizes the tragedy of intolerance, a perennial concern of creative writers. More recently, Rohinton Mistry explored similar issues in the Parsi community in India in his fine novel, *Family Matters* (Faber and Faber, 2002). The tyrannies of no choice among fundamentalist groups clash with the tyranny of a certain kind of imposed 'freedom', which some social theorists claim is another form of no choice. The exploration of these shades of grey by political philosophers or perhaps theologians is certainly better than attempting to resolve them with bullets.

16. The classic statement is G. S. Becker, *A Treatise on the Family* (Cambridge, MA: Harvard University Press, 1981). More recently, see J. Ermisch, *An Economic Theory of the Family* (Princeton University Press, 2003).

17. J. S. Coleman, *Foundations of Social Theory* (Cambridge, MA: Belknap, 1990); D. Lockwood, *Solidarity and Schism* (Oxford: Clarendon Press, 1992); W. G. Runciman, *A Treatise on Social Theory*, 3 vols (Cambridge University Press, 1983–97). A more accessible introduction aimed at undergraduates is J. Scott, *Sociological Theory* (Aldershot and Brookfield, VT: Edward Elgar, 1995).

18. Pahl and Spencer, 'Personal communities'.

19. Wellman, 'The network community'.

20. Wellman and Gulia, 'Network basis of social support'.

21. The original and most frequently cited author on this issue, particularly in relation to getting a job, is Granovetter, whose original article, 'Strength of weak ties', sparked a very lengthy debate and numerous further studies. Interestingly, although Granovetter originally defined the strength of a tie as 'a

(probably linear) combination of the amount of time, the emotional intensity, the intimacy (mutual confiding), and the reciprocal services which characterize the tie' (ibid., 1361), in practice, this was operationalized as frequency of contact. Burt has also contributed to this debate by introducing the idea that successful business managers are those who have contacts with people unlike themselves and so can then bridge what he calls 'structural holes'; see R. Burt, *Structural Holes: The Social Structure of Competition* (University of Chicago Press, 1992).

22. For a summary of research in this field, see P. Fongay, 'Patterns of attachment, interpersonal relationships and health', in *Health and Social Organisation: Towards a Health Policy for the 21st Century*, ed. D. Blane, E. Brunner and R. Wilkinson (London: Routledge, 1996).

23. As we saw in the extended endnote 1 for chapter 6, Wenger has identified five main kinds of support network for older people. She orders these from most to least supportive as follows: 'locally integrated' (large groupings, which include friends and neighbours as well as local family); 'wider community focused' (large groupings, where people rely on friends and distant kin); 'locally self-contained' (small groupings, where people are mostly reliant on neighbours); 'local family dependent' (small groupings, where people rely on close family members, often a spouse carer); 'private-restricted' (very small groupings, the person is alone or with an isolated spouse carer, and there is little reliance on local kin and minimal ties to neighbours). See 'Social networks and the prediction of elderly people at risk', paper given at the Royal College of Psychiatrists Conference, *Psychiatry of Old Age* (Windermere, 1997). Wenger's typology acknowledges the importance of friends in circumstances where relatives are unavailable for various reasons, including distance and death. While we acknowledge Wenger's pioneering work, we have not engaged with this in more detail simply because her field is gerontology, whereas, as discussed in the Introduction, we made a conscious decision not to include the elderly in our sample, but we do recognize the complementarity of Professor Wenger's approach.

24. See, for example, P.6, 'Social networks, social exclusion, social capital, and public policy', paper presented at the symposium, *Networks, Localities, and Communities: New Directions for Research and Social Policy* (Keele University, 1998).

25. See the comments on the papers by McCulloch and Paxton in endnote 86 for chapter 1.

26. The issues that we are raising in a very compressed form are discussed with great verve and lucidity by R. A. Dahl in *After the Revolution? Authority in a Good Society* (New Haven, CT, and London: Yale University Press, 1970). 'The fact that decisions on some matter affect your interests in a vital way does not mean that it is necessarily rational for you to insist upon participating' (p. 31). However, it is important to remember the cautionary tale told by Hall – see chapter 1, endnote 79.

27. Putnam does not appear to recognize the possible dysfunctional consequences of league sports. Different countries have different enthusiasms. Those countries which support soccer have to cope with associated alcoholism, violence and racism from overexcited fans. This reflects badly on the cities or countries where such behaviour takes place. Unpleasant racial behaviour by a Spanish crowd at an international 'friendly' match against England in November 2004 might have jeopardized Spain's bid to host the Olympic Games in 2012. At times of sporting fixtures between long-term rivals or during the World Cup employers may feel obliged to change their work hours or to accept a lower standard of work than normal.

28. We are encouraged by a later reformulation of Putnam's views. The authors recognize that 'social capital is necessarily a local phenomenon because it is defined by people who know one another... we are really talking about a network or accumulation of mainly local connections... trust relationships and resilient communities generally form through local personal contacts', Putnam and Feldstein, *Better Together*, 9.

29. See the discussion of homophily in chapter 7, p. 180.

30. As social network researchers have found, plotting entire social networks is a formidable, if not impossible task, and the same would be true if we were to try to plot a society of personal communities. See endnote 7 for the appendix.

31. C. Calhoun, 'Indirect relationships and imagined communities: large-scale social integration and the transformation of everyday life', in *Social Theory for a Changing Society*, ed. P. Bourdieu and J. S. Coleman (Boulder, CO: Westview Press/Russell Sage Foundation, 1991), 95–130, 98. It is as well to remember that the analytical distinction between social integration and system integration was clearly articulated by Lockwood in 1963, when he distinguished between *actors* and *parts* of the social system. The original essay is reprinted in *Solidarity and Schism*.

32. Nisbet, *Sociological Tradition*, 101.

33. Allan, 'Friendship, sociology and social structure', 699.

34. Delanty, *Community*, 144.

35. Putnam, *Bowling Alone*, 24.

APPENDIX
HOW WE CARRIED OUT OUR STUDY

1. For other accounts of our approach, see Pahl and Spencer, 'Capturing personal communities' and 'Personal communities: not simply families of "fate" or "choice" '.

2. See chapter 1 for a full discussion of these debates.

3. Wellman, 'The place of kinfolk in personal community settings', 197.

4. In qualitative research, sample units (e.g. people, organizations, settings, events, timings) are chosen because they have particular characteristics or features which will enable an in-depth exploration and understanding of the research question. Cases are information rich. This approach is known as criterion-based, judgement or purposive sampling, and is very different from probability sampling, in which elements in the population are chosen at random. For an excellent discussion of qualitative sampling, see Patton, *Qualitative Evaluation and Research Methods*; J. Mason, *Qualitative Researching* (London: Sage, 2002); J. Ritchie, J. Lewis and G. Elam, 'Designing and selecting samples', in *Qualitative Research Practice*, 77–108.

5. In purposive sampling it is important to remember that cases are chosen strategically to be information rich not to represent proportionately the distribution of characteristics in the wider population.

6. For a fuller discussion of alternative approaches, see endnote 51 for chapter 2.

7. Our decision to limit our study was based on our interest in *personal communities* – the set of significant and active ties in which people are embedded – as outlined in chapter 2, but we were also aware of the immense problems associated with the study of full personal networks. Attempting a qualitative study of such networks, exploring each link in detail, was simply beyond the scope of this study. As Van der Poel notes, 'In research so far, personal networks have been restricted to the primary star. The reasons for this limitation are mainly of a practical nature. The number of persons to be interviewed increases exponentially with every higher order star', Van der Poel, *Personal Networks*, 48. According to one approach, a random sample of 1,000 participants would produce some 18,500 persons to be interviewed in the second step and, assuming that half of the persons generated by these new participants have not been mentioned before, the size of the next sample to be contacted would be over 170,000! This procedure, known as snowball sampling, is likely to produce high non-response rates in later steps of the process. Participants are understandably reluctant to provide the interviewer with names and addresses of others whose approval and permission has not been sought. Furthermore, even in the primary star the only information that can be reliably elicited from the focal individual is whether those mentioned in his/her star know each other. The actual *content* of the relationship is not known and may be only unreliably imputed. Even the content of relationships within the focal individual's family will not be accurately known. The research methodology adopted by Van der Poel is based on L. McCallister and C. S. Fischer, 'A procedure for surveying personal networks', *Sociological Methods and Research* 7(2) (1978), 131–48. This is an admirably clear account of a method we rejected for the very reason the authors acknowledge in a serious caveat: 'It is clearly important that network researchers consciously and clearly specify what they mean theoretically by "relation". The findings of network research can be strongly influenced by the measures of "relation" used to define the

network. Therefore researchers should pay as much attention to the methods they use to identify network memberships as they do to the analysis of data describing those networks' (ibid., 146). The authors also concluded that creating personal networks (or communities) with only twenty minutes of interview time posed serious problems and they list a whole string of difficulties such as a crude naming of 'best friends' or those 'close to', without more detailed elucidation (though they did try to overcome the difficulties in such a strategy by eliciting named persons in response to specific questions and by asking interviewees to fill out a self-administered questionnaire about each person, to gather information such as how they met, where they live, their age, employment, marital status and so on). It was for this and other reasons that we chose our specific qualitative research strategy.

8. The number twenty was chosen in the light of findings from other studies. For example, Van der Poel reported an average network size of 18.5 (Van der Poel, *Personal Networks*, 53). Surprisingly, perhaps, this was exactly the same size as that reported by Fischer, *To Dwell among Friends*, 292. This latter study is particularly useful for those interested in research strategies, since the Respondent Interview Schedule for the original fieldwork carried out in 1977 is reproduced.

9. For a detailed description of Framework, see Ritchie et al., 'Carrying out qualitative analysis'.

10. For a discussion of different approaches to analysis, see, for example, E. Spencer, J. Ritchie and W. O'Connor, 'Analysis: practices, principles and processes', in *Qualitative Research Practice*, 199–218.

11. For a discussion of the problem of anecdotalism and how to overcome it see, for example, Silverman, *Doing Qualitative Research*.

12. See Mason, *Qualitative Researching*, for an excellent discussion of alternatives to variable analysis.

13. For a discussion of generalization or 'external validity' in qualitative research, see S. Kvale, *InterViews: An Introduction to Qualitative Research Interviewing* (Thousand Oaks, CA: Sage, 1996), J. C. Mitchell, 'Case and situational analysis', *American Sociological Review* 31(2) (1983), 187–211, Lewis and Ritchie, 'Generalising from qualitative research', C. Seale, *The Quality of Qualitative Research* (London: Sage, 1999), and Spencer et al., *Quality in Qualitative Evaluation*.